T0380797

Love and Loss

A Journey through Fear to Peace

Volume Five
Plumbing the Depths Above the Clouds
August 2017 to Now

Betty Hibod

BALBOA.PRESS
A DIVISION OF HAY HOUSE

Balboa Press books may be ordered through booksellers or by contacting:

Balboa Press
A Division of Hay House
1663 Liberty Drive
Bloomington, IN 47403
www.balboapress.com
844-682-1282

Because of the dynamic nature of the Internet, any web addresses or links contained in this book may have changed since publication and may no longer be valid. The views expressed in this work are solely those of the author and do not necessarily reflect the views of the publisher, and the publisher hereby disclaims any responsibility for them.

This book is a work of non-fiction. Unless otherwise noted, the author and the publisher make no explicit guarantees as to the accuracy of the information contained in this book and in some cases, names of people and places have been altered to protect their privacy.

Any people depicted in stock imagery provided by Getty Images are models, and such images are being used for illustrative purposes only.
Certain stock imagery © Getty Images.

Print information available on the last page.

Scripture quotations marked RSV are taken from the Revised Standard Version of the Bible, copyright © 1946, 1952, 1971 by the Division of Christian Education of the National Council of the Churches of Christ in the USA. Used by permission.

ISBN: 979-8-7652-5509-4 (sc)
ISBN: 979-8-7652-5510-0 (e)

Balboa Press rev. date: 10/18/2024

To conquer death, you only have to die.

– Jesus Christ Superstar

Contents

Foreword

Our task is not to leave a record of what happened on this date for those who will inherit the Earth; history will take care of that. Therefore, we will speak about our daily lives, about the difficulties we have had to face. That is all the future will be interested in, because I do not believe very much will change in the next thousand years. – Paul Coelho, *Manuscript Found in Accra* [1]

Many books have been written as histories recounting events that shaped the life of a group, society, nation, or civilization, or as biographies recounting events and achievements relating to one person's life and work. Many books have been written putting forth ideas, philosophies, and words of wisdom to live by. Some of these we call holy books, or scripture.

Fewer books have been written like this one, which go behind the scenes of history, lay bare the feelings behind the philosophies, and document the painful and joyful inner path along which historical events and philosophical ideas emerge. This book is intensely, even shockingly, personal, not clinical or abstract or detached. It is an intimate, detailed, sensual, and sometimes disturbing account of a life lived on the cusp that bridges time and eternity. Its focus is narrow; it does not reveal much at all about anyone's visible public life or accomplishments, but it explores in great depth the invisible contents of minds, hearts, and souls.

The books of history, biography, religion, and philosophy transmit the end results of the spiritual process, the visible outward effects of invisible inner struggles. This book goes inward, looks directly at the inner struggles and makes visible the invisible forces that shape the end result. It is not a recitation of historical or biographical facts. It speaks "about our daily lives, about the difficulties we have had to face," and in so doing traces the line drawn by the finger of God from darkness to light.

The scriptures and scriptural commentaries of most religions describe a path to salvation or inner peace, and provide instructions or guideposts for moving along the path, but they are still only theoretical, hypothetical, mythical, or metaphorical accounts. This book seeks to show how theories and hypotheses play out in real time and space, how myths come alive in the flesh, how metaphors become the very things they symbolize. How does daily life look from inside someone in the throes of awakening? How does she know who or what she is? How is her destiny revealed? How do seemingly ordinary mundane events become miracles?

Joseph Campbell said: "Words can act as barriers…. There's a saying that appears both in Lao-tzu's work and in the Upanishads: 'Those who know do not speak. And those who speak do not know.' That's hard for one giving a lecture."[2] It's also hard for one writing a book. Can indescribable occurrences and perceptions, sensory and extrasensory, nevertheless be described somehow in thoughts and words? This book is an attempt to find out.

A Reader's Guide

The journal from which this book is excerpted spans over thirty years and in its unabridged form occupies thousands of pages. It is a true story, and all the characters in this drama are real people. To protect the privacy of these people and their families, most names, locations, and dates are fictitious. Some characters may be composites of more than one real person.

There are many words used throughout the book that can be defined in various ways, words like "God," "spiritual," "consciousness," "miracle," "time," "love," "heaven," and "hell." These words are intentionally left amorphous. As you progress through this story, the meanings of words will change, come into sharper focus, or you will see that precise definitions really don't matter and can even be counterproductive, having a limiting effect if applied to the mind-expanding metaphors in which they are often used.

This book begins with two concurrent threads. One is a chronological account of powerful events and sensory perceptions that propelled the author's mystical journey. The other is the author's intellectual analysis of those events and perceptions, and of the art, science, religion, and philosophy that informed and gave meaning to her experience. Eventually a third stream joins the other two, which represents the emergence into consciousness of a hidden force beyond the sensory body and analytical mind which we discover has been directing this process all along.

The basis of this book is a very personal diary which, like most diaries, was not meant for public consumption. This is the author's view not into the world, but into herself, a voyage of discovery in which no social proprieties were observed and no dark backwaters were left unexplored. Many of the statements herein would be considered audacious, boastful, embarrassing, or offensive in polite company and would never have been uttered in public. These private utterances are now made public in this book because the author's spiritual call demands it.

This book is not intended to teach or preach, but simply to describe in great detail one person's journey to awakening. If you question some of the opinions and conclusions expressed in the beginning of the book, just wait – the author's views often changed with new experiences and new insights. This story evolves through many amazing twists and turns, and as with all journeys worth taking, this one is not so much about the point of arrival, if there is one, as about the process of getting there.

Prologue

I was twenty-one years old when I graduated from college and embarked on a great adventure. Armed with only my diploma and one steamer trunk of belongings, I set out to begin a new job in a strange, distant land. I was exhilarated, anxious to see and learn and experience new things.

I loved my new home, but expected to stay only a couple years and then move on. I also expected to remain single and independent. I had such high standards and expectations for a life partner that I figured I would never marry, never find a man who could live up to my impossibly high standards. Maybe I would have a boyfriend from time to time, but no commitments.

Within weeks of my arrival in my new home, I met the man I would marry, the love of my life, Louis. There were many obstacles to our love, many social and cultural differences, but our glorious connection as star-crossed lovers was undeniable, and all the obstacles were finally overcome. Our shining path of destiny was clear. After a seven-year courtship, we were married.

Then, after a seven-year marriage, Lou died. My grief was devastating, sending me into a dark abyss. With Lou's death I came to know that my marvelous adventure with him was not just a finite earthly journey, but also an infinite spiritual one. In an effort to heal my broken spirit, I began to spew my thoughts, feelings, and revelations into a journal – a spiritual journal, a cathartic chronology of my quest for healing and restoration. This book is taken from that journal, my travelogue through life, love, loss, and eternity.

PART 51

Marking Time

August 2017 – October 2017

~ 1222 ~

HAPPINESS AND JOY

My intuitive friend Martha gave me a scroll that says, "There is no way to happiness. Happiness is the way." About the same time, I read an article in a Buddhist magazine that tried to explain the difference between happiness and joy. The article left me more puzzled than I was before. That is not surprising; these words are so hard to define. Even revered teachers have trouble describing the indescribable. The scroll made more sense to me.

Happiness as most people know it is earthbound; it is the dualistic opposite of sadness, as nirvana is the opposite of samsara. We feel happy when we are successful in satisfying our desires or allaying our fears, acquiring or averting that which the Three Poisons tempt us to pursue or avoid. Sadness is what we feel when we fail in the attempt.

Joy is eternal. It is immune to the poisons and their temptations in this world. It is one of the four qualities of a buddha, along with Loving-kindness, Compassion, and Equanimity. (~1030~) Like the other divine qualities, Joy represents the fusion of opposites, standing at a higher hermetic level, in the vortex, beyond cravings and aversions. Joy – St. Francis' "perfect joy" (~743~) – remains unperturbed, and is in fact perfected, through pain and suffering.

Joy is simple contentment, with gratitude for all that life brings, regardless of circumstances. To be more than just happy – to be joyful – is to know unshakable peace in this world, to rise above the struggles and strains of life. Joy is reflective of being on the path. To be as Jesus was – the Way and the Truth and the Life – to be the unnamed *Way* as the Dao is known; to be *Truth* as Allah is known; to live now, in this world, awake in eternal *Life* as the Buddha's enlightenment is known.

To know happiness in this way, as the conscious realization of Joy, means that when sadness enters, happiness does not depart. The soul remains content in the presence of both pleasure and pain, serene in the knowledge that all thoughts and emotions, like the physical body, are but transitory illusions, and that only one thing – divine Love – is ever-present, reflected in Loving-kindness, Compassion, Equanimity, and Joy.

In this passage, especially in the last two sentences, C.S. Lewis, perhaps unwittingly, explains the suffering of Job in the Bible and why bad things happen to good people:

> Everyone has noticed how hard it is to turn our thoughts to God when everything is going well with us. We 'have all we want' is a terrible saying when 'all' does not include God. We find God an interruption. As St. Augustine says somewhere, 'God wants to give us something, but cannot, because our hands are full—there's nowhere for Him to put it.' Or as a friend of mine said, 'We regard God as an airman regards his parachute; it's there for emergencies but he hopes he'll never have to use it.' Now God, who has made us, knows what we are and that our happiness lies in Him. Yet we will not seek it in Him as long as he leaves us any other resort where it can even plausibly be looked for. While what we call 'our own life' remains agreeable we will not surrender it to Him. What then can God do in our interests but make 'our own life' less agreeable to us, and take away the plausible source of false happiness? – C.S. Lewis, *The Problem of Pain* [56]

Joy – true happiness – cannot be found until pain reveals the true colors of false happiness and gives us no choice but to look to God. When we jettison both pleasure and pain, happiness and sadness, we find God … and Joy.

~ 1223 ~

A friend of mine who just celebrated her 60th birthday posted on Facebook a photo of herself as a young adult. Her image was so pure and innocent, as we all were at that time of life.

I, too, have some photos of myself at that young age, and I look at them with a wry smile. Do we ever ask ourselves questions about the babe in the picture, like, "Where is she now?" Do we try to educate her: "If only she knew then what I know now!" Do we cry over her lost innocence, or over her latent potential still, even now, unrealized?

Or do we remember how far we have come: "I've grown so much since those days," or "My life since then has been like a beautiful flower opening." I have become what I was meant to be.

~ 1224 ~

In an article about the impossibility of teaching Zen, Norman Fischer perfectly describes the bodhisattva condition, and my condition with Emily:

> Of course, the Zen teacher, an imperfect human being, is going to disappoint a fair number of those who come to practice. You will say and do things that are hurtful, even if you never intend to. Meaning to straighten someone out (always a dubious proposition), you will completely botch the job, reinforcing the behavior or view you were trying to soften. You will have all kinds of complicated and contradictory feelings about people who come to practice with you—loving them, worrying about them, dreading them, seeing them make terrible mistakes you can't prevent, watching as they manipulate you and set you up for all sorts of falls. In the end, you will realize you can't help them at all and will have to watch them suffer, or watch them make you suffer, and maintain your composure even so. – Zoketsu Norman Fischer, "No Teacher of Zen," *Buddhadharma*, Spring 2014, Fall 2017

Emily did not come to me looking for a Zen teacher, but she found one, anyway. So did I.

~ 1225 ~

I discovered another factor in Emily's personality disorder – the amygdala and its role in brain chemistry. From two independent sources I found the amygdala referenced as the part of the brain that responds physiologically to fear (the etiological basis of Emily's psychosis) and controls emotional regulation (her irrational anger that expresses her fear). From Kaia Roman, "Is That Your Intuition Talking (Or Just Your Fear)?":

> Fear feels bad, uncomfortable, and it activates the brain's amygdala, which is a sensor of sorts that's there in our brains to help keep us safe. When the amygdala is activated, it gives us three response options: fight, flight, or freeze. To make sure we have all of the brain power we need to carry out this instinctual response, the amygdala limits activity in the prefrontal cortex—which happens to be where logical thought, clear decisions, and rational choices are generated.[128]

And from Rochelle I. Frank, PhD and Joan Davidson, PhD; *The Transdiagnostic Road Map to Case Formulation and Treatment Planning*:

> Emotion regulation deficits are core features of bipolar spectrum conditions (Goodwin & Jamison, 2007) and borderline personality disorder (BPD) (Linehan, 1993a). Disruptions in dopamine and serotonin systems responsible for regulating emotion are associated with many of the hallmark symptoms of bipolar disorder, including depression, mania, and increased

appetitive behavior (Miklowitz & Johnson, 2006). The characteristic emotional hypersensitivity and associated behavioral dysregulation in BPD have been linked to increased amygdala activation (Herpertz et al., 2001). Trauma-related changes in neural structures are associated with hyperarousal, dissociation, and emotional numbing and dysregulation in PTSD (Malta, 2012).[129]

I asked myself years ago when my body chemistry became more acidic in my fear-driven post-Lou PTSD, and again later when each resurgence of divine love brought a resurgence of sex hormones: Does psychology change physiology, or the other way around? Do thoughts and feelings change body chemistry, or the other way around? I think it can go either way, but the ultimate way is when the love of the spirit moves the body and mind together as one.

Of course, I have always seen through Emily's abusive behavior to her buddha-nature underneath, and have instantly forgiven her for every affront. But with this new biological knowledge I am even less tempted to hold Emily responsible for her actions. Being a victim of psychological and physical abuse along with her probable genetic predisposition for mental illness stacks the deck against her. It is easy to see why her emotional dysregulation is not easily brought under control. Her mind and her body both work against her as she tries to calm her angry amygdala. Deep inside she wants to be a good person; she wants to be able to love and be loved in a healthy, mature way. But her demons have her by the throat.

~ 1226 ~

How do you know when you are born again, as the Christians say, or in Buddhist terminology, when you are enlightened? The answer is really very simple: When everything you do comes from divine love. When you hear your life instructions coming from your higher self, your God-self, your buddha-nature, not from base desires, emotions, and urges. When you know intuitively that you are doing God's work and God's will with your every thought, word, and deed. Even if you say or do things that may seem sinful to others, you are acting from God's love in their service, not your own. (see Walter Hilton's *The Ladder of Perfection*: ~1012~)

And when harm is done to you, even unto death, you can turn the other cheek, and thoughts of vengeance and retaliation never even enter your mind. When you can viscerally understand what drove Jesus to say, "Father, forgive them, for they know not what they do," knowing that the darkness which leads people to do harm is necessary in this world of duality, but will eventually dissipate with everything else into the invisible light of eternal love.

People who know this divine love, for whom the pleasure and pain of worldly life no longer hold power over them, are mystics. But one must use caution in declaring oneself a mystic, a bodhisattva, a shaman, or a "born again" Christian. In addition to one's own intuitive knowledge of one's enlightenment comes the reflection of it from the outside; other people also see it and respond to it. In many places in this journal I describe my hesitancy to ascribe to myself these titles, but my mystic suspicions are validated when others reflect them back to me.

How did Jesus respond when asked if he was the Son of God? In one account he said, "I am." In another account he said, "You have said so." Validation from inside and outside.

~ 1227 ~

Ignacio's discussion group is exploring mysticism, reading an article by Jay McDaniel, "Process and Mysticism." McDaniel did as well as he could to bring process thought to bear on mysticism, but it was inevitably a futile attempt. Process thought is totally earthbound; the concept of "process" only has meaning in the framework of time, events unfolding one after another in a sequential "process." Mysticism, on the other hand, is about realms beyond space and time. Mysticism cannot be known in terms of process.

A large part of McDaniel's confusion seemed to be about the difference between *makyo* and *satori*. He describes as mystical experiences occurrences that might not rise to the level of *satori*, but be only *makyo*. I was again led to synchronistic readings from Buddhist sources that made clear the distinction between *makyo* and *satori*. Here is a summary of the difference:

Makyo (nyam, in Tibetan)	**Satori (tokpa)**
1. Usually sudden, unprepared, not related to other signs or events.	1. Prepared via study, meditation, contemplation, prayer; convergence of synchronicities; the prepared "zap" described by Trungpa (~1211~)
2. Hallucination, illusion, figment of the imagination, little or no deep meaning.	2. More than hallucination, a change of consciousness, seeing into one's true nature, seeing emptiness.

3. No lasting effect. A desire to hang on to or repeat the experience may arise, which is the temptation to cling or grasp – the first poison.

3. Everlasting effect. One is fundamentally, involuntarily, and irreversibly changed. No craving or need to repeat the experience.

4. Usually happens in meditation, perhaps being a phantom of the mind caused by sitting still for a long time.

4. Can happen anytime, anywhere, in sleep or meditation, at home or at work, in the course of ordinary life.

5. May or may not have relevance to spiritual journey.

5. Always has relevance to spiritual journey, points the way.

6. May be pleasant or frightening, possibly evoking emotion.

6. Neither pleasant nor frightening, but always awesome, liberating, beyond emotion, infused with eternal presence.

The definition of a mystic is someone who communicates directly with Source, not needing an intermediary like scripture, clergy, or ritual. *Makyo* are usually passing illusions sometimes attributed to altered brain chemistry. *Satori* are true spiritual messages coming into consciousness from beyond consciousness. Therefore true mystic experiences must be *satori*, not *makyo*.

Makyo are not unimportant; they can be precursors of *satori*, the first opening of a portal that, with spiritual maturation, could lead to awakening. *Anuttara samyak sambodhi* is the highest state of awakening, generally believed to be unattainable until death, the earthly body being an impediment to complete liberation from *dukkha*.

My biggest disappointment with McDaniel's account of mysticism came when he said, "Mysticism can be evil, too." *Not so*. All mystics awaken to and arrive at the same Source. Christian, Buddhist, Sufi, Hindu, Jewish, Daoist, and shamanic mystics take different paths but all find the same truth, the same oneness, which is beyond the dualistic concept of good and evil. Mysticism cannot be evil, and by the same token, cannot be good. Once you have experienced *satori*, even a little one, you never look at the world the same way again. The mystic always sees this world of duality from the perspective of, in the context of, the timeless eternal oneness.

Based on the above criteria, I consider the three events in my life that I call epiphanies (~232~/~340~/~604~) to be true mystical experiences, *satori*, that revealed eternity and set me on a lifelong spiritual path. Weaving in and around these pillars of awakening have been many dreams, visions, trances, animal and human encounters, some of which may fall into the category of *makyo*. These *makyo* do not increase my level of awakening, but they give me comfort and encouragement along the path. Through these *makyo*, God and the spirits let me know they are still with me.

In his book *Mysticism*, F.C. Happold lists seven characteristics of mystical states (~933~), which I can validate from my own experience. But is everyone who has had a mystical experience a mystic? I have added to Happold's list the following additional criteria to determine whether the sum total of a person's experience adds up to being a full-fledged mystic:

1. **Multiple spiritual experiences**. Communication with the spirits is ongoing. Spiritual experiences, both *satori* and *makyo*, happen repeatedly, often piling up to the point that one's life is engulfed and defined by them. Some of these events can be ordinary natural phenomena – feathers, rainbows, opening to a random passage in a book, shoulder straps breaking – but which have special meaning to the mystic.

2. **Loving-kindness, Compassion, Joy, and Equanimity** – the defining characteristics of a buddha. Divine love spontaneously drives every thought, word, and deed. Emotions arise but are channeled into higher purpose. Even anger is put to constructive, loving use.

3. **Total surrender.** No ego-driven behaviors. Chögyam Trungpa Rinpoche said, "Enlightenment is ego's ultimate disappointment." No law, no sin. Automatic, unintentional, effortless practice of the Five Precepts, the Six Perfections, the Eightfold Path, the Ten Commandments, and other such moral guidelines.

4. **External recognition.** The mystic's love, compassion, and wisdom are visible to others. Some mystics in the early stages don't know that they are mystics, but they are known as such to others by their auras and their actions. Some people feel comforted by the mystic's light and seek to bask in it; others feel threatened by it and seek to extinguish it. But the mystic's expression of divine love remains constant toward both his disciples and his destroyers.

The above criteria, which describe the permanent changes that take place in an individual's life after *satori*, might be helpful in deciding whether an isolated spiritual experience is *makyo* or indeed satori. There are degrees of mysticism, as in the ten bhūmi of the bodhisattva, and satori can come in degrees, each successive satori leading to a higher level of awakening. This progression can perhaps be seen as "process" from the worldly perspective, but with each new *satori*, time recedes farther into the background until it disappears in *anuttara samyak sambodhi*.

Some but not all mystics possess psychic or healing powers, can walk on fire without being burned, or levitate, but every true mystic can be known by the indestructible and irreversible presence of divine love, which exudes from every pore.

~ 1228 ~

Last night was the first concert I have played in a while. I struggled to get motivated to practice for it, procrastinating mightily and fighting my ever-shortening attention span. I wondered if it is time to retire completely, if my spiritual path might no longer include my musical vocation.

But I played well. Not perfectly, but well enough that a dozen audience members gave me glowing reviews and congratulatory hugs afterward. One of my fellow performers said, "You are fantastic! I love playing with you. You make it seem so easy."

How do I reconcile this evidence of continuing competence with my declining motivation? My musical career is like Velcro – I keep trying to pull away from it, but it won't let go. There are more concerts in my near future. Let's see where they take me.

~ 1229 ~

Another great book has crossed my path, given to me by Martha: *Why People Don't Heal and How They Can*,[160] by Caroline Myss. In this book Caroline gives me yet another insight into the psyche of Emily:

> In addition to her painful childhood history, Mary also had a history of chronic ailments. She was always in pain—some days emotional, some days physical. Though she was kind and always ready to support her friends, she much preferred the company of people who had also had abusive childhoods. That day at our lunch, I realized that Mary needed to be with people who spoke the same language and shared the same mindset and behaviors. I immediately began to think of this attitude as "woundology." I have since become convinced that when we define ourselves by our wounds, we burden and lose our physical and spiritual energy and open ourselves to the risk of illness.

I remember a time early in our friendship when Emily asked me if I had a difficult relationship with my mother. She seemed to want me to relate incidents of discord, so I told her about my mother's angry outburst at me over a minor infraction. Emily seemed pleased to hear this; she clutched at my story as if she needed us to share some kind of childhood trauma to bind us together. This desire for camaraderie between us as fellow victims also explains her habit of projecting onto me so many of her own past injuries. And Emily's ongoing ailments, physical and emotional, validate Caroline's observation that defining oneself by one's wounds can lead to chronic illness.

I have often wondered, given Emily's unhealed woundedness and her apparent denial of her severe social dysfunction, if she could be any good at her job of marriage and family counseling. Her own life is littered with abusive and failed relationships. She has never known any other kind. Is it possible for someone who has never known a healthy relationship to help others find one? But perhaps she practices "woundology" with her clients and finds with them, and they with her, preferred company. Perhaps in that comfortable company of people who "speak the same language and share the same mindset and behaviors" she can offer some real help.

Caroline continues:

> So many people in the midst of a "process" of healing, I saw, are at the same time feeling stuck. They are striving to confront their wounds, valiantly working to bring meaning to terrible past experiences and traumas, and exercising compassionate understanding of others who share their wounds. But they are not healing. They have redefined their lives around their wounds and the process of accepting them. They are not working to get beyond their wounds. In fact, they are stuck in their wounds. Now primed to hear people speak woundology, I believe I was meant to challenge the assumptions that I and many others then held dear—especially the assumption that everyone who is wounded or ill wants the full recovery of their health.

Here, too, is a spot-on description of Emily – the wounded one stuck in her wounds. And me – the empath who, at least in the beginning, assumed that Emily wanted to be healed. She knows what it is to be sick and stuck, and she responds to that kinetic reality. I know what it is for her to be healed and free, and I respond to that latent potentiality.

The power of woundology is so strong that sometimes we make up wounds to gain sympathy. C.S. Lewis describes a *faux* woundology that can be found in the social repertoire of many people:

> Did we pretend to be angry about one thing when we knew, or could have known, that our anger had a different and much less presentable cause? Did we pretend to be "hurt" in our sensitive and tender feelings when envy, ungratified vanity, or thwarted self-will was our real trouble? Such tactics often succeed. The other parties give in. They give in not because they don't know what is really wrong with us but because they have long known it only too well … It needs surgery which they know we will never face. And so we win; by cheating. But the unfairness is very deeply felt. Indeed what is commonly called "sensitiveness" is the most powerful engine of domestic tyranny, sometimes a lifelong tyranny. – C.S. Lewis, *Reflections on the Psalms* [161]

~ 1230 ~

A couple days ago I sent a package to Emily's office address. It came back from the post office marked undeliverable. I re-sent the package to her home address and asked her if she had given up the office. "Yes, I gave up that office this summer," she replied.

Back in April I had a dream that Vincent was negotiating the lease for the office they had shared. I wonder if he is still there. Emily wouldn't say.

~ 1231 ~

I attended the Yom Kippur service at the Jewish temple this evening. It was a fine service, and reminded me that Judaism is the root of Christianity. Especially the guilt part. Yom Kippur is particularly guilt-ridden, being the Day of Atonement, for confession and forgiveness of multitudinous sins.

Jesus was not the first to forgive sins. The Jews were already forgiven before Jesus came along:

> Moses prayed to God:
> "As you have been faithful to this people ever since Egypt,
> Please forgive their failings now,
> In keeping with your boundless love."
> And God responded: "I forgive, as you have asked."
>   (Numbers 14:19-20 RSV)

I noticed the name of my fire god, Adonai, who spoke to Moses from the burning bush, sprinkled throughout the Hebrew liturgy:

> Baruch atah, Adonai Eloheinu …
> Hear, O Israel, Adonai is our God, Adonai is One!
> Blessed is God's glorious majesty forever and ever.
> May God's great name be blessed to the end of time.

Jesus' prayer, the Lord's Prayer, also invoked the name of God: "Our Father, who art in heaven, hallowed be thy name." But there is the wise saying in the *Dao De Ching*: "The Dao (Way) that can be named is not the Dao." So which is it, does God have a name, or not?

What is your name?" Moses asked the god that summoned him from the burning bush. It was *ehyeh asher ehyeh*: "I am what I am." This enigmatic phrase was a Hebrew idiom of deliberate vagueness, which meant, in effect, "Never mind who I am!" or even "Mind your own business!" In the ancient world, to know somebody's name meant that you had power over him. God was not to be controlled and manipulated in this way. – Karen Armstrong, *The Great Transformation*

God refused Moses' request for a name by which to identify him. The voice in the burning bush simply said, "I am." Not really a name, but a statement of eternal truth, of simply "being" in the worldly sense. Adonai condescended to Moses and the limited understanding of earthly beings by giving him descriptive words to use to identify God, but the true God, the Godhead, the Dao, the Source, cannot really be named. God is revealed on earth in formless, nameless waves – in wind, in water, in light, and in our invisible, unnamable souls which transcend this life, our physical bodies, and our earthly egos and identities.

By giving God a name, whether Adonai, Emanuel, or even Yahweh (translation of "I am" [i]), we limit God and separate "him" from "us" – from all the people and things who also have names and separate identities. We topple God from his eternal throne and bring him down to earth in fragments, chips off the old block, like us.

But God the Source is never split, or named, remaining one and indivisible in eternity, in the third realm above the realms of good and evil – above the dualistic pairs of opposites where everything is given a name, in the eternity that is inside and outside all things.

The Buddhists explain this better than the Christians or the Jews:

> [Enlightenment] is not transcendent of our ordinary way of being; it's more like we've been living in two dimensions, and now there are three. Strawberries still taste like strawberries and harsh words are still harsh, but now we're aware of how everything interpermeates everything else, and that even the most difficult things are lit from within by the same undivided light. – Joan Sutherland, "What Is Enlightenment?"[131]

~ 1232 ~

In an interview with Caroline Myss at the Hay House World Psychic Summit 2017, Caroline described "woundology," the wounded condition that likely contributes to Emily's psychotic behavior, and the conscious recognition of it that would be necessary for her to be liberated:

---

[i] The word "Lord" when spelled with capital letters, stands for the divine name, *YHWH*, which is here connected with the verb *hayah*, to be. (footnote to Exodus 3:15 RSV)

A person who is a wounded child, the wounds in that person, give a person permission to behave in a certain way: I can use my wounds to control other people. And one day that person has to become conscious of the fact that I like using my wounds to control other people. I may not have financial power. I may not have political power. I may not have any other power in my family, but I do have this, and I can make people feel bad for me. And I can use the wounds in my childhood, and every time I play that card, I get my way.

And one day, maybe that person will become conscious of the fact that they're doing that. Now it's conscious. Now I have to own it. And now at that point, it's a game-changer. Now I have to take responsibility for the fact that I am consciously choosing to hurt you using my wounds.

I can blame my childhood. I can do whatever I want. I can make up things. That, too, is conscious. I'm choosing to come up with excuses to allow me to get away with this. I can hold my mother responsible, but guess what, she's not here and that was forty years ago. I am still of my own free will choosing to make a dark choice, and it's hurting another person, but it suits me.[130]

Caroline then went on to describe the narcissist and the entitlement of suffering:

We also have a society in which suffering is rewarded. I suffered and, therefore, I am owed something. I am owed more respect, I am owed more sympathy, I'm owed more tenderness, I am owed something, and therefore, if I give up the facts, the stories of my suffering, if I let them go, either through forgiveness or simply by stopping the telling of my stories of suffering, then I let go of a whole identity. And if I can't bring suffering to the party, then who will I be? And I, then, will not have permission to make others suffer. I have to keep this string of suffering alive because it gives me authority to do what I do.[130]

And then the meaning of suffering in the life of Christ and how such suffering can be transmuted into perfect joy:

To me, religion is nonsense, but Jesus is, to me, the greatest spiritual teacher that ever walked the Earth. He and Buddha, but Jesus for me is the greatest teacher of healing and cosmic truth. And it wasn't about some mythic god sending down a mythic son who would hang on a cross and now God's happy, now I'm happy. It was about a man who said, you know what, I am going to go through all the things you use as an excuse to kill each other, and I'm going to show you a different option, and it was a mystical option, a journey into mystical law. It was an archetypal mystical cosmic drama that, unless you look through your soul, it will never make any sense.

He said, I'm going to be betrayed by friends, I'm going to be abandoned by God, I won't hear him for the first time in my whole journey on Earth. Will you take this away from me? I don't hear you; okay, then I'll do it. I'll be beaten to shreds. It'll be the most brutal death of the time, and I won't fight back. I'll absorb all of this, the humiliation, the pain, the grief, I'll accept it all. There's a reason greater than I can understand because I'm being directed to this.

There's a law greater than the one that you see in front of you. It's not about your petty justice. It's about listening to whatever commands are commanding your soul. And if you can get this, you will not kill each other because of an action that happens in front of you immediately. That is the pain I'm trying to save you from, your own foolishness.[130]

Caroline, who says religion is nonsense (even though she is a practicing Catholic), has explained the meaning of Christ's crucifixion and the subordination of civil law and Mosaic Law to the soul's divine command as well as any theologian has.

~ 1233 ~

GOOD AND EVIL, Part 10

God does really in a sense contain evil—i.e., contains what is the real motive power behind all our evil desires. He knows what we want, even in our vilest acts: He is longing to give it to us. He is not looking on from the outside at some new "taste" or "separate desire of our own." Only because He has laid up real goods for us to desire are we able to go wrong by snatching at them in greedy, misdirected ways. The truth is that evil is not a real thing at all, like God. It is simply good spoiled. That is why I say there can be good without evil, but no evil without good. You know what the biologists mean by a parasite—an animal that lives on another animal. Evil is a parasite. It is there only because good is there for it to spoil and confuse. – C.S. Lewis, *The Collected Letters of C.S. Lewis, Volume II* [85]

From a certain perspective, Lewis is right. Lucifer was a fallen angel, good spoiled. But Lewis, like many others, confuses or conflates earthly good – the temporal opposite of evil – with eternal Goodness, in which both earthly opposites are contained. When Lewis says, "The truth is that evil is not a real thing at all, like God," he really means like the Godhead. Worldly good and evil are both unreal, having these equal and opposite characteristics/descriptors:

Good: heaven – pleasure – happiness – light
Evil: hell – pain – sadness – darkness

Goodness has none (or all) of these characteristics. A better word for divine "good" is divine "love." Its prime characteristics are Loving-kindness, Equanimity, Compassion, and Joy, which are unchanging amid the ever-changing maelstrom of worldly good and evil.

Lewis says, "there can be good without evil, but no evil without good." Here is the other side of that coin:

Good arises with evil. To have good, there must also be evil. Lewis' point is also correct – to have evil, there must be good. Lewis argues the converse of National Geographic's point: Without good, how would we have developed our human characteristics – meanness, cruelty, vengeance? Both views are true. Interdependent co-arising demands that for one to arise, there must be the other.

Are "human characteristics" confined to humans? Do good and evil exist outside the human realm? Events take place in nature among non-humans that, when they happen among humans, we call evil. Animals engage in brutal wars of conquest; they fight and sometimes kill for territory or mates; the female praying mantis bites off the head of her male partner; spiders torture their prey; dogs bite; bees sting; pack rats steal.

To the extent that non-humans understand these instinctive behaviors as humans do, as evil, they must also possess the positive virtues of kindness, mercy, and forgiveness. This raises the question of whether good and evil behaviors in both humans and non-humans arise from instinct, conscious choice, or semi-conscious choice coerced by physical, emotional, or spiritual factors such as fear, mental illness, or demons. (Animals, like humans, can be fearful, mentally ill, or possessed.)

One knows my demand of philosophers that they place themselves *beyond* good and evil – that they have the illusion of moral judgment *beneath* them. This demand follows from an insight first formulated by me: *that there are no moral facts whatever.* Moral judgment has this in common with religious judgment that it believes in realities which do not exist. – Friedrich Nietzsche, *Twilight of the Idols*

We often do evil things to accomplish what we think are good things – to protect and provide for our ourselves, our families, and our communities. Lying, cheating, stealing, unfair competition in business, and warfare are reflective of greed getting ahead of good.

Jesus placed himself beyond good and evil, above moral judgment, when he said, "Judge not, lest ye be judged." I think the rest of the biosphere understands earthly dichotomous behaviors as Nietzsche, Jesus, Jung, and the Buddha understood them, not as good and evil, but simply as the way life is – the Source expressed in equal and opposite archetypal patterns.

Instinct and intuition override thought and sensation. Enlightened behavior, whether in animals or humans, is directed not by analysis and intention, but by simple "knowing," which sublimates the desires and fears of the mind and body. When we arrive at this "knowing," we return to the Garden of Eden via the narrow gate.

~ 1234 ~

HEALTH, *Part 17*

The patient is enraged and feels something akin to despair. If she's honest with herself, what she wanted from this appointment was not in the doctor's power to give her. She wanted to be cured of what she has come to know and cannot ever seem to fully forget: her body will fail her. What she's interpreted as the shocking fallibility of her doctors is more accurately interpreted as a normal rite of passage—her move from the world of health into the world of unfixable ailments and, eventually, her demise. No doctor will be able to prevent death from happening to her.

She recalls a question she was asked by the very first ear doctor, the one who thought she might have Ménière's disease. The doctor was curious about the ringing. She said, "Before the ringing started, what did it use to sound like in your ear?"

The patient had tried to remember what it used to sound like in her ear before the ringing started. She couldn't. Now the irony of this failure strikes her. She should try to hear what she's previously ignored. She should try to register what the absence of illness sounds like while she's lucky enough to be able to appreciate all that's not there. She stops on the sidewalk. She closes her eyes. She listens. – Heidi Julavits, "Diagnose This: How to be your own best doctor," *Harper's Magazine*, April 2014

I used to ask myself, "Why do I have tinnitus?" I never asked, "Why did I *not* have tinnitus before?" People often ask, "Why is there pain and suffering in the world?" but rarely ask, "Why is there pleasure and comfort in the world?" We think that getting what we want and avoiding what we don't want is the default condition of life, and when we don't get what we want, something has gone wrong. Then we spend the rest of our lives trying to reset the defaults. Eventually life shows us that there are no default settings. Anything goes.

There are millions of people for whom pain and suffering seem to be default settings – the disabled, the homeless, those with chronic mental or physical illness, those who have lived through famine, torture, or abuse. Satisfaction, contentment, and happiness are measured very differently for these people than for those who are comfortable and fully functional.

The answer to all "Why?" questions is the same – because that's just the way it is. Pain, suffering, pleasure, comfort, sickness, and health are all part of every life, and are defined differently from different perspectives. Each person's suffering is uniquely his own.

When you change the way you look at things, the things you look at change. Accept both pleasure and pain, sound and silence, with equanimity. Change the way you look at them, the way you listen to them.

~ 1235 ~

TIME AND ETERNITY, Part 6

Messages have been coming to me about the elasticity of time, its relation to space, and the relationship of space and time to eternity. From a Hay House Psychic Summit 2017 interview with Collette Baron-Reid:

> So you have to just be—that's the other thing about linear time. Okay, so we all think that we're living in a world with time that goes from A to B, that our experience goes, here's my now and there's my future down there. But the truth is, that's a man-made construct. And time is so elusive. It expands, it contracts. You could be thinking you're seeing something two weeks down the road and then you forget about it and it happens two years later, so you have to give up your attachment to timing on anything.

Existentialist philosopher Søren Kierkegaard understood that each moment contains all of time. He said, "The moment is not properly an atom of time but an atom of eternity." Alan Watts said much the same thing in *The Way of Zen*, "It is rather the past and future which are the fleeting illusions, and the present which is eternally real." C.S. Lewis also touched on this idea in *The World's Last Night*, "The taking up into God's nature of humanity, with all its ignorances and limitations, is not itself a temporal event, though the humanity which is so taken up was, like our own, a thing living and dying in time." And Jorge Luis Borges in *Labyrinths*, "Time is the substance I am made of. Time is a river that carries me away, but I am the river; it is a tiger that mangles me, but I am the tiger; it is a fire that consumes me, but I am the fire." And Hermann Hesse in *Siddhartha*, "Have you also learned that secret from the river; that there is no such thing as time? That the river is everywhere at the same time, at the source and at the mouth, at the waterfall, at the ferry, at the current, in the ocean and in the mountains, everywhere and that the present only exists for it, not the shadow of the past nor the shadow of the future."

Space and time are the same thing, the same infinity/eternity viewed from different angles. This is the miraculous discovery of Einstein's Theory of Relativity: At the speed of light, time and space implode into each other. Imagine a piece of stretchy fabric being pulled apart; as the whole cloth expands, its separate threads visibly separate from each other. The oneness of the cloth is then perceived as a collection of interwoven components – as the fabric of eternity is pulled apart, but without being torn asunder, to reveal its separate elements in space and time, the separate jewels in Indra's Net.

Part of the reason that we have such a hard time understanding time is that we have no language or thought processes to adequately describe it. Maria Popova comments on Alan Burdick's book *Why Time Flies: A Mostly Scientific Investigation*:

> Burdick asks: For argument's sake, I'll accept that perhaps the universe did not exist before the Big Bang—but it exploded in something, right? What was that? What was there before the beginning? Proposing such questions, the astrophysicist Stephen Hawking has said, is like standing at the South Pole and asking which way is south: "Earlier times simply would not be defined."
>
> Perhaps Hawking is trying to be reassuring. What he seems to mean is that human language has a limit. We (or at least the rest of us) reach this boundary whenever we ponder the cosmic. We imagine by analogy and metaphor: that strange and vast thing is like this smaller, more familiar thing. The universe is a cathedral, a clockworks, an egg. But the parallels ultimately diverge; only an egg is an egg. Such analogies appeal precisely because they are tangible elements of the universe. As terms, they are self-contained—but they cannot contain the container that holds them. So it is with time. Whenever we talk about it, we do so in terms of something lesser. We find or lose time like a set of keys; we save and spend it like money. Time creeps, crawls, flies, flees, flows, and stands still; it is abundant or scarce; it weighs on us with palpable heft.[133]

Ignacio says that our thoughts are more than our words, and our experience is more than our thoughts. Words cannot completely convey our thoughts, and thoughts cannot completely capture our experience. Michael Carroll, a Vajrayana Buddhist and student of Chögyam Trungpa, explains the difference between thought and experience: "Coffee is a thought. Drinking is an experience. You have an experience, then you name it." You think about it, talk about it, name it, and the mystery disappears.

This is why "knowing" is indescribable. No metaphor, analogy, symbol, or any construct of language or even nonverbal thought can accomplish the quantum leap that is required to "know" the ultimate truth. Sufi poet Jalāl ad-Dīn Muhammad Rumi said, "I wonder why I ever thought to use language." (So … why did I ever think to write this book?)

PART 52

Prayer

October 2017 – January 2018

~ 1236 ~

Buddhist author Mark Unno writes about the difference between prayers *for* and prayers *of*.[134] Reflecting on his words, I see that prayers *for* are about *getting* something – health, wealth, comfort, victory, peace. Prayers *of* are about *giving* something – gratitude, acceptance, reverence, forgiveness, sympathy, love.

Prayers *for* beg to be answered, and when they aren't, we feel abandoned by God. Prayers *of*, says Unno, "are the prayers of buddhas and bodhisattvas – that is, prayers arising out of the awakened mind." Awakened minds do not pray *for* anything, because in the blessed poverty of unsupported thought, there is nothing they need or want. They know that they cannot be abandoned by God because they have awakened to the ever-present God within them. Prayers *of* need no answer, because the prayer is its own completion. Prayers *for* seek action or change on the earthly plane; prayers *of* simply acknowledge the unchanging condition on the eternal plane.

Caroline Myss sends a similar message from the Christian point of view:

> One day as I was saying the rosary, I realized that I did not have an agenda as such. I was just praying for the sake of praying. It had to be one of the most mind-blowing experiences of my life. I couldn't think of a thing to ask for—which was a bit like sitting on Santa's lap and drawing a blank. I started to float in the experience of praying without an agenda. The feeling was truly euphoric. And then I knew that this was the first time I had experienced an unconditional sense of faith and trust in God. I had no complaints to state, no wish list, no this or that. I only wanted to float in this light space of trust. – Caroline Myss, https://www.myss.com/the-essence-of-faith

The last day of Jesus' life gives us instruction in the transition from prayers *for* to prayers *of*. In Gethsemane he prayed for deliverance from the horror he was about to face: "My Father, if it be possible, let this cup pass from me;" and then he moved to a prayer of acceptance: "Thy will be done." On the cross he fell back into fear: "My God, my God, why hast thou forsaken me?" But he also rose above his worldly self with his prayer of forgiveness: "Father, forgive them, for they know not what they do."

Prayers *of* arise out of the eternal stillness of the awakened mind, but righteous prayers *for* can be no less awakened, arising not from greed or fear but from the high hermetic levels of ever-changing duality: "Thy kingdom come, thy will be done, on earth as it is in heaven." As utterances of the God-self, prayers for peace and healing call upon the Power of Intention and the Law of Attraction to strengthen and empower loving, healing connections here on earth:

> The Hebrew word *davar* means both deed and word, and the *davar* of prayer is a worded action and a doing speech. We put those words out into the world, hone our energies as tools for wellbeing and affirmed belonging. We elevate and focus our *kavanah*, our intention. Prayer gives God the gifts of our intention, our energy, our hope to use to create deeper human belonging, greater engagement, richer connection.
>
> In such a world, prayer for healing is meeting in a depth more resonant and aware than our normal consciousness. We focus the vibrations of our minds and hearts and direct that intention to God and, through God, toward the resilient, vibrating patterns of energy that are our loved ones, the objects of our concern. We strengthen the us-ness of them. We raise to explicit consciousness the vague concern for the other and we sharpen that concern into praise, petition and empathy. – Rabbi Bradley Shavit Artson, "What Are We Doing When We Pray?"[ii]

Honen Shonin, founder of the Buddhist Jodo sect, said that illness is the result of unwholesome residual karma. As such, one cannot prevent illness through prayer to any deity: "If prayer could heal and prolong life, there would be no illness, there would be no death." No matter how hard we pray, we cannot change this reality.

The only thing we can do is in Nichiren's teaching of Tenju-Kyoju, lessening one's karmic retribution: "If one's heavy karma from the past is not expiated within this lifetime, one must undergo the sufferings of hell in the future, but if one experiences extreme hardship in this life, the sufferings of hell will vanish instantly." Prayer cannot change the current reality, but because of the prayer, through our trust in the great compassion of the Buddha, we can let go of fear and have peace of mind. We can turn prayers *for* into prayers *of*.

Another understanding of Tenju-Kyoju is to spread the heavy burden over many people. The heavy burden stays heavy if one person tries to carry it alone, but when more people hold it, the burden can be lighter. This is strengthening the "us-ness" of Rabbi Artson.

[ii] https://www.openhorizons.org/what-are-we-doing-when-we-pray1.html

~ 1237 ~

Theologians have sometimes asked whether we shall 'know one another' in Heaven, and whether the particular love-relations worked out on earth would then continue to have any significance. It seems reasonable to reply: 'It may depend on what kind of love it had become, or was becoming, on earth.' For, surely, to meet in the eternal world someone for whom your love in this, however strong, had been merely natural, would not be (on that ground) even interesting. Would it not be like meeting in adult life someone who had seemed to be a great friend at your preparatory school solely because of common interests and occupations? If there was nothing more, if he was not a kindred soul, he will now be a total stranger. You no longer want to swap your help with his French exercise for his help with your arithmetic. In Heaven, I suspect, a love that had never embodied Love Himself would be equally irrelevant. For Nature has passed away. All that is not eternal is eternally out of date. – C.S. Lewis, *The Four Loves* [125]

Jesus said that in the resurrection we neither marry nor are given in marriage. Lewis explains why this is. Marriage is a social contract which may or may not embody "Love Himself." I take Lewis' "merely natural" love to mean a selfish attachment that comes from instinct and ego, driven by one's own worldly needs and desires. This is not love at all. Like lust that leads to marriage, it is not in service to the other, and so is "eternally out of date."

If Lewis had applied the same logic to good and evil (~1233~) that he used here regarding "love-relations worked out on earth," he would have seen that, as earthly love has no relevance in heaven, so it is with earthly good and evil. "For Nature has passed away."

~ 1238 ~

My fear of pain and disability is the last hurdle I must clear before I can pass through the narrow gate. Selfishness is still with me. I want spiritual elevation because, as Jesuit mystic Anthony de Mello says, I want relief – relief from discomfort, but more important, from my fear of discomfort.

I can engage in intellectual philosophical pursuits and find meaning, truth, and satisfaction, joyfully pondering spiritual matters of time and eternity – as long as my body is not struggling or in pain, demanding my attention. But when even a minor ailment sets in, all my otherworldly awareness goes away and I am pulled back into preoccupation with self.

My imagination works overtime; I project myself into a future of terror that flashes back to the terror of my past. My empathic nature causes me to respond viscerally, emotionally, and sometimes irrationally when I contemplate the potentially major suffering that might ensue if my minor ailments go rogue. I feel the pain of my hypothetically suffering self even though the feared physical suffering, so far, hasn't happened.

Suffering is our response to fear. I suffer not from actual pain, but from fear of pain. I am still seeking freedom *from* pain; better would be freedom *in* pain, peace in the midst of the storm.

~ 1239 ~

Early in my spiritual journey, I sensed that *agape*, the love of God, was spooky – detached, cold, emotionless, like the humanoids in the film *The Invasion of the Body Snatchers*. (~7~) In the intervening years I have found a deeper understanding of *agape*. The calm, peaceful bliss of divine love is not the absence of all emotion; it is the presence, acceptance, and transcendence of all emotion. It is the substitution of Compassion, Joy, Loving-kindness, and Equanimity for the passions; detachment from the tug of war between the pairs of opposites, but fully and eternally attached to the God-self/buddha-nature at the heart chakra. I don't fear the body snatchers anymore.

~ 1240 ~

HALLOWEEN

My dear Emily,

On Halloween four years ago, we discovered that we share a great love. That love has not changed. Even though our daily lives are not intertwined as they used to be, our spiritual union is as close as ever. I am still your good shepherd, loving you just as you are, anger and all. I am not perfect, but my love is.

~ 1241 ~

I attended an all-day conference for fundraising professionals. At the luncheon I looked around for an open seat at a table in the back of the room. I found one beckoning to me. As I sat down and began to eat my salad, I noticed that the tables were numbered. I had inadvertently chosen table #44. The angels, known by the Angel Number 4, are still with me.

~ 1242 ~

Delight is a bell that rings as you set your foot on the first step of a new flight of stairs leading upwards. Once you have started climbing you will notice only the hard work: it is when you have reached the landing and catch sight of the new stair that you may expect the bell again. – C.S. Lewis, *The Collected Letters of C.S. Lewis, Volume II* [85]

C.S. Lewis once again comes to my rescue as I wonder why the miracles seem to have stopped in my life. I pine for the bell to ring again, but Lewis tells me to be patient. I am standing on the landing, having climbed one set of stairs; another bell will ring to signal my climb to the next level of elevation … Ohhh … the back of my neck is tingling … spiritual input through the 5th chakra … bell ringing.

~ 1243 ~

A blind man has few friends; a blind man who has recently received his sight has, in a sense, none. He belongs neither to the world of the blind nor to that of the seeing, and no one can share his experience. After that night's conversations Robin never mentioned to anyone his problem about light. He knew that he would only be suspected of madness. When Mary took him out the next day for his first walk he replied to everything she said, "It's lovely—all lovely. Just let me drink it in," and she was satisfied. She interpreted his quick glances as glances of delight. In reality, of course, he was searching, searching with a hunger that had already something of desperation in it. Even had he dared, he knew it would be useless to ask her of any of the objects he saw, "Is that light?" He could see for himself that she would only answer, "No. That's green" (or "blue," or "yellow," or "a field," or "a tree," or "a car"). Nothing could be done until he had learned to go for walks by himself. – C.S. Lewis, *The Dark Tower* [135]

God has no image. God is invisible light. God is invisible wind. God is not a color or a tree or a car. Yet God is made visible in the images projected to the seer when he looks at all these God-given things. Yes, the blind man who receives his sight is a seer, one who sees. And yes, the seer must walk alone, because others who cannot see as he does suspect him of madness.

The more I read of C.S. Lewis, the more I respect him as a great 20th century mystic, along with Joseph Campbell, Thich Nhat Hanh, and Anthony de Mello. He is a seer.

~ 1244 ~

APOLOGY AND FORGIVENESS, Part 5

The rabbi at the Jewish temple described three kinds of forgiveness in the Jewish tradition:

The first kind of forgiveness is *mechilah*, "forgoing the other's indebtedness." This is not a reconciliation of heart or an embracing of the offender; it is simply reaching the conclusion that the offender no longer owes me anything for whatever it was that he or she did. The tradition, however, is quite clear that the offended person is not obligated to offer *mechilah* if the offender is not sincere in his or her repentance and has not taken concrete steps to correct the wrong done. Without good grounds, the offended person should not forgo the indebtedness of the sinner; otherwise, the sinner may never truly repent and evil will be perpetuated.

The second kind of forgiveness is *selichah*, "forgiveness." It is an act of the heart. *Selichah*, too, is not a reconciliation or an embracing of the offender; it is simply reaching the conclusion that the offender, too, is human, frail, and deserving of sympathy. It is closer to an act of mercy than to an act of grace.

The third kind of forgiveness is *kapparah*, "atonement or purification." This is a total wiping away of all sinfulness. It is an existential cleansing. *Kapparah* is the ultimate form of forgiveness, but it is only granted by God. No human can "atone" the sin of another; no human can "purify" the spiritual pollution of another. *[This is one reason why the Pharisees condemned Jesus, because he forgave sins, which only God could do.]*

Mechilah seems to be a quest for justice, a lower chakra elemental first step toward the idea of true forgiveness. Justice requires repentance and restitution. The rabbi said, "God does not forgive a wrongdoing that was done against another until that person forgives him first." This is like the tit-for-tat forgiveness in the Lord's Prayer; to be forgiven we must forgive those who sin against us. Forgiveness for our sins co-arises as we forgive others.

Selichah is like the forgiveness requested from the cross by Jesus for his torturers – an expression of compassion at the 4th chakra, the next step after justice. It is the realization that life's actions and events are directed at a higher level than the human will. The rabbi quoted Joseph in Genesis 50, forgiving his brothers, "As for you, you meant evil against me; but God meant it for good, to bring it about that many people should be kept alive, as they are today." The rabbi continued, "One does not decide what happens to him; one decides what he wants to do with what happens to him."

Kapparah rises above both the law and sin, as Paul described in Romans, the state of sinless grace achieved when one is "born again." It is not just forgiveness, but *agape*, the ultimate cleansing, the place where sin and forgiveness are irrelevant – beyond compassion to perfect oneness, "at-onement" – a higher chakra condition – *shekinah,* divine light, the presence of God in the world.

~ 1245 ~

SEX, Part 32

After Lou died, I became asexual. Sex for its own sake had no meaning to me; it was no longer effective as a means of either pleasure or escape. The only sex I wanted going forward, if any, was the same tantric sex I knew with Lou. Nothing less would do.

Then divine love was reawakened in me with The Unnamed One, and again with Emily. Although both felt mysteriously drawn to me and professed to love me, neither of them recognized our tantric love as something entirely different from the other loves they had experienced. Our love had a sexual aspect, as all tantric love does, but I knew I could not express this sexuality with their physical forms unless they, too, were awakened to the same metaphysical love. Both of them misunderstood my professions of love as simply a desire for sex, not understanding sexuality as the effect, not the cause, of our loving attraction.

~ 1246 ~

THE PARABLE OF THE TALENTS

For it will be as when a man going on a journey called his servants and entrusted to them his property; to one he gave five talents, to another two, to another one, to each according to his ability. Then he went away. He who had received the five talents went at once and traded with them; and he made five talents more. So also, he who had the two talents made two talents more. But he who had received the one talent went and dug in the ground and hid his master's money.

Now after a long time the master of those servants came and settled accounts with them. And he who had received the five talents came forward, bringing five talents more, saying, "Master, you delivered to me five talents; here I have made five talents more." His master said to him, "Well done, good and faithful servant; you have been faithful over a little, I will set you over much; enter into the joy of your master." And he also who had the two talents came forward, saying, "Master, you delivered to me two talents; here I have made two talents more." His master said to him, "Well done, good and faithful servant; you have been faithful over a little, I will set you over much; enter into the joy of your master."

He also who had received the one talent came forward, saying, "Master, I knew you to be a hard man, reaping where you did not sow, and gathering where you did not winnow; so I was afraid, and I went and hid your talent in the ground. Here you have what is yours." But his master answered him, "You wicked and slothful servant! You knew that I reap where I have not sowed, and gather where I have not winnowed? Then you ought to have invested my money with the bankers, and at my coming I should have received what was my own with interest. So take the talent from him, and give it to him who has the ten talents. For to every one who has will more be given, and he will have abundance; but from him who has not, even what he has will be taken away. And cast the worthless servant into the outer darkness; there men will weep and gnash their teeth." (Matthew 25:14-30 RSV)

Two statements in this parable caught my attention:

1) "… to one he [the master] gave five talents, to another two, to another one, *to each according to his ability*." The master knew in advance which of his servants would best handle his money, knowing their abilities and assigning responsibility to them accordingly; and

2) "Well done, good and faithful servant; you have been faithful over a little, *I will set you over much*; enter into the joy of your master." The servants got to keep for themselves neither the talents the master entrusted to them nor the interest earned. All belongs to the master. The faithful servants were not rewarded with riches or fame or a well-earned vacation, but with even more responsibility.

Much is expected from those to whom much is given. The most was expected from the servant who was entrusted with five talents. Little was expected from the servant who buried his one talent in the ground. The master assured the faithful servants that by furthering the master's cause and dutifully accepting their increased responsibilities, they will enter into the joy of their master. Trusting and acting based on this assurance is true faith.

The Parables are powerful because they have meaning on many levels – on the surface, in the temporal relationships of the people in the story; under the surface, in the relationship between Man and God; and deeper, in the eternal unity of God, Man, Heaven, Hell, Earth, Time, Space, and Things. It is important that a parable not involve real people; identification of a character in the story with a real person creates a boundary, a limit on the imagination, and blocks access to the deeper universal meaning of the story.

The lesson I learned from this Parable is about the opposite effects of behaviors motivated by love versus fear. The servants who invested their talents accepted their calling to a life of service and surrender to the master's will even with its risks, finding strength and courage in the power of divine love. The servant who buried his one talent acted out of fear, knowing the master to be a "hard man." He misunderstood the nature of the master's sowing and reaping ("Consider the lilies, how they grow; they neither toil nor spin; yet I tell you, even Solomon in all his glory was not arrayed like one of these."), and did not hear the call to send the gospel out into the world and help it grow. In his fear he hid his talent, hid his light under a bushel, seeking safety rather than growth, much as Peter who, in his fear, sought safety when he hid his truth and denied Jesus three times.

The first two servants had fully surrendered to the master's will and had lost all fear of him; the third servant was not so fully committed and therefore was afraid (as Adam and Eve were afraid and hid from God after eating of the Forbidden Tree), seeing only the worldly master of vengeance and punishment, the "hard man," not the ultimate God which is beyond vengeance and fear. Because the faithless servant saw only a punishing master, punishment is what he got.

At the deepest level, the worthless servant was not cast into the outer darkness in the time sequence presented in the story as a consequence of his actions. In eternity, karma and time are not linear; cause is effect; effect is cause. In the timelessness of eternity, the worthless servant was already in darkness before he was given any talents, his behavior arising in duality out of that state of darkness. By the same token, the faithful servants were known to be such before they acted faithfully, thus were entrusted with more talents; they were given much according to their foreknown ability, and accordingly, had already entered the joy of the master.

All the servants in the story represent ever-present potentialities, different routes on the journey to God. Both potentialities – to be the faithful servant or the fearful servant – now exist inside each of us. Our degree of awakening to the master's will determines which route we will take.

In each moment we make the choice anew to be faithful or fearful; faithful one moment, fearful the next. In the moment we reach the eighth bhūmi, however, there is no backsliding; our route of faithfulness is irreversible, and the master hands us five talents.

~ 1247 ~

GOOD AND EVIL, Part 11

In the beginning, God was perfect, complete, being love itself in the stillness of eternity. But God was lonely, so he created his creation out of himself so that he could have an object for his love. He wanted to create movement in the stillness, to allow his love to flow. He created

Man in his own image, implanting divine love within, so that he could behold his love reflected back to him and to all creation. God gave Man dominion over the earth, so that through Man's obedient stewardship in divine love, the unity of all things in God could be maintained even in the separation of space-time.

But God knew that by splitting off one polarity, the opposite polarity would also be released. Interdependent co-arising. With good there would also be evil. With beauty, ugliness. With joy, sorrow. God planted the Tree of the Knowledge of Good and Evil and gave Man access to it, but warned Man that there was danger in eating its fruit. The rest is history.

~ 1248 ~

The fable about the moth in the flame, attributed to Sufi poet Farīd ud-Dīn Attar (1145-1220) has been on my mind:

> One night, the moths gathered together, tormented by their longing to unite themselves with the candle. They all said, "we must find someone to give us news of that for which we long so earnestly."
>
> One of the moths then went to a castle and saw the light of a candle within. Upon returning he reported what he saw, but the wise moth said, "He has no real information to give about the candle." Then another moth visited the candle, passed close to the light, drawing near to it and touching the flame with its wings. He too came back and explained something of what union with the candle meant, but the wise moth said to him, "Your explanation is really worth no more than your comrade's."
>
> A third moth rose up and threw himself violently into the candle's flame. As he entered completely into its embrace, his members became glowing red like the flame itself. The wise moth saw from afar that the candle had identified the moth with itself and had given the moth its light. He said, "This moth alone understands that to which he has attained. None other knows it, and this is all."[136]

This is the Jewish atonement, the Christian and Islamic surrender to God, the Jungian annihilation of the ego, the Buddhist no-self, Campbell's identification with the divine (~646~), Plato's emergence from the cave into the sunlight (~1131~), and the Hindu salt doll dissolving in the ocean (~612~). The end of the journey is the same regardless of the route taken to get there. And the metaphors are the same: the Source represented by light, the seeker's longing for unity with the light, the loss of self in the unity, and the impossibility of understanding for those who do not share the experience. Neither the moth nor the salt doll returns to report.

Even in the pagan polytheistic culture of ancient Rome, the Stoic philosopher Seneca (1-65 A.D.) grasped the essence of the one eternal Source, which he calls "fortune." Man's temporary custody of all that he has, including himself, is acquired without his knowing, and all that he has, and is, is inevitably returned to unity with the Source. Seneca even echoes Jesus' "Parable of the Talents" (~1246~):

> The wise man does not need to walk about timidly or cautiously: for he possesses such self-confidence that he does not hesitate to go to meet fortune nor will he ever yield his position to her: nor has he any reason to fear her, because he considers not only slaves, property, and positions of honor, but also his body, his eyes, his hands, everything which can make life dearer, even his very self, as among uncertain things, and lives as if he had borrowed them for his own use and was prepared to return them without sadness whenever claimed. Nor does he appear worthless in his own eyes because he knows that he is not his own, but he will do everything as diligently and carefully as a conscientious and pious man is accustomed to guard that which is entrusted in his care. Yet whenever he is ordered to return them, he will not complain to fortune, but will say: "I thank you for this which I have had in my possession. I have indeed cared for your property—even to my great disadvantage—but, since you command it, I give it back to you and restore it thankfully and willingly."
>
> If nature should demand of us that which she has previously entrusted to us, we will also say to her: "Take back a better mind than you gave; I seek no way of escape nor flee; I have voluntarily improved for you what you gave me without my knowledge; take it away." What hardship is there in returning to the place whence one has come? That man lives badly who does not know how to die well.[137]

~ 1249 ~

The psychic James Van Praagh differentiates the Soul from the Spirit, saying that the Soul is the part of us that lives after we die, that travels from incarnation to incarnation, that carries our karma, that makes us recognizable as we move through eternity and the collective unconscious. The Spirit, on the other hand, is the Holy Spirit, the eternal God-self in us. The Spirit energizes the Soul.

I like this distinction. I came to the same conclusion a while ago in my description of the four souls (~403~) and later with Ignacio's group (~754~). It explains the metaphor of the salt doll dissolving in the ocean as the Soul, NaCl remaining separate from H_2O even though invisible in the water; and the iceberg melting into the ocean, H_2O into H_2O, as the Spirit. When we achieve unexcelled complete awakening, the Soul, along with the body-mind-ego, melds into the Spirit and becomes one with it, finally dissolving into emptiness.

Religious scriptures and other spiritual writings can be confusing because they often conflate the Soul and Spirit together. Here is how they are different:

	SOUL (finite, in duality)	SPIRIT (infinite, in eternity)
John Wesley	servant of God (John the Baptist)	son of God (Jesus)
Joseph Campbell	6th chakra – God with form	7th chakra – God without form
	Christ Crucified	Christ Triumphant
	"transparent to transcendence"	"identification with the divine"
Carl Jung	God	Godhead
Wayne Dyer	God is in me. (panentheism)	I am God. (pantheism)
Ramakrishna (Hindu)	salt doll (NaCl) melts in ocean (H_2O)	iceberg (H_2O) melts in ocean (H_2O)
Buddhism	bodhisattva	buddha
Attar (Sufi)	moth around the flame	moth in the flame
astrology, alchemy	Moon – reflecting light	Sun – the light itself

The great mystics are known by their direct knowledge of the spirit realm as depicted in the right-hand column. They are, as Jesus said to Nicodemus, "born of the spirit."

First we put aside the ego, then the body-mind, then finally the soul. We become pure spirit. We become nothing. And everything.

~ 1250 ~

GOOD AND EVIL, Part 12

The Christian "Affirmation of Baptism" contains the following pledge:

> Do you renounce the devil and all the forces that defy God?
> *I renounce them.*

> Do you renounce the powers of this world that rebel against God?
> *I renounce them.*

> Do you renounce the ways of sin that draw you from God?
> *I renounce them.*

Thus, the baptized Christian aligns himself with the "good guy" aspect of God and renounces the "bad guy" side. This alignment, however, firmly rooted as it is in the duality of this world, does not bring him any closer to the Source, the one eternal God, who does not renounce the devil, the rebel, or the sinner, but embraces them as equally beloved parts of the divine creation.

> I form light and create darkness,
> I make weal and create woe,
> I am the Lord, who do all these things.
>   (Isaiah 45:7 RSV)

The dictionary definition of "renounce" is "to give up, refuse, or resign, usually by formal declaration; to refuse to follow, obey, or recognize any further; repudiate." By this definition, to renounce the devil, rebel powers, and sin is to refuse to "recognize any further" an essential part of the eternal God. Renouncing evil, repressing it, rejecting it, repudiating it, leads not to goodness, but to ignorance. It is taking the third Buddhist poison.

Imagine if everyone was baptized and vowed to renounce evil. Would everybody pile up on the "good" side of the teeter-totter and catapult the devil into outer space? As appealing as that sounds, thousands of years of failure to eradicate evil show us that the world doesn't work that way. No matter how good we try to be, somewhere the devil still lurks; greed and fear, the law and sin, are still around to tempt us. Whenever we try to push evil down, it rises up somewhere else. Desire for good, fear of evil, and the refusal to face both good and evil head-on – the Three Poisons – keep the world forever at war.

> When you renounce something, you're stuck to it forever. When you fight something, you're tied
> to it forever. As long as you're fighting it, you are giving it power. You give it as much power
> as you are using to fight it. – Anthony de Mello, S.J., *Awareness*

It is the renunciation of evil that keeps evil alive. Renunciation of evil does not increase goodness; it widens the gulf between opposite poles and makes evil stronger. By the same token, renouncing goodness – "going to the devil," as we say – does not increase evil. Everything is in perfect balance and constantly in flux; the categorization of thoughts, actions, things, and people as good or evil is always shifting. One person's good is another person's evil; one person's sincere belief is another person's heresy. When someone leaves an apparently sane environment to join a terrorist group, he is not necessarily turning to evil; from his perspective, he is redefining what "good" is.

In this dualistic world we can't eradicate evil without taking good away with it. We can, however, elevate both good and evil to the place of unity where everything melds into divine love. Acknowledging the existence of evil (however you define it), facing it, accepting it, and drawing it toward the center where love is at the 4th chakra, is the only way to find peace and understanding. Jesus met evil on its own terms; he brought "bad" people – prostitutes, lepers, and tax collectors – into his sphere and showed them the way to divine love, and in so doing he incurred the wrath of the priests and Pharisees, the "good" people.

Jesus brought divine love to the earth, but he did not end evil. If evil could be ended, why did Jesus not destroy the demons in the possessed man, rather than send them into swine? He said resist not evil, turn the other cheek, go the extra mile – not returning evil with evil, but in a kind of spiritual aikido, using the power of evil against itself. Accept good and evil with equanimity, knowing that both are part of God. Accept the pain that evil inflicts, bear witness to evil, and by so doing, bear witness to the good that must arise in opposition to it. As good and evil are both unleashed and pulled toward the center, they both surrender their separate identities and assume their place in the unity that is God.

Reaching the Source, the place of divine love, requires a leap of faith that allows Judas (a piece of God revealed in space-time, like all of us) to be loved just as Jesus is; that breeds compassion for the rebellious powers and the ways of sin; that replaces renunciation with loving-kindness; that enables the bodhisattva to joyfully participate in the sorrows of the world.

No one is purely good or purely evil. Martin Luther seemed to understand this, declaring that the human being is *simul justus et peccator*, at the same time saint and sinner. In the same sense, the Buddhists say there is no purely good or evil act. Even perfectly skilled behavior, in humble service and intending no harm, cannot but contain elements that some would deem evil.

Because of this, Buddhists can be frustratingly aloof when it comes to addressing someone's claim of having been wronged. Even when there appears to be clear injustice or unskilled behavior, they sometimes hesitate to intervene, even for the sake of justice, believing that karma dictates everything, and whatever happens is supposed to happen. In every experience there is a lesson to be learned that couldn't be learned any other way. To intervene would be to counteract or interrupt the karma, in fact impeding the victim's spiritual development. (see "The Trolley Problem:" ~1205~)

This is akin to Hank Wesselman's view of Sophia, the personification of Wisdom:

> Having dreamed the anthropos into being, the Sophia loves us and wants the best for us … and she feels concern for the dark force patterning adrift in our world and attached to our leadership. She watches to see what we will do to rectify our situation. She will not intervene, however. It is up to us … and always has been.[112]

At the beginning of our spiritual journey we have choices, and we can choose not to do evil as we understand it in the worldly sense. When we are born again, however, freed from the law and sin, there is no longer a choice. We are one with God's love; our every act is God's will. We are God just as Jesus was. When divine love takes over, no vow of renunciation is necessary. Skilled behavior is automatic, even in the face of evil, even when tested by the harshest adversary. C.S. Lewis explains why:

> "I suppose there are two views about everything," said Mark.
> "Eh? Two views? There are a dozen views about everything until you know the answer. Then there's never more than one."
>
> – C.S. Lewis, *That Hideous Strength* [139]

~ 1251 ~

The phone rang. Caller ID said "private caller." I don't normally answer unidentified calls, but this time I was tempted. Then I remembered a strange, similarly unidentified call I had answered years ago that I sensed was Emily's dissociative personality. (~921~) This time I said to myself, "Best leave it alone." The caller left a hurried message, in a familiarly chilling voice: "It was fun."

~ 1252 ~

> For if we take the imagery of Scripture seriously, if we believe that God will one day give us the Morning Star and cause us to put on the splendour of the sun, then we may surmise that both the ancient myths and the modern poetry, so false as history, may be very near the truth as prophecy. ... When human souls have become as perfect in voluntary obedience as the inanimate creation is in its lifeless obedience, then they will put on its glory, or rather that greater glory of which Nature is only the first sketch. For you must not think that I am putting forward any heathen fancy of being absorbed into Nature. Nature is mortal; we shall outlive her. When all the suns and nebulae have passed away, each one of you will still be alive. Nature is only the image, the symbol; but it is the symbol Scripture invites me to use. We are summoned to pass in through Nature, beyond her, into that splendour which she fitfully reflects. – C.S. Lewis, *The Weight of Glory* [86]

I understand what Lewis is saying about Nature, and I agree in principle, but he uses the pronoun "we" imprecisely. We as physical beings are part of Nature and mortal in the same sense as the rest of Nature is. (The jury is still out on the spirituality of Nature. Does a dog have buddha-nature? Is there nothing else in Nature that outlives Nature as we do? Perhaps everything does.) The part of us that outlives Nature is the "we" that Lewis describes, differentiating the temporal body-mind from the timeless soul:

> And in there, in beyond Nature, we shall eat of the tree of life. At present, if we are reborn in Christ, the spirit in us lives directly in God; but the mind and, still more, the body receives life from Him at a thousand removes—through our ancestors, through our food, through the elements. The faint, far-off results of those energies which God's creative rapture implanted in matter when He made the worlds are what we now call physical pleasures; and even thus filtered, they are too much for our present management. What would it be to taste at the fountainhead that stream of which even these lower reaches prove so intoxicating? Yet that, I believe, is what lies before us. The whole man is to drink joy from the fountain of joy. As St. Augustine said, the rapture of the saved soul will "flow over" into the glorified body.[86]

Lewis' reference to St. Augustine jumped out at me. "The rapture of the saved soul" flowing over into the glorified body is Tantra – the body being infused with the divine love of the spirit. What neither Lewis nor Augustine may have fully grasped is that the "whole man" and "glorified body" who drink from the fountain of joy exist now in this life, in Nature, on earth as it is in heaven, without waiting for death. In awakening, what Lewis calls "physical pleasures" can rise above pleasure to joy, from intoxication to bliss, not just in the hereafter, but here and now.

I am bothered by the bumper sticker that says, "HE > i." Jesus made it clear that everyone has the potential to realize the God-self within as he did, to be born again. In the Thomas Gospel Jesus said, "The kingdom is inside of you and outside of you." He said something similar in Luke 17:20-21 RSV:

> Being asked by the Pharisees when the kingdom of God was coming, he answered them, 'The kingdom of God is not coming with signs to be observed; nor will they say, 'Lo, here it is!' or 'There!' for behold, the kingdom of God is in the midst[iii] of you.'

Humbling oneself before God may seem to be a virtue, but can lead to self-loathing unless it is accompanied by the arising of the God-self within, which leads to divine self-love. Jesus would have us say, "HE = ME." When we truly understand the truth of this equality – when we identify with the divine, as Joseph Campbell put it – we are born again. To equate oneself with God in this way is not ego glorification; it is ego annihilation.

[iii] ἐντός entos – inside, within, in the midst of

I am as great as God, and he as small as I;
He cannot me surpass, or I beneath him lie.
God cannot, without me, endure a moment's space,
Were I to be destroyed, he must give up the ghost.
Nought seemeth high to me, I am the highest thing;
Because e'en God himself is poor deprived of me.
– Angelus Silesius (1624-1677)

~ 1253 ~

CHRISTMAS

As I was carving my Christmas turkey, I felt a wave of gratitude coming over me. I thanked the turkey for giving its life for me. I gave thanks for the wonder that the world is, that life is, and especially for the unknowable knowledge that allows me to grasp the wonder.

The Buddhists say that it is a great honor to be born into the human realm. It is an even greater honor to be in the human realm and at the same time see beyond it. This is the miracle of Christmas, of the Word made Flesh. Jesus brings that invisible realm into view for those on earth who are ready to see it.

~ 1254 ~

At the Buddhist service today, while listening to the chanting, I felt another wave of panic sweep over me. I had to leave the service and walk around to relieve the stress, and to prove to myself that I could still, in fact, walk around. I played a game on my phone for a few minutes to reset my mind and then returned to the service.

The downside of knowing the freedom of eternity is feeling imprisoned in the body. My last great fear is that as I age, my increasing infirmity will lock me in even tighter. This feeling of imprisonment in the body was a major aspect of my suffering after Lou died. I ask my spirit guides for help, but I often feel that my connection to the spirits is like a garbled phone connection; I know they are speaking to me, but I can't quite make out the message. My body, my sensory sending and receiving machine, fails me. My frustration over this adds to my fear. Not only is my body giving out, but the spiritual forces that could support me are incommunicado.

I am weighed down by a strange weariness, feeling as if I am straining against my limitations, as if my body, my life, is itself an obstacle, a restraint on my spirit. Death will be such a blessed relief, or so I think.

I know that my spirit is free, always has been, and always will be. When I can understand this truth not just intellectually, but in the way of unknowable knowing, when I am able to be comfortable in my body whatever its condition, then I will be free to leave it.

I deeply admire the severely disabled, like Stephen Hawking and Helen Keller, who stayed grounded in the world and kept functioning despite their disabilities. They learned how to ignore the body parts that didn't work and make the most of the parts that did. They learned how to live in the moment, to be attuned to life energy as it is, not as it was, or could have been, or should have been. They looked outward toward the world, not inward toward their own hopes and fears. If they felt trapped in duality as I do, their exemplary lives showed no sign of it.

After the service, my spiritual guide relayed this message: *The question "Why?" is coming up … whatever happens, good or bad, is sent as a challenge to you because you are ready for it … don't be afraid … don't hesitate … trust your buddha-nature."*

~ 1255 ~

Gnosticism (from Ancient Greek: γνωστικός gnostikos, "having knowledge," γνῶσις gnōsis, knowledge) is a modern name for a variety of ancient religious ideas and systems originating in Jewish milieus in the first and second century A.D. Based on their readings of the Torah and other Biblical writings, these systems believed that the material world is created by an emanation of the highest God, trapping the Divine spark within the human body. This Divine spark could be liberated by gnosis of this Divine spark.

Gnosis refers to knowledge based on personal experience or perception. In a religious context, gnosis is mystical or esoteric knowledge based on direct participation with the divine. In most Gnostic systems, the sufficient cause of salvation is this "knowledge of" ("acquaintance with") the divine. It is an inward "knowing," comparable to that encouraged by Plotinus (neoplatonism). – *Wikipedia*

If I can be described as anything religious, I suppose I am a Gnostic. Gnosticism is almost synonymous with mysticism and intuition, and thus finds commonality with spiritual practitioners of all times, places, and religions. It is easy for me to accept the truth of the gnostic gospels like the Thomas Gospel, rather than be skeptical of them, as are so many others who are not in the "know."

As has happened so many times, comforting information comes to me just when I need it. In the course of my research on Gnosticism, I came upon an explanation for my discomfiture in the prison of the body:

> The term *demiurge* derives from the Latinized form of the Greek term dēmiourgos, δημιουργός, literally "public or skilled worker." This figure is also called "Ialdabaoth," Samael (Aramaic: sæmʻa-'el, "blind god"), or "Saklas" (Syriac: sækla, "the foolish one"), who is sometimes ignorant of the superior god, and sometimes opposed to it; thus in the latter case he is correspondingly malevolent. Other names or identifications are Ahriman, El, Satan, and Yahweh.
>
> The demiurge creates the physical universe and the physical aspect of humanity. The demiurge typically creates a group of co-actors named *archons* who preside over the material realm and, in some cases, present obstacles to the soul seeking ascent from it. The inferiority of the demiurge's creation may be compared to the technical inferiority of a work of art, painting, sculpture, etc., to the thing the art represents. In other cases it takes on a more ascetic tendency to view material existence negatively, which then becomes more extreme when materiality, including the human body, is perceived as evil and constrictive, a deliberate prison for its inhabitants.
>
> Moral judgments of the demiurge vary from group to group within the broad category of Gnosticism, viewing materiality as being inherently evil, or as merely flawed and as good as its passive constituent matter allows. – *ibid.*

Satan and Yahweh are both demiurges? This bolsters Campbell's assertion that the early Christians considered Yahweh a lesser god, a worldly god, the creator of the universe but not the Supreme Being. Yahweh's technically inferior creation presents just a rough approximation of the reality of God, but in fleeting glimpses I can see behind the façade. The entire universe, including me, is infused with and powered by the perfect eternal light of divine love. I see past God to Godhead.

I am in the final round of my battle with Mara/Satan, the demiurge and its archons. When I can fully know the illusion of the body and the material world, to understand the "merely flawed" universe and allow my "passive constituent matter" to make it good, I will rise above the limitations of my body and escape this "deliberate prison for its inhabitant" even while still in it.

~ 1256 ~

NEW YEARS EVE

Morning in church with the Christians, afternoon watching football, evening enjoying downtown holiday lights, midnight ringing the temple bell with the Buddhists.

Tonight as I walked along the sidewalk enjoying the festive lights, I looked down, noticed a small white feather, picked it up, and put it in my wallet. An angel feather, or just an accident?

In the last thirty years I have heard, seen, read, and studied the spiritual work of dozens of sages from around the world, spanning thousands of years and myriad cultures. I have written hundreds of thousands of words about my experiences. And yet, I know that none of my words or those of the others mean anything compared to the power of the refiner's fire – the direct experience of God.

This journal will end not when words tell me to stop, but when visions, voices, and feathers do.

~ 1257 ~

As I once said to Baker—my mystical friend with the crowded poetry—the trouble about God is that he is like a person who never acknowledges one's letters and so, in time, one comes to the conclusion either that he does not exist or that you have got the address wrong. What was the use of going on dispatching fervent messages—say to Edinburgh—if they all came back through the dead letter office: nay more, if you couldn't even find Edinburgh on the map. His cryptic reply was that it would be almost worth going to Edinburgh to find out. – C.S. Lewis, in a letter to his brother, Warren Lewis [140]

This is what our spiritual journey is, and mystics are especially good at – going to Edinburgh.

~ 1258 ~

Another book, *Hours with the Mystics* [138] by Robert Alfred Vaughan, has appeared before me, another gift rescued from the library's throwaway pile. It has given me another mystical view of interdependent co-arising:

I saw and knew the Being of all Beings, the Byss and the Abyss: the birth of the Holy Trinity; the origin and primal state of this world and of all creatures through the Divine Wisdom. Moreover, I saw and had cognizance of the whole Being in good and evil—*how each had its origin in the other*, and how the Mother did bring forth; and this all moved me not merely to the height of wonder, but made me to rejoice exceedingly. – Jacob Behmen [Boehme], Polish-German mystic (1575-1624)

And of the mystic's aloneness:

Mysticism is heard discoursing concerning things unutterable. It speaks, as one in a dream, of the third heaven, and of celestial experiences, and revelations fitter for angels than for men.

Its stammering utterance, confused with excess of rapture laboring with emotions too huge or abstractions too subtle for words, becomes utterly unintelligible. Then it is misrepresented: falls a victim to reaction in its turn; the delirium is dieted by persecution, and it is consigned once more to secrecy and silence. The mystic, after all his pains to reduce himself to absolute passivity, becomes not theopathetic, but *anthropopathetic*—suffers, not under God, but man.

In the above passage, Vaughan aptly described the life of Christ and all prophets who are misunderstood, scorned, and rejected by those they are sent to liberate.

Angelus Silesius bids men lose, in utter nihilism, all sense of any existence separate from the Divine Substance—the Absolute *[Silesius' poem: ~1252~]* … Thus individuality must be ignored to the utmost; by mystical death we begin to live; and in this perverted sense he that loseth his life shall find it.

Humanity is a divine evolution, and each true man (to use Emerson's apt illustration), a façade of Deity. Even Angelus would have acknowledged that it was in some sort through Christ that his boastful sonship became possible. But the believer in the Oversoul will admit no such medium, and owns a debt to Christ much as he owns a debt to Shakespeare. Mysticism of this order usurps the office of the Holy Ghost, and directly identifies the spirit of man with the Spirit of God.

[Ralph Waldo Emerson:] "I, the Imperfect, adore my own Perfect. I am somehow receptive of the great soul, and thereby I do overlook the sun and the stars, and feel them to be but the fair accidents and effects which change and pass. I become a transparent eyeball. I am nothing. I see all. The currents of the Universal Being circulate through me; I am part or particle of God."

Here again is the idea of identification with the divine as expressed by two mystics, Angelus Silesius and Ralph Waldo Emerson. When I studied the writings of Emerson in school, his spirituality never came up, because only teachings from the canon of Christian orthodoxy were acceptable. Emerson's views, like those of most mystics, were heretical. Only now have I come to know him fully, not just as a poet, but as a holder of mystical truth.

It is scarcely necessary to observe that Behmen and the mystics are partly right and partly wrong in turning from books and schools to intuition, when they essay to pass the ordinary bounds of knowledge and to attain a privileged gnosis. It is true that no method of human wisdom will reveal to men the hidden things of the divine kingdom. But it is also true that dreamy gazing will not disclose them either. Scholarship may not scale the heights of the unrevealed, and neither assuredly may ignorance.

[Behmen] teaches that the Divine Unity, in its manifestation or self-realization, parts into two principles, variously called Light and Darkness, Joy and Sorrow, Fire and Light, Wrath and Love, Good and Evil. Without what is termed the Darkness and the Fire, there would be no Love and Light. Evil is necessary to manifest Good. Not that anything is created by God for evil. In everything is both good and evil: the predominance decides its use and destiny. What is so much pain and evil in hell is, in heaven, so much joy and goodness. The bitter fountain and the sweet flow originally from one divine Source. The angels and the devils are both in God, of whom, and in whom, all live and move. But from their divine basis, or root, the former draw joy and glory, the latter shame and woe. The point of collision is the gate of anguish and of bliss.

The Buddhist concepts of duality, karma, interdependent co-arising, and the singularity of good and evil are explained above by Behmen, a Christian, as well as any Buddhist could – as long as we understand Behmen's Divine Unity to be not God, but Godhead.

Like most of those attempts to explain the inexplicable which have proved more than usually attractive, this theory has its truth and its falsehood. It is true that the harmonious development of life is neither more nor less than a successive reconciliation of contraries. The persistent quality, representing our individuality and what is due to the particular self, must not exist alone. The diffusive quality, or fluent, having regard only to others, must not exist alone. The extreme of either defeats itself. Each is necessary to, or, as Behmen would say, lies in the other. The two factors are reconciled, and consummated in a higher unity when the command is obeyed— 'Thou shalt love thy neighbour as thyself.' Towards this standard all moral development must tend. Pairs of principles, like the Personal and the Relative, the Ideal and the Actual, etc.—at once twin and rival—where each is the complement of the other, are very numerous. They are designed for union, as heat and cold combine to produce a temperate or habitable clime. Had Behmen confined his theory of contraries within such limits, we might have questioned his expressions; we must, I think, have admitted his principle. …

Opposites are reduced in amplitude together as they approach unity (hot becomes warm, cold becomes cool), or are unified when they meet at the far side of the orb, or are exploded to oblivion when they reach their extremes and fly off their hinges. So far, so good, but then Vaughan goes off the rails:

… But when he takes good and evil as the members of such an antithesis, he is deceived by an apparent likeness. It would be a strange thing should anyone declare courage and meekness, lowliness and aspiration, the work of God and the work of man, incapable of harmony. It is still more strange to hear any man pronounce any harmony possible between good and evil, sin and holiness. The former set of terms belong to one family; the latter are reciprocally destructive, totally incompatible. Here lies Behmen's fallacy.

In his statements, "Behmen and the mystics are partly right and partly wrong in turning from books and schools to intuition," "… this theory has its truth and its falsehood," and "Here lies Behmen's fallacy," Vaughan exemplifies the well-meaning scholar who can bring a wealth of book-learning to his subject matter, but little or no direct personal experience. He goes to great lengths to argue the fallacies in Behman's views, not understanding that what we call truth and falsehood, right and wrong, from the intellectual perspective are meaningless from the mystical perspective.

Vaughan was a devoted student of mysticism, but not a mystic himself. If he were, he would not question and over-analyze the alleged truth or falsehood of Behmen's teachings. The mystical experience is beyond intellect and analysis. Behmen is so sure of his truth because it was delivered to him by divine revelation, not study or logic. Vaughan was correct when he wrote: "The mystic, after all his pains to reduce himself to absolute passivity, becomes not theopathic, but *anthropopathic* – suffers, not under God, but man." Vaughan, in his vain criticism, is one of the men under whom the mystic suffers.

Mystics are perfectly in tune with each other, and are fine with what appear to be contradictions in worldly terms; they all know that their apparently contradictory explanations are fully reconciled in the one eternal Unity that they have all directly experienced. Like Vaughan, I am a scholar and student of mysticism, but because I approach the subject from within rather than from without, I celebrate and revel in the eternal consonance that I find among all the great mystics, seeing beyond their seemingly dissonant or contradictory worldly expressions.

~ 1259 ~

APOLOGY AND FORGIVENESS, Part 6

I don't have much respect for TV evangelists because most of the time they seem to be more interested in putting on a show and making money than helping people or finding truth. There are a few however, who have given me something to think about, Ravi Zacharias[iv] being one. Yesterday he said something that caught my attention, that Christianity is the only religion that offers salvation. Not Islam, Buddhism, or Hinduism, where karma is what it is and there is no release from it.

[iv] I am intrigued by the different ways that Hindus-turned-Christians reconcile, or not, the Eastern and Western approaches to spirituality. Anthony de Mello found commonality in the teachings of Jesus and the Hindus, and used these teachings to reinforce each other. Ravi Zacharias did not. He got caught in the secular trappings of Hinduism with which he grew up, and missed its deeper truth, which he eventually found in the new clothes of Christianity. The same thing happens to Christians, Jews, Muslims, Buddhists, and others who cannot find the spiritual truth of their ancestral culture and gravitate instead to the same truth wrapped in a new package which is free of the social and psychological overlays that clouded their youthful religious experience.

But there *is* release from karma in Buddhism – it is called enlightenment. Jesus described the same thing when he talked about being born again. Most Christians don't understand that Jesus did not save them directly; he showed the Way by which they could save themselves. By following the Way of Jesus, one can be freed of sin. By following the Way of the Buddha, one can build merit, repair one's karma and eventually be liberated from it.[v]

Jesus said, as did the Buddha, that the Way is not easy. Few will enter through the narrow gate, as few will know the dharma that the blind turtle finds in the hole in the log in the vast ocean. Ravi acknowledges that the road to salvation requires suffering, not unlike the Buddhist view of suffering expressed in the Four Noble Truths. In all great religions the key to spiritual growth is surrender – letting go of ego and giving oneself back to the Source, to God.

Much of Judeo-Christian theology is built on guilt. It is guilt over allegedly sinful acts and fear of the punishment that awaits, not the acts themselves, that makes Jews and Christians crave forgiveness. In Buddhism there is no guilt because there is no judgment; no act is purely good or evil, right or wrong. Unskilled behavior, unlike sinful behavior, carries no baggage of guilt.

The Lord's Prayer says that our sins will be forgiven as we forgive those who sin against us. In Christianity, forgiveness is often selfish, to build merit, gain favor with Man and God, and clear the path to heaven. We forgive others not out of compassion for them, but so that we might be forgiven and thus gain access to heavenly rewards.

In Buddhism, forgiveness takes place on a higher plane. As the Buddhist elevates toward enlightenment, he discovers that all his acts are part of the eternal matrix, and that he was already forgiven for unskilled behavior before any acts were committed. As merit is built over many incarnations, bad karma is balanced by good karma, and our eternally present forgiveness is revealed, along with Compassion, Joy, Equanimity, and Loving-kindness. When Jesus said, "Your sins are forgiven you," he was referring to this already-conferred forgiveness that awaits all of us, once we find the Way to it.

~ 1260 ~

One reason why many people find Creative Evolution so attractive is that it gives one much of the emotional comfort of believing in God and none of the less pleasant consequences. When you are feeling fit and the sun is shining and you do not want to believe that the whole universe is a mere mechanical dance of atoms, it is nice to be able to think of this great mysterious Force

---

[v] The Buddha taught that bodhisattvas do not cling to the merits they generate (~474~); they don't need merits, because to the extent they are awakened they are already beyond the action of karma in their lives. Their karma is fully repaired and then tossed aside. This is the same liberation from sin, no longer being under the law, that Paul described in Romans.

rolling on through the centuries and carrying you on its crest. If, on the other hand, you want to do something rather shabby, the Life-Force, being only a blind force, with no morals and no mind, will never interfere with you like that troublesome God we learned about when we were children. The Life-Force is a sort of tame God. You can switch it on when you want, but it will not bother you. All the thrills of religion and none of the cost. Is the Life-Force the greatest achievement of wishful thinking the world has yet seen? – C.S. Lewis, *Mere Christianity* [76]

Indeed, many people find the idea of a quasi-animate Life-Force an attractive explanation for the operation of the universe; but then, many devoutly religious people view their hallowed God in equally simplistic, superficial terms. Eventually, at a certain point along the mystic path, from whatever discipline you come, the Source is understood for what it really is, whether you call it God, or Life-Force, or any other name, or no name at all.

I have to believe that with the arrival of his wife Joy, Lewis gained greater insight into God. Before he directly experienced divine love, his writings have that hallmark Judeo-Christian confusion between the worldly God of mind and morals, and the eternal Godhead that subsumes and rises above mind, morals, and the mere mechanical dance of atoms.[vi]

When divine love enters, when you learn to surrender to the great mysterious God-Force-Source and ride on the crest of its wave no matter where it takes you, doing something shabby never occurs to you. Morals and mind are limits that are exploded in the All.

~ 1261 ~

GOOD AND EVIL, Part 13

God's love is not a reward for being good. Neither is happiness. Goodness can bring as much pain as evil can, as evidenced by the persecution of Jesus and so many other righteous prophets and mystics. Extreme goodness, like extreme evil, causes people to feel threatened and fearful. It increases the separation between people; it makes the average sinner feel inferior, and worried that the Good One, perhaps even more effectively than the Evil One, will diminish him, beat him in competition for a job, a spouse, a leadership role, or the respect of his peers.

Divine love closes the gap. It is what we experience when we become conscious of our eternal connection to the Source and to all that emanates from it – when we can love Judas as we love

---

[vi] How differently Lewis and I used the dancing atomic metaphor! Lewis described the universe as a "mere mechanical dance of atoms;" I described my vision of eternity as miraculous "dancing molecules," not mere mechanics, but a marvelous manifestation of God alive and dancing in his universe. Lewis saw atoms in worldly terms, bound up in the laws of physics; I saw them in eternity, liberated and flying free.

Jesus; when we can see through the veil of earthly good and evil to the buddha-nature/God-self in all people and all things, including all who do us harm.

Emily came into my life to lift the 3rd Perfection out of the dry hypothetical realm and dramatically demonstrate this principle to me in real life. No matter how much good I did for her, nothing could stop the torture she inflicted on me. Nothing could stop her archetypal expression of the deep psychosis that governs her behavior.

As evil escalated in her, I felt the corresponding good rising in me. And then I saw neither good nor evil, just my vision of God with form at the 6th chakra. As I made tantric love to my God with form, good and evil dissolved into the ether. Divine love kept me intimately with her and holds me with her still.

~ 1262 ~

FORGIVENESS, GRATITUDE, AND PERFECT JOY

We often say we should be grateful and forgiving, not angry or resentful. But we cannot control the presence or absence of emotions; we cannot prevent the ugly ones from arising, nor can we conjure up the pleasant ones anytime we want them. However, we *can* control how we respond to emotions, our own and those of others. At the highest mystic levels our responses become automatic, reflective of the unimpeded operation of our internal God-self/ buddha-nature.

Forgiveness is a means to liberate us from the past, and gratitude to liberate us from the future. They enable us to be in the moment, without regret for the past or fear of the future. But only true forgiveness and gratitude, arising as a result of coming to terms with the pain of the past and uncertainty of the future, can have this effect.

Feigned gratitude and feigned forgiveness – façades that evade the underlying issues without resolving them – do not release us from the discomfort of the past or the future; they just repress it. The surface is smooth, but the turbulence underneath remains. C.S. Lewis described this phenomenon: "The real trouble about the duty of forgiveness is that you do it with all your might on Monday and then find on Wednesday that it hasn't stayed put and all has to be done over again."[87]

True forgiveness and gratitude cannot be forced and cannot be willed. They must be spontaneous. Anita Moorjani made a distinction between playacting at loving and actually being loving. In the same sense, merely acting grateful does not necessarily demonstrate true gratitude. The appearance of gratitude or forgiveness can sometimes be a mask, a way of dismissing, deflecting, or denying tension rather than dealing with it.

It is easy to be grateful when we are blessed by acts of kindness, and to forgive when we are not personally harmed by acts of cruelty. I can easily be grateful for the kindness of friends, and I can pretty easily forgive Adolph Hitler, for instance, because I was not personally a victim of Nazi atrocity. Gratitude and forgiveness are easy when they are just intellectual exercises.

We have no problem being genuinely grateful for good friends and the beauties of nature, but can we be just as grateful for a friend's betrayal as for his kindness? Can we be grateful for beautiful sunsets and also for devastation when nature turns on us with hurricanes and shark attacks? Our ability to be grateful even for pains that hurt us personally, and to forgive those who trigger our own suffering, is the test of true gratitude and forgiveness versus the feigned kind.

True gratitude is counterintuitive. Gratitude for suffering only makes sense when one understands the equality of both sides of the pairs of opposites. It is only possible to know this kind of gratitude when you can approach the matter from a higher hermetic plane, from the position of eternal unity where both extremes are equally sacred and profane.

True gratitude, which includes gratitude even for hurtful and destructive people and events, thus has meaning only in the context of spiritual elevation, when one realizes that the lessons to be learned from suffering are more powerful than those learned from no suffering, and are absolutely necessary for spiritual growth. This is St. Francis' "perfect joy" (~743~), the "appreciative joy" of the Buddha (~1030~), the 3rd Perfection of Patience (~506~), and the 27th Practice of the Bodhisattva:

TWENTY SEVEN

To Bodhisattvas, who desire the wealth of virtue, all agents of harm
Are like a precious treasure. Therefore, cultivating
The patience that is free from hatred and animosity
Towards all is the practice of Bodhisattvas.
— from *The Thirty-Seven Practices of a Bodhisattva* [78]

PART 53
Life and Death
January 2018 – March 2018

~ 1263 ~

TO MARY WILLIS SHELBURNE, 8 January 1963: I don't mind betting that the things which 'had to be done' in your room didn't really have to be done at all. Very few things really do. After one bad night with my heart—not so bad as yours, for it was only suffocation, not pain—my doctor strictly rationed me on stairs, and I have obeyed him. Of course it is hideously inconvenient: but that can be put up with and must. What worse than inconvenience would have resulted if you had left those 'things' undone? Do take more care of yourself and less of 'things'! – C.S. Lewis, *The Collected Letters of C.S. Lewis, Volume III* [87]

TO MARY WILLIS SHELBURNE, 17 June 1963: Pain is terrible, but surely you need not have fear as well? Can you not see death as the friend and deliverer? It means stripping off that body which is tormenting you: like taking off a hair-shirt or getting out of a dungeon. What is there to be afraid of? You have long attempted (and none of us does more) a Christian life. Your sins are confessed and absolved. Has this world been so kind to you that you should leave it with regret? There are better things ahead than any we leave behind.

Remember, though we struggle against things because we are afraid of them, it is often the other way around—we get afraid because we struggle. Are you struggling, resisting? Don't you think Our Lord says to you 'Peace, child, peace. Relax. Let go. Underneath are the everlasting arms. Let go, I will catch you. Do you trust me so little?'

Of course, this may not be the end. Then make it a good rehearsal.

Yours (and like you a tired traveler near the journey's end),
Jack [87]

TO MARY WILLIS SHELBURNE, 6 July 1963: I live in almost total solitude, never properly asleep by night (all loathsome dreams) and constantly falling asleep by day. I sometimes feel as if my mind were decaying. Yet, in another mood, how short our whole past life begins to seem! … Well, we shall get out of it all sooner or later, for even the weariest river winds somewhere safe to sea. [87]

Many years ago, I wondered how C.S. Lewis handled his own illness and death. In these letters to Mary Shelburne, Lewis gives me a clue. Lewis' wife Joy died on July 13, 1960; Lewis himself died on November 22, 1963. These letters were thus written in the sunset of his life, after Joy's death and just before his own. When I first read *A Grief Observed*, I suspected that Lewis was just marking time after losing Joy, allowing his weary body to accelerate its winding to the sea, his mind decaying in the bardo between consciousness and unconsciousness.

In 1961, shortly after Joy's death, Lewis was diagnosed with nephritis, leading to renal failure which killed him in 1963. It seems that after Joy, the process of life turned into the process of death for him, as if the end of Joy marked the end of his life purpose. A long time ago I wrote, "Have I been forced to experience this trial [Lou's death], and to live beyond three years of it, so that I might pick up where Lewis left off?" (~3~)

In the thirty years since I was introduced to the writings of C.S. Lewis, I have gotten to know him as a dear friend, mentor, and fellow traveler on the spiritual path. Lewis' mysticism emerged gradually in his writings, his early journey preparing him to know divine love in human form later in life through his wife. My journey took place in the opposite sequence: I found divine love early through my husband, and my mysticism became kinetic from the point of Lou's death. Although at the time I had wished that Lou's death would be the beginning of the end for me as Joy's death was for Lewis, in fact it marked a new beginning. For both Lewis and me, the loss of our beloved spouse was the catalyst, the psychic catastrophe, that prepared us for the quantum leap to awakening.

Lewis and I are like two runners on a relay team – Lewis passed his baton of awakening to me near the end of his leg of the race, and I took it up near the beginning of mine. Indeed, I have followed in the footsteps of Lewis. Am I nearing the end of my leg? What other assignments are in store for me before I'm done? There are many more runners on our relay team, and I will surely pass the baton to others, perhaps through this tome, as Lewis passed the baton to me through his writings.

~ 1264 ~

PRIDE AND THE EGO, Part 4

> Then the Lord said to Samuel, "Behold, I am about to do a thing in Israel, at which the two ears of every one that hears it will tingle. On that day I will fulfil against Eli all that I have spoken concerning his house, from beginning to end. And I tell him that I am about to punish his house forever, for the iniquity which he knew, because his sons were blaspheming God, and he did not restrain them. Therefore I swear to the house of Eli that the iniquity of Eli's house shall not be expiated by sacrifice or offering forever." (1 Samuel 3:11-14 RSV)

Didn't Jesus bring the good news that forgiveness and salvation come by grace, not works? Are Eli's sins (which are not so much his as his sons') still not expiated, Christ's sacrifice notwithstanding? The infraction seems so small, the father being held responsible for his sons' blasphemy.[vii] The Hebrew God doles out harsh punishment for seemingly minor infractions, like Moses being denied entry into the Promised Land because he failed to give God the credit for making water come out of a rock in the wilderness of Zin.[viii] Raping and pillaging at Jericho was okay, but not neglecting God's demanding ego.

This God possesses the worst traits we ascribe to Man, including the selfish ego. It's no wonder, since the Hebrew God was created by Man in his own image, reflecting everything that Man desires and fears. All the anthropomorphic gods, by whatever names they are given, are but dualistic aspects of the Godhead.

What this means is that the curse God put on the house of Eli "forever" is superseded and overruled by the timeless grace of the Godhead, which liberates all that exists in space-time, which is where "forever" is. This is the good news that Jesus brought.

Thich Nhat Hanh told a story about a Buddhist monk who rose high in stature among his people, and then lost it when his ego arose. But then his savior brought redemption:

> Below and all around him, many thousands of people were bowing low, in awe—the king among them. It was indeed extraordinary for a monk, one who had forsaken everything for the Way, to have reached such a lofty place among mortals. And so, for a moment, for the batting of an eye, he felt pride in himself. Immediately, a strange fire surged to his face, and he knew that evil had penetrated him. He shook himself lightly and tried to regain control, but it was too late.
>
> "Look at me: I am Trieu Pho. And you are no one but Vien An, the slanderer, the murderer! You did me a terrible wrong, and for many lives I have chased after you to make you pay for your crime. For ten lifetimes, I have pursued you, but I have not been able to take revenge because in each existence you have been a great monk, even a saint, and your ways and conduct have been so blameless I could find no opening for an attack. But Vien An, I finally caught up with you! The king's devotion and the people's worship brought you down. You exposed yourself to pride and egotism, and I found a way in. I am the sore you have been carrying on your body!"

[vii] The Hebrew God sometimes contradicts himself: "The son shall not suffer for the iniquity of the father, nor the father suffer for the iniquity of the son; the righteousness of the righteous shall be upon himself, and the wickedness of the wicked shall be upon himself." (Ezekiel 18:20 RSV)

[viii] And the Lord said to Moses that very day, "Ascend this mountain of the Ab'arim, Mount Nebo, which is in the land of Moab, opposite Jericho; and view the land of Canaan, which I give to the people of Israel for a possession; and die on the mountain which you ascend, and be gathered to your people, as Aaron your brother died in Mount Hor and was gathered to his people; because you broke faith with me in the midst of the people of Israel at the waters of Mer'i-bath-ka'desh, in the wilderness of Zin; because you did not revere me as holy in the midst of the people of Israel. For you shall see the land before you; but you shall not go there, into the land which I give to the people of Israel." (Deuteronomy 32:48-52 RSV)

"In so many existences, I have myself suffered because of this desire for revenge. I have sunk into darkness because of my hatred for you. But the Most Venerable Kanishka proposed using this miraculous water to wash your sore, and doing so has washed away my hatred. I will no longer chase after you. It is your great blessing to have met holy Kanishka and to be saved by him. Our karmic debt to one another is released!" – Thich Nhat Hanh, "The Giant Pines"[25]

The moral of both the Hebrew and Buddhist stories is that pride comes before a fall. When God commanded, "You shall have no other gods before me," he banished the ego-god within each of us. When pride in what we think are our own accomplishments denies God as the ultimate source of all accomplishments, the God-self inside us, knowing the truth, afflicts us.

> Pride goes before destruction, and a haughty spirit before a fall.
> (Proverbs 16:18 RSV)

~ 1265 ~

I feel true gratitude for the blessings that have been bestowed upon me, and I have received the greatest blessing there is – the knowledge of divine love operating in my life. But life itself is not so precious to me. I can take it or leave it. I appreciate the miracle of my existence, but I can see beyond it. My death, whenever and however it comes, will be welcomed.

Much of the time now I feel as though I am sleepwalking through life, as if I am dreaming, watching someone else living my life. I am more and more detached from my work, finding less reward in it. My friends are still wonderful, but even as I tell them my deepest thoughts and hear theirs, they are not penetrating my depths. There is a persistent distance, isolation, aloneness, that is becoming more obvious, and perhaps ominous, to me.

I am an old soul. Perhaps I am just getting tired of my oft-repeated human existence. Does this mean I am coming to the end of incarnations, the end of karma? Am I a "once-returner," with one more incarnation to go? Am I a salt doll, dissolving into the ocean but destined to be precipitated again onto the beach? Or am I an iceberg, ready to dissolve into the ocean as H_2O, lose my soul identity, and rejoin the indivisible unity of spirit – to graduate from bodhisattva to buddha? *Anutpattica dharma shanti*. Patience. I am waiting to find out.

~ 1266 ~

Today at church Ignacio took my hand and held it, saying, "I want to thank you."

"Okay. For what?" I asked.

"For bringing Buddhist concepts into our theology discussion group. It is important to have that perspective."

Ignacio is sick and almost blind. Death is not far away, but he drags himself out of the house and into the discussion group whenever he can. Leading this group is what keeps him going. I am so grateful for his work and his indomitable spirit, not to mention his role as the catalyst for my 1/1/09 epiphany. I lap up his wisdom like a thirsty dog.

~ 1267 ~

My cell phone rang. I looked at the caller ID. It was Emily. It has been over a year since we have seen each other. The last time she called was eight months ago. And yet, even now, my heart jumps in fear reflex when I see her name. I did not answer. I am not yet healed.

She left a message. Her voice was light and cheery, in the same persona as her texts and emails, with small talk and superficial expressions of light and good energy. Her happy façade is still in place. She doesn't want me close, but she still wants me around. She is not yet healed, either.

~ 1268 ~

I went to the beach to watch the full moon rise in the east. The clouds cleared long enough for me to get a few photos. It was a "blue moon," the second full moon of the month, and in a few hours would become a red moon in full lunar eclipse.

When I came home I got word that my dear colleague Patrick had just died. He rose with the moon this evening, in spectacular form.

~ 1269 ~

Yet the circle is not less round than the sphere, and the sphere is the home and fatherland of circles. Infinite multitudes of circles lie enclosed in every sphere, and if they spoke they would say, For us were spheres created. – C.S. Lewis, *Perelandra* [141]

Here is the wonderful circle/sphere metaphor again. Lewis describes so well the relationship between God and his creation: "For us were spheres created." All of us, all we circles, together comprise the sphere in which we are all contained. Earlier I quoted Angelus Silesius' audacious poem (~1252~): "… God cannot, without me, endure a moment's space, Were I to be destroyed, he must give up the ghost."

Lewis and Silesius present us a great and irresolvable paradox: Who created Whom? If the sphere was created for the circles, then the idea of circles must have preceded the sphere. If God must be destroyed along with us, does that mean we created God? Is the existence of God as dependent on us as our existence is dependent on him? This paradox can only be resolved by knowing that creator and creation are both without beginning or end, inseparable and interlocking, inside each other, eternally one.

~ 1270 ~

HEALTH, Part 18

A few days ago I rubbed my eyes especially hard, and big black blotches appeared in my field of vision. Floaters dislodged into the vitreous humor of my left eye. Very annoying, and frightening. The floaters seem to be dissolving, but there are still dark lines and spots that pop up and distract me when I look at a blank wall or computer screen.

Two kinds of fear come up when my body starts to malfunction: fear of pain and fear of disability. Pain is an issue when I get a cold or flu with the usual sore throat and difficulty breathing. I want the discomfort to go away, and I fear that it never will. Panic sets in.

Disability is the issue when my senses malfunction, as happened when the floaters in my eye appeared, or when my ears get clogged, or my tinnitus seems deafening. I fear losing my bearings, my orientation to the outside world, and I fear that my sensory dysfunction will be permanent. Panic sets in.

So far, my pains and disabilities have been minor and mostly temporary. But someday they will be severe and permanent. My knowledge of that is the source of my panic. Babies and animals don't panic. They don't project into the future; they live in the moment, letting each moment's pain last only a moment, directing their thoughts to the life to be lived in the moment mindless of the pain. Pain can be indulged, ignored, or accepted. The monk who was in pain did not suffer because he did not fight the pain; he accepted it. (~725~)

Helen Keller, blind and deaf, was able to use the senses she still had – touch, smell, taste, and most important, thought – to reorient herself to the world. In the TV series *Kung Fu*, there was a blind Shaolin monk whose lack of sight gave heightened sensitivity to his other senses, and to forces beyond the senses. Perhaps the less dependent we are on the physical senses, the more attuned we can be to extrasensory input. This is the silver lining of disability that I pray will carry me through the fear of it.

Reinforcing that idea, Zen Buddhist Norman Fischer reminds me that my physical body and its sensations are not real:

> The Buddhist teachings on the workings of mind, called Abhidharma, teach us that there isn't a body per se, just a variety of momentary mental events. Some of them we think of as "physical," even though they're not. When I feel an ache in my right leg, the Abhidharma analysis goes, this sensation is a mental event produced in consciousness when an object I call a leg activates inner sensors that awaken awareness in a particular way. Likewise, seeing, hearing, and all sense perceptions are mental events stimulated by apparently physical objects.
>
> Contemporary cognitive science agrees. All experiences arise when consciousness is activated by a sense organ meeting an internal or external object. (Here, the mind itself functions like a sixth sense organ in relation to emotion and thought.) We assume we are "experiencing" the object that gave rise to the event in our consciousness. But the truth is that the only thing we can verify is the experience itself, however we may be misconstruing it. The idea of the body is like this. It is an idea based on unwarranted assumptions about the coherence of our conscious experience.
>
> In Buddhist analysis, then, there is no body. What there is, is form (*rupa*)—some kind of illusory arising that appears to be solid and that forms a basis for experience we call physical. But in actual fact it's just a continuous flow of momentary conscious events.[121]

As my sensory powers diminish, I grasp for them, clutch what is left of them and fear the unknown territory that lies beyond them. When they are totally gone and there is nothing left to grasp, I can be at peace in the dark, silent, intangible realm of spirit. This is the lesson that Helen Keller and Norman Fischer are teaching me.

~ 1271 ~

TO BEDE GRIFFITHS, 25 May 1944: About the past, and nothing being lost, the point is that 'He who loses his life shall save it' (Matthew 10:39) is totally true, true on every level. Everything we crucify will rise again: nothing we try to hold onto will be left us.

I wrote the other day [in *The Great Divorce*, Chapter 9, which he was writing at the time], 'Good and evil when they attain their full stature are retrospective. That is why, at the end of all things, the damned will say we were always in Hell, and the blessed we have never lived anywhere but in Heaven.' – C.S. Lewis, *The Collected Letters of C.S. Lewis, Volume II* [85]

Everything we try to hold onto slips through our fingers; everything we give up comes back to us, including health, wealth, and life.

I love Lewis' ability to connect past and future. Indeed, as I think about it, I see that we do judge good and evil by their effects in the past. And just as surely, the dark side of dualism is always in hell as the light side is always in heaven. This gives new weight to the creed that says Jesus descended into hell before he ascended into heaven. He was always in both places, and also rising above the dichotomy.

~ 1272 ~

Emily likes her tempestuous life. Lots of travel, barhopping, dancing, carousing, competitive and manipulative social interactions. Wild, impulsive sex. Claims of spirituality, but no behavioral evidence of it. Her life moves fast, but rarely breaks the spiritual surface. She seeks companions who will keep up her pace and follow her rules.

My life is quiet, peaceful, and deep. I like to stay in one place and enjoy a few close friends in cooperative, supportive relationships. Only the highest tantric sex will do. My spirituality came to me unbidden, and is reflected in every aspect of my life. I seek no companions, but when they come to me, they find no pace to be kept nor rules to be followed.

We are exact opposites. Together we are everything. I can be joyfully motionless with her in that completeness. She finds such motionlessness to be alternately frightening or boring. She does not understand the depth of our eternal union as I do. In this life she is unable surrender to our love, and I dare not surrender to it unless and until she reaches my tantric understanding. Duality can be so stubborn.

~ 1273 ~

SEX, Part 33
Valentine's Day

In "Buddhism and Sexuality: It's Complicated," Jeff Wilson commented on the book *Sexuality in Classical South Asian Buddhism* by José Cabezón. Wilson wrote:

Behind sex, of course, lies desire. Cabezón explores Buddhist theories of desire in great detail, offering this basic summary: experiencing pleasure "creates a predisposition to desire that pleasure again—to put ourselves, consciously or not, in situations where the pleasure can once again be enjoyed. The greater the pleasure, the stronger the imprint it leaves on the mind, and the more likely we are to seek it anew. And the more often we experience the pleasure, the more this becomes an ingrained psychic pattern. All sense pleasure is in this sense addictive." This is a serious problem for Buddhists intent on reaching nirvana, as attachment to momentarily pleasurable but ultimately painful desires becomes a never-ending feedback loop of fruitless chase and frustration.[142]

The worldly kind of sexuality, lust, is indeed a first poison desire. Uncontrolled sexuality, like gluttony, is an addiction, "momentarily pleasurable but ultimately painful." Anything that brings sensual pleasure and causes a craving for more is in this category.

C.S. Lewis shows us the Christian counterpart to the Buddhist view:

Screwtape twists the gift of pleasure: Never forget that when we are dealing with any pleasure in its healthy and normal and satisfying form, we are, in a sense, on the Enemy's ground. I know we have won many a soul through pleasure. All the same, it is His invention, not ours. He made the pleasures: all our research so far has not enabled us to produce one. All we can do is to encourage the humans to take the pleasures which our Enemy has produced, at times, or in ways, or in degrees, which He has forbidden. Hence we always try to work away from the natural condition of any pleasure to that in which it is least natural, least redolent of its Maker, and least pleasurable. An ever-increasing craving for an ever-diminishing pleasure is the formula. – C.S. Lewis, *The Screwtape Letters* [95]

When I started to read this, I began to think that Lewis got it wrong. Pleasure is the first Buddhist poison, not on the Enemy's (God's) ground, but on Screwtape's. But as I read on, I saw Lewis' true understanding emerge. Pleasure is indeed God's invention, all parts of duality being God's invention. And then, as Screwtape instructs his followers to lead men to the extremes of pleasure away from the Middle Way, the essence of the first poison is revealed – "an ever-increasing craving for an ever-diminishing pleasure" – which is the same as Wilson/Cabezón's "never-ending feedback loop of fruitless chase and frustration."

But the sexuality that arises from divine love is different. It is not merely a pleasure; it is a physical response to spiritual joy. It is not a sensation that goes away and drives the addict to grab for it again. It is a continuous state of being, Tantra, the expression of which ebbs and flows with the spiritual energy that creates it, but is itself constant and unchanging. It is not sought; it arrives without being beckoned, without craving.

Cabezón offers a lengthy exploration of sex in relation to the heavenly and hellish realms. ... In a dry understatement, Cabezón notes, "Buddhism clearly comes off as a religion that is deeply skeptical about sexed bodies and sexual acts. Sentient beings, these texts tell us, were better off in their androgynous phase at the beginning of the world cycle than they are now; and they are far better off in the upper reaches of the universe—in the higher-god realms, where one does not have to worry about sex—than in the realm of desire." He adds, "Our biologically sexed bodies, rampant sexual desires, and polysensual sexuality are clearly seen as obstacles to the goal of human perfection." In other words, sex gets in the way of buddhahood.[142]

The Buddhists and Christians agree that the physical body can be a spiritual obstacle. But the Buddhists, like the Christians, went astray over the centuries trying to address the problem, creating scripture, dogma, and doctrines, like the celibacy demanded of priests and nuns, that actually made the problem worse. All religions that build walls around sex, making rules and restrictions in an attempt to corral lust into a safe, chaste practice, do not recognize the highest love that God provides, a love that rises to "the upper reaches of the universe" above "the realm of desire." Once tantric sex is discovered, all religious orthodoxy and teachings based on worldly phenomena become irrelevant. Sex happens as divine love dictates. There are no rules.

Emily is spending Valentine's Day with Danny. Early this morning I thought of her, and invoked her spirit in tantric sex. But it wasn't there. At the beginning of her relationship with Danny, my body reflected her ardor with him. Perhaps now the glitter of lust has worn off for them, and my body reflects that, too, as it did when her relationship with Arthur cooled. (~980~)

When the sexual impulse wanes in tantric love, there is no sorrow. Tantric lovers know that the spirit, eternally present, will return to the body in due time. There is no grasping or desire for mere pleasure. Once you know sex in tantric love, simple worldly pleasure – which, like pain, is a source of suffering – holds no more attraction.

~ 1274 ~

ANGER

When the energy of anger serves ego, it is aggression. When it serves to ease others' suffering and make the world a better place, it is wisdom. – Melvin McLeod, "The Wisdom of Anger," *Lion's Roar*, March 2017

Anger is often associated with the second Buddhist poison. Like the other two poisons of desire and ignorance, we all experience these feelings to some degree. Is there a way to turn these poisons to helpful rather than harmful use? McLeod explains that when anger is not driven by ego, it can bring good to the world. When directed into constructive channels, anger is the energy that drives great movements for freedom and social justice. Righteous anger, as opposed to aggressive anger, is expressed without doing harm, with the realization that aggression is usually someone's maladaptive response to his own suffering. McLeod says, "When we are the targets of aggression ourselves, knowing that it may come out of the other person's pain helps us respond skillfully." So it was when Emily's aggressive anger exploded upon me.

> A teaching I heard Thich Nhat Hanh offer many times is that people who are difficult, people who say and do mean and offensive things, are not evil. They act that way because they suffer deeply and lack the understanding and skills to act differently. So rather than responding to them in anger, our responsibility as practitioners is to understand why they suffer, nourish our capacity to respond with compassion, and help them learn to transform the roots of their suffering.
>
> I came to understand Thich Nhat Hanh's teaching more deeply one day when I realized that the difficult people around me—those who were critical, judgmental, easily irritated, short-tempered, and so on—were like that not just to me and others, but also to themselves. If they were being hard on me, they were making themselves suffer even more. I could separate myself, mentally and physically, from their meanness; they could not. It became easier not to take the mean things people said or did personally, and my compassion grew. – Mitchell Ratner, "Difficult People Are Suffering People," *Lion's Roar*, May 2018

In my social justice work I have often found it necessary to speak truth to power, and I have felt the sting of many aggressive attacks. My revelatory truth also raised up demons in both The Unnamed One and Emily.

When the state of unsupported thought is reached, when there is nothing to lose, nothing held by the ego to protect or defend, it is possible to respond to the attacks of aggressors not with retribution or defensiveness but with compassion and equanimity, in the spirit of the 3rd Perfection. We can turn the other cheek, give up our cloak as well as our coat, and walk the extra mile with our aggressors, reflecting the peace that passes understanding and rises above anger.

Through all aspects of my life and work over the years, my relationship with anger has gradually evolved, from my early bitter rages to acceptance of vicious retaliation as the price of truth-telling, to my current state of compassionate forgiveness and loving service to my aggressors. It has not been an easy journey, but it was fruitful; my anger is no longer a source of suffering for myself or others.

When I read, "I could separate myself, mentally and physically, from their meanness; they could not," I recognized the cause of my continuing sorrow for Emily. For the wounded child inside her, there is no respite, no escape, no separation from the pain that drives her anger. Emily's torment is so much worse than mine, even though she says she is just fine.

~ 1275 ~

Indeed the safest road to Hell is the gradual one—the gentle slope, soft underfoot, without sudden turnings, without milestones, without signposts. – C.S. Lewis, *The Screwtape Letters* [95]

Billy Graham, the legendary Christian evangelist, died a few days ago. Now articles are coming out about the unsavory side of his life and work – his anti-Semitic, homophobic, racist, anti-communist, pro-war stance, and the multimillion-dollar empire he built by playing, praying, and preying on people's fear. Billy did a better job than most hucksters of covering up his dark side, but his preaching and especially his politicking were as laden with fear and hate as any.

I do not doubt the sincerity of Graham's Christianity. I think he honestly believed that he was bringing people to God with his ministry. Evil knows the truth of goodness just as goodness knows the truth of evil. Which side of Billy, the good or the evil side, was supreme in him? The fear-based Christian cults that have arisen around the world – and with them the rise of the hateful Religious Right that has wreaked havoc in politics and government – were built largely on Graham's message.

There must be evil in the world as there must be good. Billy's evil was God's will, just as his goodness was. Billy was a dramatic demonstration of the inseparability of good and evil in this world, and how evil often comes wrapped in godliness.

Billy Graham preached of being lifted up to Heaven, but I fear that he has glided down Screwtape's gentle slope to Hell.

~ 1276 ~

I recently attended a seminar presented by leaders of four different Buddhist sects representing Mahayana, Theravada, and Vajrayana traditions. The subject of the discussion was the various ways that Buddhist sutras and doctrines have been interpreted and practiced from one tradition to another, with emphasis on the Eightfold Path, meditation, practicing the Six Perfections, and taking the bodhisattva vow as means to achieving enlightenment.

None of these sincere but misguided Buddhists understands the true nature of enlightenment or the way to find it. None of the techniques they described can produce enlightenment – not meditation, or living the Eightfold Path, or practicing the Perfections, or taking a vow. In fact, these behaviors can be counterproductive. Attempting to strengthen capacities of love, wisdom, and compassion through one's own willpower and effort can reinforce that which Buddhism has always aimed to transcend: attachment to an autonomous, enduring self. To paraphrase Anita Moorjani: Acting as if one is a buddha does not mean one is *actually* a buddha. Huai-jang asked, "How could sitting in meditation make a buddha?" (~295~) Living a virtuous life is commendable, but it will not in itself bring enlightenment.

The required first step to enlightenment is not skilled behavior; it is surrender. Letting go of everything – money, control, fame, possessions, pleasure, safety, security, all desires and fears – letting go of ego. When that happens, the enlightened being that is already inside us, the God-self/buddha-nature, is free to emerge, and with it, divine love.

Often a major crisis, catastrophe, or catharsis is necessary to break the ego-dominated will and enable surrender. An increase of suffering must be experienced before nirvana – no suffering – can be exploded out of it. In my case, the horrific battle with grief and abandonment that I suffered at Lou's death was the catalyst I needed to jumpstart my surrender.

Once even a brief glimpse of enlightenment, a sneak preview of what lies beyond the narrow gate, is experienced, one's life is utterly changed. Living according to the Five Precepts, the Eightfold Path, and the Six Perfections becomes automatic and unintentional. These behaviors are not the cause of enlightenment, but the effect of it. Trying (and usually failing[ix]) to live according to these moral rules without the underpinning of divine love only produces frustration, impatience, and more suffering. Once the divine underpinning is there, however, everything just falls into place. As Yoda said, "There is no try."

~ 1277 ~

Emily wants to rekindle our relationship. I wrote to her, "Yes, a rekindling would be wonderful, but I am not yet ready. Doesn't mean I love you any less." It breaks my heart to say this, knowing what we are together in eternity, but I must balance my own health and safety against my sacrificial love for her. I must shore myself up now if I am to be around to serve her later, if and when she awakens and wants a best friend who deeply understands.

I would instantly sacrifice myself for her if doing so would indeed save her. But as long as she is comfortable in her life of depravity, nothing that I or anyone else might do can save her, only provide narcissistic supply and enable her continuing darkness. As I live the life of Christ, I must remember that Jesus' sacrifice did indeed accomplish his mission of demonstrating the Way to salvation. My sacrifice must do the same.

[ix] I can will what is right, but I cannot do it. For I do not do the good I want, but the evil I do not want is what I do." (Romans 7:18-19 RSV)

I am an empath. I cannot always differentiate my own pain from the pain of others. During the last couple weeks my chronic backache has become acute, making every movement difficult. Whose pain am I feeling? Mine, or Emily's?

It is clear to me now that Emily came into my life more for my benefit than hers. I needed to see just how vile and vicious the dark side can be. Having shown me the lightest of the light, God could not help but show me the darkest of the dark. And show me how divine love runs through both light and dark, into every nook and cranny.

~ 1278 ~

Here's my Christiane Northrup empath quiz result:

> You are a BALANCED EMPATH.
>
> Overall, you are moderately empathic. You can sense other people's emotions and you can understand how they are feeling, but you don't let their feelings affect your emotional state. What this translates into is a balanced life with few extremes. You're generally healthy. Your worldview is mostly positive. You're helpful but not to the point where it negatively affects you. You have good boundaries, even if you sometimes consciously choose to overstep them.
>
> Your relationships work well because of your ability to see how others are feeling without getting drawn in to their emotional ups and downs. While you believe that most people are good, you also understand not everyone is. You can see the bad ones coming from a mile away, so you don't engage with them.
>
> All in all, life works well for you.[143]

Balanced, though sometimes I lose my balance. But then, that's because I teeter on the razor's edge, the Middle Way.

> To energy vampires, trauma and drama are comfortable. If there was no drama, the energy vampire would have to look at the spiritual side of life. They are afraid of it. ... Old-soul empaths generally have a very solid relationship with the divine, with their faith in divine source. We feel bad for those who don't, and we're eager to share that deep and abiding faith with another. But they don't want to do the work of contacting that divine within. They'd rather just get a hit of our energy to keep them afloat until the next time. And if we don't recognize our own role in keeping this drama going, which is attempting to be their higher power by being available all the time and having all the answers, then we risk losing ourselves, getting sick and enabling them to stay stuck.[143]

This so perfectly describes my journey with Emily, and explains why I need to stay away from her now, both to protect myself and also to stop enabling her stuckness. I am a balanced, old-soul empath. If and when Emily decides to get unstuck and do the painful and scary work of "contacting that divine within," I will be there for her. Until then, there is nothing I can do.

I am different from the typical empath in that I entered and stayed in the abusive relationship with my eyes wide open, knowing what it was, knowing that there was a divine reason for it. This is, as Christiane described, the balanced empath consciously choosing to overstep her boundaries.

Because of my 11/17/13 epiphany (~604~), I was able to see both the horror of Emily's pain and also the boundless divine love that exists for her in the spirit, the unchained buddha-nature released from the bondage of her demons. But in another way, I am no different from other empaths: There is nothing I can do to effect her release unless and until Emily seeks it herself, and discovers her precious buddha-nature not in my narcissistic supply, but in her release from narcissism.

~ 1279 ~

Dear Betty,

Received your lovely card, thank you. Life is a series of events made up of moments, I am living in the moment these days, no thought of the past or future. Blessed to have so much love in my life, blessed to love so much in my life. I will always remember your kindness and forget the other stuff.

Light,
Emily

Other stuff? What "other stuff"? Her own offenses that she projects onto me? Even now, she must make our estrangement my fault. And yet, I understand. In a way, it is.

~ 1280 ~

THE THREE FORKS

The pastor was really on his game this morning at church. The scripture readings included some of my favorite passages: Moses' healing snake on a stick (Numbers 21:4-9) and Jesus' talk with Nicodemus (John 3:1-15).

But the best part was the sermon, in which the pastor told a story about three men who rode their horses through the woods into a clearing where they met a wise man. The road diverged into three forks, and the men asked the wise man which fork led to the treasure they sought. The wise man couldn't give them an answer. One man took the left fork, which led to a dead end in deep darkness. The second man took the right fork, which led to another dead end, this one a field of bright light. The third man pleaded with the wise man to help him decide which road to take. The wise man asked him what it was like in the place from which he came. The third man turned around and rode back home, whence he came.

The moral of the story is obviously that there's no place like home, the place you came from, where God is. But, I asked the pastor, where did the third road, the middle fork, go? He didn't know. *But I do.*

The middle fork, the Middle Way, is the road the Buddha took, the Way between the dualistic opposites of dark and light. At the end of the Middle Way is the Bodhi Tree of Enlightenment, which is the same as the Tree of Eternal Life, guarded by the cherubim's fiery sword, the backdoor into the Garden of Eden, just beyond the narrow gate through which few may enter. The middle fork is the "Way and the Truth and the Life; no one comes to the Father but by me." This road turns the corner around and over both dead ends and finds its way home at a higher hermetic level, a higher dimension.

The ride of the three men is symbolic of our journey through life. The clearing represents the bardo, the junction between states of being – between light and dark, life and death, and between duality and eternity. The wise man represents the priest, prophet, bodhisattva, or guru who can provide wisdom and support but cannot make your choice for you. The left fork leads to a place of fear and darkness – samsara, suffering, hell – and the right fork to a place of love and light – nirvana, no suffering, heaven. Both roads, however, are stuck in the field of duality. The left fork represents fear, pain, and aversion: a second poison weakness. Although it may seem that the right fork is a better route, it represents desire, pleasure, and attachment: a first poison weakness.

By turning around and riding back home the same way he entered the clearing, the third man set himself up for future incarnations. He remained in the realm of duality. He did not gain any new insights or experiences; he only retraced the steps his life had already taken. He returned home to God, but not by the route that would free him from karma. He found his way back to the place of exile east of Eden, close to God, and through merit transfer perhaps in closer communion with him, but not back into the Garden.

The Middle Way is not easy – living the life of Christ is not easy – but it is the one and only path that leads back into the Garden, to the Great Void, to the end of the law and sin and karma, to the fusion of the pairs of opposites into oneness with the Godhead who cannot be named, to awakening and surrender to the God-self within us, to the emptiness and fullness of eternity, to being "born of the spirit" as Jesus described it to Nicodemus.

~ 1281 ~

GOODBYE, IGNACIO

Dear Betty,

Ignacio made the decision to stop medical treatment and let go of his life. He has been hospitalized for a week, unable to eat, complete weakness and fatigue. He is just worn out. I'm actually relieved for him. It's been such a tough year; now he will not have to struggle further and can just sink into the reverie.

Love,
Cecilia

Three days later …

Dear Betty,

Ignacio passed from this world last night. Very peacefully, as had been the previous couple of days. Of course the really hard days have yet to fall. Doesn't seem real yet, maybe that's good; shield the pain for a while.

Love,
Cecilia

~ 1282 ~

Stephen Hawking died today. He was 76, a ripe old age for someone with ALS. The great power of his mind was reflected in his work as a physicist, but even more in his ability to thrive in a devastatingly disabled body and even retain a fine sense of humor in that humbling physical condition.

We don't generally look to scientists for great spiritual lessons. And yet, Hawking, like Einstein, without intending to, lit the path to God. And sometimes the people we look to for spiritual guidance, like Billy Graham, without intending to, obscure the path to God.

Stephen Hawking who, like Einstein, claimed no particular devotion to any religion, was nevertheless, like Einstein, inadvertently but necessarily spiritual and, like Einstein, said some wonderfully provocative things:

> Even if there is only one possible unified theory, it is just a set of rules and equations. What is it that breathes fire into the equations and makes a universe for them to describe?

> I regard the brain as a computer which will stop working when its components fail. There is no heaven or afterlife for broken down computers; that is a fairy story for people afraid of the dark.

> The past, like the future, is indefinite and exists only as a spectrum of possibilities.

> So long as the universe had a beginning, we could suppose it had a creator. But if the universe is really completely self-contained, having no boundary or edge, it would have neither beginning nor end: it would simply be. What place, then, for a creator? [144]

~ 1283 ~

PRIDE AND THE EGO, Part 5

> There is one vice of which no man in the world is free; which everyone in the world loathes when he sees it in someone else. There is no fault which makes a man more unpopular, and no fault which we are more unconscious of in ourselves. And the more we have it ourselves, the more we dislike it in others.

> The vice I am talking of is Pride or Self-Conceit: and the virtue opposite to it, in Christian morals, is called Humility. You may remember, when I was talking about sexual morality, I warned you that the centre of Christian morals did not lie there. Well, now, we have come to the centre. According to Christian teachers, the essential vice, the utmost evil, is Pride. Unchastity, anger, greed, drunkenness, and all that, are mere fleabites in comparison: it was through Pride that the devil became the devil: Pride leads to every other vice: it is the complete anti-God state of mind. – C.S. Lewis, *Mere Christianity* [76]

Lewis was quite right in saying that the center of Christian morals is not sex, but Pride – and this is also true in non-Christian religions. Everything he says about the Christian view of Pride is just as true about the Buddhist view of the self. His last sentence above could just as easily have been written by a Buddhist. In fact, Buddhist monk Ajahn Brahmavamso wrote something similar:

> In the first *jhana* mostly, and in the higher *jhanas* completely, the potential to do, will, and make choices – what I call "the doer" – has disappeared. The five hindrances are no longer able to prevent you from seeing that there is no one at the controls of your body and mind,

to put it bluntly. Will is not a self, or a product of a self. Will is just an impersonal natural process that can come to an absolute cessation. This insight is the most certain that you have ever known: free will is a delusion.

Consequently, sensory experience will never again be taken as evidence of a knower or a doer, such that you will never again imagine a self or a soul at the centre of experience, or beyond, or anywhere else. "Just this," concluded the Buddha "is the end of suffering."[145]

Lewis says, "Pride leads to every other vice." Ajahn says "the doer" – the self and its five hindrances – raises up all that we consciously know about the sensory body and mind, and is the main obstacle to awareness of our true nature. They put us in Lewis' "complete anti-God state of mind." What Lewis calls Humility in Christian terms is what Ajahn calls the cessation of the will in Buddhist terms.

Lewis understood very well the Buddhist concept of no-self, the demise of "the doer." From *Mere Christianity*:

The more we get what we now call 'ourselves' out of the way and let Him take us over, the more truly ourselves we become. The more I resist Him and try to live on my own, the more I become dominated by my own heredity and upbringing and surroundings and natural desires. In fact what I so proudly call 'Myself' becomes merely the meeting place for trains of events which I never started and which I cannot stop. What I call 'My wishes' become merely the desires thrown up by my physical organism or pumped into me by other men's thoughts or even suggested to me by devils. ... I am not, in my natural state, nearly so much of a person as I like to believe: most of what I call 'me' can be very easily explained. It is when I turn to Christ, when I give myself up to His Personality, that I first begin to have a real personality of my own.[76]

And how the eternal dance subsumes the ego into *agape,* from *The Problem of Pain*:

The golden apple of selfhood, thrown among the false gods, became an apple of discord because they scrambled for it. They did not know the first rule of the holy game, which is that every player must by all means touch the ball and then immediately pass it on. To be found with it in your hands is a fault: to cling to it, death. But when it flies to and fro among the players too swift for eye to follow, and the great master Himself leads the revelry, giving Himself eternally to His creatures in the generation, and back to Himself in the sacrifice, of the Word, then indeed the eternal dance 'makes heaven drowsy with the harmony'. All pains and pleasures we have known on earth are early initiations in the movements of that dance: but the dance itself is strictly incomparable with the sufferings of this present time. As we draw nearer to its uncreated rhythm, pain and pleasure sink almost out of sight. There is joy in the dance, but it does not exist for the sake of joy. It does not even exist for the sake of good, or of love. It is Love Himself, and Good Himself, and therefore happy. It does not exist for us, but we for it.[56]

And even more Buddhist-like, from *Present Concerns*:

> There are three kinds of people in the world. The *first class* is of those who live simply for their own sake and pleasure, regarding Man and Nature as so much raw material to be cut up into whatever shape may serve them.

> In the *second class* are those who acknowledge some other claim upon them—the will of God, the categorical imperative, or the good of society—and honestly try to pursue their own interests no further than this claim will allow. They try to surrender the higher claim as much as it demands, like men paying a tax, but hope, like other taxpayers, that what is left over will be enough for them to live on. Their life is divided, like a soldier's or a schoolboy's life, into time 'on parade' and 'off parade', 'in school' and 'out of school'.

> But the *third class* is of those who can say like St. Paul that for them 'to live is Christ'. These people have got rid of the tiresome business of adjusting the rival claims of Self and God by the simple expedient of rejecting the claims of Self altogether. The old egoist will has been turned round, reconditioned, and made into a new thing. The will of Christ no longer limits theirs; it is theirs. All their time, in belonging to Him, belongs also to them, for they are His.[79]

Lewis does a great job of describing the progression from free will to God's will, from chance to predestination, and from self to no-self. Lewis' "third class" is Ajahn Brahmavamso's higher *jhana* where "the doer" has disappeared and there is no one at the controls. Once we let go of pride/self/ego and surrender the controls to God, we recognize the illusion of the pride/self/ego-inspired free will, find alignment with the true center, enter a complete *pro*-God state of mind, and discover that vice, virtue, and free will are merely sensory illusions, and that behind the illusion is God's eternal will. Our real personality emerges.

In this sense we understand that the ego is not really annihilated. It is, as a dualistic expression of the soul, harmonized and homogenized with its eternal self, the God-self, which also dwells within. By the Law of Three (~968~), the negative and positive polarities join in the eternal dance, the singularity which is the Godhead.

~ 1284 ~

I haven't visited my angel cards in a while, but today I glanced at them and wondered if they had a message for me. I began shuffling the cards, moving them around, getting used to feeling them in my hands again. Sure enough, after several shuffles two cards jumped out of the deck:

"Chakra Clearing" – Archangel Metatron: "Call upon me to clear and open your chakras, using sacred geometric shapes."

"Clear Your Space" — *Archangel Jophiel: "Get rid of clutter, clear the energy around you, and use feng shui."*

I have been demoralized lately by several thorny problems in my work and personal life that refuse to be resolved. Emily is still estranged. There are interpersonal feuds among my friends and colleagues. Several organizations that I serve are struggling. I am weighed down by the deaths of Patrick and especially Ignacio, feeling the sorrow of their families left behind. The political state of the world, choked in greed and fear on a massive scale, is a constant background irritant.

My third eye no longer comes into view, and the little signs that the spirits are with me — rainbows, feathers, dreams — that buoyed me up through past difficulties seem to have stopped. But today I am reassured that all is well. With the cards the spirits found a way to reach me. How is it that two cards with similar messages find themselves side by side in the deck, and both jump out together? Okay, I get the message. My job for now is keeping it simple, narrowing my focus and staying in the moment, clearing away clutter in the house and in the mind.

PART 54
Thinking
March 2018 – May 2018

~ 1285 ~

THINKING AND THE MIND, Part 2

> The Naturalists have been engaged in thinking about Nature. They have not attended to the fact that they were thinking. The moment one attends to this it is obvious that one's own thinking cannot be merely a natural event, and that therefore something other than Nature exists. The Supernatural is not remote and abstruse: it is a matter of daily and hourly experience, as intimate as breathing. – C.S. Lewis, *Miracles* [27]

Bishop George Berkeley (1685-1753), a major influence on Lewis, taught that thoughts create the material world, and that God, something other than Nature, must exist as the source of our thoughts. The answer to the question of whether an object continues to exist even when we are not thinking about it is captured in this pair of limericks attributed to Roman Catholic priest Ronald Knox:

> There was a young man who said God
> must think it exceedingly odd
> if he finds that the tree
> continues to be
> when no one's about in the Quad.

> Dear Sir, your astonishment's odd
> I am always about in the Quad
> And that's why the tree
> continues to be
> since observed by, Yours faithfully, God.[146]

The God-self, the Supernatural in us, is also in Nature. God and Nature look at each other as in a mirror. Thich Nhat Hanh goes deeper into the phenomenon of thought and discovers not Berkeley's and Lewis' supernatural God that thinks, but the Godhead that unifies the thought and the thinker:

When Descartes said, "I think, therefore I am," his point was that if I think, there must be an "I" for thinking to be possible. When he made the declaration "I think," he believed that he could demonstrate that the "I" exists. We have the strong habit of believing in a self. But, observing very deeply, we can see that a thought does not need a thinker to be possible. There is no thinker behind the thinking—there is just the thinking; that's enough.

Now, if Mr. Descartes were here, we might ask him, "Monsieur Descartes, you say, 'You think, therefore you are.' But what are you? You are your thinking. Thinking—that's enough. Thinking manifests without the need of a self behind it." Thinking without a thinker. Feeling without a feeler. – Thich Nhat Hanh, "Four Layers of Consciousness"[147]

I am facing obstacles in one of my work projects, causing many delays. I am becoming frustrated and demoralized by this situation, having to jump through hoop after hoop. Thich teaches me that this frustration comes from the remnant of my ego, the thinker that thinks it thinks thoughts.

Don't think. Wait, then act. The delays that are holding back the project are not to annoy me, but in fact to protect me. Just ride the wave without thinking. Act as God's will, not my prideful will, directs. When the time is right, the path will be clear.

> Do you have the patience to wait until your mud settles and the water is clear?
> Can you remain unmoving until the right action arises by itself?
> —Lao-tzu, *Dao De Ching*

~ 1286 ~

THINKING AND THE MIND, Part 3

I attended a lecture by a disciple of Trungpa Rinpoche on mindfulness meditation, letting go of thoughts, and making friends with anger and fear so that they will no longer be in control. He warned us that corralling our thoughts and taming the mind is hard work. Trungpa called it "warrior's work:"

> The ground of fearlessness, which is the basis for overcoming doubt and wrong belief, is the development of renunciation. Renunciation here means overcoming that very hard and tough, aggressive mentality which wards off any gentleness that might come into our hearts. Fear does not allow fundamental tenderness to enter into us. When tenderness tinged by sadness touches our heart, we know that we are in contact with reality. We feel it. That contact is genuine, fresh, and quite raw. That sensitivity is the basic experience of warriorship, and it is the key to developing fearless renunciation.

The idea of renunciation is to relate with whatever arises with a sense of sadness and tenderness. We reject the aggressive, hard-core street-fighter mentality. The neurotic upheavals created by overcoming conflicting emotions, or the *kleshas*, arise from ignorance, or *avidya*. This is fundamental ignorance that underlies all ego-oriented activity. Ignorance is very harsh and willing to stick with its own version of things. Therefore, it feels very righteous. Overcoming that is the essence of renunciation: we have no hard edges.

Warriorship is so tender, without skin, without tissue, naked and raw. It is soft and gentle. You have renounced putting on a new suit of armor. You have renounced growing a thick, hard skin. You are willing to expose naked flesh, bone, and marrow to the world. – Chögyam Trungpa Rinpoche, "The Tender Heart of the Warrior" [148]

Trungpa's "fearless renunciation" is a great description of the unresisted vulnerability of divine love. I understand what Trungpa is saying. It is the same thing Jesus said when he told us to turn the other cheek, and what he did by rejecting the "aggressive, hard-core street-fighter mentality" (personified by Barabbas) and submitting to crucifixion.

We shall draw nearer to God, not by trying to avoid the sufferings inherent in all loves, but by accepting them and offering them to Him; throwing away all defensive armour. If our hearts need be broken, and if He chooses this as the way in which they should break, so be it. – C.S. Lewis, *The Four Loves* [125]

It was a mystery to my friends why I peacefully accepted Emily's abuse, did not run from it or put up any defense against it. I went to war with her demons without a suit of armor, exposing naked flesh, bone, and marrow to the world. My sad and tender heart was broken, as it had to be.

We can let the circumstances of our lives harden us so that we become increasingly resentful and afraid, or we can let them soften us and make us kinder and more open to what scares us. We always have this choice. – Pema Chödrön, *The Places That Scare You: A Guide to Fearlessness in Difficult Times*

Young people, at the height of their health and strength, think they are invincible. They take risks, play violent sports, drive fast cars. They acquire Trungpa's "aggressive mentality" and consider tenderness a sign of weakness. With age and infirmity they discover the underlying fear that drove their youthful aggression and learn that tenderness, gentleness, and soft edges are signs of a greater kind of strength. To be fearless they must face and embrace all that they fear. Total invincibility comes with total vulnerability. Jesus demonstrated this when he conquered death by dying.

Most people go to God for relief, as Tony de Mello said, religion being the opium of the people, as Karl Marx said. They want something – peace, comfort, healing, support, money, a spouse, a job – and they are told that if they pray, do good works, confess their sins, repent, and give lots of money to the church, they will get what they want. And salvation, to boot. No renunciation or exposing of naked flesh necessary.

But this kind of relief is just a placebo. Sometimes we get what we want, but not because our selfish prayers activated the supernatural hand of God. Nor is the hand of God being withheld when our prayers are not answered. Nothing happens, good or bad, by the intervention of some external force, be it God or Satan, but by the power of our own thoughts and their alignment, or not, with the eternal God-self within us.

> "Do you not see that whatever goes into a man from outside cannot defile him, since it enters not his heart but his stomach, and so passes on?" (Thus he declared all foods clean.) And he said, "What comes out of a man is what defiles a man. For from within, out of the heart of man, come evil thoughts, fornication, theft, murder, adultery, coveting, wickedness, deceit, licentiousness, envy, slander, pride, foolishness. All these evil things come from within, and they defile a man." (Mark 7:18-23 RSV)

Our own thoughts and actions, not the thoughts or actions of others, are what hurt and defile us. The only freedom that cannot be taken away, said Victor Frankl, is the freedom to choose one's attitude in any given set of circumstances. It was St. Francis' attitude, not anyone's outward behavior, that changed his hardship into perfect joy. "There is nothing either good or bad," said Shakespeare, "but thinking makes it so." Tibetan Buddhist Yongey Mingyur Rinpoche presents the same idea:

> We choose ignorance because we can. We choose awareness because we can. Samsara and nirvana are simply different points of view based on the choices we make in how to examine and understand our experience. There's nothing magical about nirvana and nothing bad or wrong about samsara. If you're determined to think of yourself as limited, fearful, vulnerable, or scarred by past experience, know only that you have chosen to do so. The opportunity to experience yourself differently is always available. – Yongey Mingyur Rinpoche, "We Always Have Joy," https://www.lionsroar.com/we-always-have-joy/?mc_cid=67f49dc8a9&mc_eid=84a461539f

From the time we are small children we are taught to look outside ourselves for help – to parents, teachers, friends, doctors, lawyers, employers, governments, and God. These helpers can help in a way, to a point. Even the external God that our childhood religions introduced to us will come to our rescue to the extent that our programmed belief in him is not shattered by the reality that he is an illusion. Karl Marx explained this illusion in *A Contribution to the Critique of Hegel's Philosophy of Right (1844)*:

Religious suffering is, at one and the same time, the expression of real suffering and a protest against real suffering. Religion is the sigh of the oppressed creature, the heart of a heartless world, and the soul of soulless conditions. It is the opium of the people.

The abolition of religion as the illusory happiness of the people is the demand for their real happiness. To call on them to give up their illusions about their condition is to call on them to give up a condition that requires illusions. The criticism of religion is, therefore, in embryo, the criticism of that vale of tears of which religion is the halo.

Karl Marx is saying much the same thing as Carl Jung when he said, "The foundation of all mental illness is the unwillingness to experience legitimate suffering. Religion is a defense against the experience of God." A religion that keeps up the illusion, feeding its people the pleasant placebo, defends people against the truth and turns them away from the necessarily painful path to God.

The true God who dwells within us, the God-self/buddha-nature, our linkage from duality to eternity, is the only one we can count on when we really need help. But first we must find this eternal Godhead as Victor Frankl did when, in the midst of his suffering as a prisoner in a Nazi concentration camp, he joined the angels in the "contemplation of an infinite glory" that rises above and beyond worldly pain. We can change our thoughts, but first we must change the nature of our prayers, from prayers *for* to prayers *of.* (~1236~)

The path to God provides exactly the opposite of what we think we want. First we must weather the storms of fear, pain, poverty, dishonor, rejection – the Buddha's "unsupported thought," Bonhoeffer's "dishonorable suffering," St. Francis' "perfect joy" – before the true peace that passes understanding can be found through the narrow gate, in the hole in the log in the vast ocean. Once we have weathered the storm, we find the place where we have no wants or needs, and our prayers need no answers.

~ 1287 ~

THINKING AND THE MIND, Part 4
Miracles and Magic

In the morning, as he was returning to the city, he was hungry. And seeing a fig tree by the wayside he went to it, and found nothing on it but leaves only. And he said to it, "May no fruit ever come from you again!" And the fig tree withered at once. When the disciples saw it they marveled, saying, "How did the fig tree wither at once?" And Jesus answered them, "Truly, I say to you, if you have faith and never doubt, you will not only do what has been done to the fig tree, but even if you say to this mountain, 'Be taken up and cast into the sea,' it will be done. And whatever you ask in prayer, you will receive, if you have faith." (Matthew 21:18-22 RSV)

The Bible is full of fantastic claims for the power of faith like the one above. Another one is in Matthew 17:20 RSV: "For truly, I say to you, if you have faith as a grain of mustard seed, you will say to this mountain, 'Move from here to there,' and it will move; and nothing will be impossible to you."

Did these highly improbable space-time events really happen, or are they metaphors conveying a reality beyond space-time consciousness? What is the truth that these Bible verses are meant to reveal?

My wall plaque says, "Faith is not belief without proof, but trust without reservations." This is surrender. Most Christians think they have faith much greater than a mustard seed and wonder why mountains don't move for them. The problem is that, although they believe in God, they don't quite trust him. They haven't fully surrendered. Muriel Esther said, "Faith produces miracles; miracles don't produce faith." Having faith – trust – opens us to participation in miracles; believing in miracles may strengthen our belief in God, but does not increase our trust in him.

> Beloved, we are God's children now; it does not yet appear what we shall be, but we know that when he appears we shall be like him, for we shall see him as he is. And every one who thus hopes in him purifies himself as he is pure. (1 John 3:2-3 RSV)

I am taken by this translation of the phrase "hopes in him." Not "believes (πιστεύω pisteuō) in him," but "hopes (ἐλπίς elpis) in him." Hope in this sense is more like trust than belief. More like surrendering than thinking. To be purified as God is pure, to see him as he is, is to let go of thinking and believing.

> Not a single star will be left in the night.
> The night will not be left.
> I will die and, with me,
> the weight of the intolerable universe.
> I shall erase the pyramids, the medallions,
> the continents and faces.
> I shall erase the accumulated past.
> I shall make dust of history, dust of dust.
> I am looking on the final sunset.
> I am hearing the last bird.
> I bequeath nothing to no one.
>   — Jorge Luis Borges, "The Suicide"

When you have found the true God, when you live in complete accord with God's will, when you live in the spirit while still on earth and the spirit directs your every thought, word, and deed, you pray in gratitude for what you have already received, your prayers having been answered before you uttered them. Fig trees wither and mountains are cast into the sea. Your ego commits suicide, and as Borges described, all the thoughts the ego created are erased. Every moment is born anew. John Milton said, "A mind is its own place, and in itself can make a heaven of hell, a hell of heaven."

The Buddhists look at miracles in a similar way:

> What is the miraculous view? … Outer objects don't truly exist. We can't find any objectively existent particle of matter. The things that appear to us are like appearances in dreams and, therefore, just as in a lucid dream, we can effect changes in the environment. The sort of person who has certainty in the view, and also realization through meditative experience, can indeed manipulate appearances in the outer world, and perform what we would call miracles for the benefit of others. Nagarjuna said, "To whomever emptiness is possible, all things are possible."

> Milarepa was approached by philosophers who thought he was just a stupid person claiming to have realization, and that he had no education and was a charlatan. He inquired whether he could ask these learned men a question, and they agreed. So he asked them, "What is the definition of earth?" They laughed and said everybody knows that but you: earth is hard and obstructing. Then he asked them for the definition of space. Once again, they laughed and mocked him and said that space allows for movement, it's unobstructing. Milarepa then walked on space and walked through a mountain. He cut through their concepts that projected an objective reality of fixed characteristics, and he also cut through their arrogance. Even though I can't do that myself, I have at least intellectual certainty that the mountain is like a mountain in a dream. – Ari Goldfield [149]

Miracles are not the suspension of the laws of nature; they are the effect of being lifted out of nature while still in it, as in a dream, to a higher dimension. During my 1/1/09 epiphany, I saw solid matter dissolve into pure energy; dancing molecules and timelessness entered my consciousness. For me, fig trees withered and mountains moved, but to everyone else in the same space and time with me, the façade, the illusion of the natural world of form and substance, remained intact. In the fullness of biological and geological time, all fig trees wither and all mountains are cast into the sea. To see these things happen is to compress all of time and space into eternal oneness. In this sense, Jesus saw the fig tree's future withered state in eternity and brought its present physical form into conformity with that state.

Sometimes evidence of connection to the higher dimension can manifest on the physical plane, as my body's hormone balance changed in response to my karmic loves; or in miraculous healing, as Anita Moorjani experienced in her near-death experience; or in the appearance of stigmata; or in levitation, seeing visions, hearing voices, or speaking in tongues. Sometimes these manifestations are perceptible by others, and sometimes not, as when Bernadette saw the Virgin at Lourdes but others did not.

Jesus, the Buddha, and all the great miracle workers were literally awakened as from a dream, aware that life is a lucid dream, the features of which can be manipulated when one has access to the higher realms. For them, the boundary between reality and illusion, natural and supernatural, ordinary and extraordinary, time and eternity, is a slippery slope. The difference between me and the great sages is that I cannot (yet) bring about miracles; I can only stand in awe of them when they inexplicably happen to me. I have known flashes of awakening, but I keep falling back to sleep. I have visited the higher realms, but I haven't been able to stay there long enough to absorb their full power. I know that this power exists; I have felt it.

> What many see we call a real thing, and what only one sees we call a dream. But things that many see may have no taste or moment in them at all, and things that are shown only to one may be spears and water-spouts of truth from the very depth of truth. – C.S. Lewis, *Till We Have Faces* [150]

However miracles happen, be they large or small, whether perceptible by others or not, whether through the synchronous operation of the laws of nature or elevation beyond nature, I take them seriously. I know someone's miraculous claim is real, whether I perceive it or not, when the result is an increase of love and a decrease of fear. God moves in a mysterious way, his wonders to perform. I believe in miracles.

~ 1288 ~

THINKING AND THE MIND, Part 5
Heaven and Hell

> There are only two kinds of people in the end: those who say to God, 'Thy will be done' and those to whom God says, in the end, 'Thy will be done.' All that are in Hell choose it. Without that self-choice, there could be no Hell. No soul that seriously and constantly desires joy will ever miss it. Those who seek, find. To those who knock, it is opened.

> Hell is a state of mind—ye never said a truer word. And every state of mind, left to itself, every shutting up of the creature within the dungeon of its own mind is, in the end, Hell. But Heaven is not a state of mind. Heaven is reality itself. All that is fully real is Heavenly.

A damned soul is nearly nothing: it is shrunk, shut up in itself. Good beats upon the damned incessantly as sound waves beat on the ears of the deaf, but they cannot receive it. Their fists are clenched, their teeth are clenched, their eyes fast shut. First they will not, in the end they cannot, open their hands for gifts, or their mouths for food, or their eyes to see. – C.S. Lewis, *The Great Divorce* [101]

Lewis' assertion that Hell is a state of mind but Heaven is reality reminds me of the differing views among Buddhists about nirvana relative to eternity. Both heaven and nirvana are considered by some to be states of mind, worldly conditions – the "good" side of duality, hell and samsara being the opposite "bad" side. Those who understand Heaven in this way would disagree with Lewis when he says, "And every state of mind, left to itself, every shutting up of the creature within the dungeon of its own mind is, in the end, Hell." There is no consciousness, be it of Heaven or Hell, that is not in the mind. When that consciousness is of Heaven, the mind is not a dungeon, but a beautiful garden where the soul is free, not shut up.

Others consider heaven and nirvana to be states of full enlightenment, beyond worldly duality to oneness with God, unity in eternity. Hell and samsara are outside that place of unity. This may be close to Lewis' view, the view of most Christians, and the view of most Buddhists.

Others, like me, consider heaven and nirvana to be states of special awareness straddling or encompassing the other two views, operating in the world of duality and yet conscious of a realm beyond it; a spiritual condition that enables one to see reality as it unfolds in space-time and also to know reality in its spaceless timeless unity. This is the paradoxical triangulation I have so often described, in duality but beyond it, on the cusp, in the bardo between thoughts where duality and eternity meet.

I recognized Emily in this passage: "A damned soul is nearly nothing: it is shrunk, shut up in itself … First they will not, in the end they cannot, open their hands for gifts." God has said to Emily "Thy will be done" in this life, but he also sent her a wake-up fairy to show her the gift of divine love that her clenched fists cannot receive, and to be with her in Hell until she is ready to open the dungeon of her mind and climb out.

~ 1289 ~

THINKING AND THE MIND, Part 6
Consciousness

"There is nothing to forgive, for these people are acting from a place of unconsciousness." – Eckhart Tolle

As I watched my eighteen-month-old grandnephew doing what toddlers instinctively do to get what they want, I commented to his mother, "At this age children are not fully conscious."

"I think that's true," she said.

Young adults are not fully conscious, either. The excellent musical performances I delivered thirty years ago were played mostly unconsciously, without my full awareness of what I was doing, how I was doing it, where my music was coming from, or the daemonic forces that created all the aspects of the sound that emanated from my instrument. It is the same with my writing; my early writings already contained the essence of spiritual truth, but in fuzzy, nebulous form. The deeper meaning, the details of that truth, are just now coming into conscious focus.

Sam Littlefair quotes Jim Tucker, a psychiatrist who is a leading researcher on reincarnation, who suggests that all of life is made up of various levels of dreaming:

> "The mainstream materialist position is that consciousness is produced by the brain," he says, so consciousness is what some people would call an *epiphenomenon*, a byproduct. He sees it the other way around: our minds don't exist in the world; the world exists in our minds. Tucker describes waking reality as like a "shared dream," and when we die, we don't go to another place. We go into another dream.
>
> Tucker's dream model parallels some key Buddhist concepts. In Buddhism, reality is described as illusion, often compared to a sleeping dream. In Siddhartha Gautama's final realization, he reportedly saw the truth of rebirth and recalled all of his past lives. Later that night, he attained enlightenment, exited the cycle of death and rebirth, and earned the title of "Buddha"—which literally means "one who is awake." – Sam Littlefair, "Do You Only Live Once?" *Lion's Roar*, May 2018

How conscious am I now? Are my thoughts really delusions, obstacles to greater awareness of reality, or just the opposite? The Buddhist author Zenju Earthlyn Manuel describes the relationship of enlightenment and delusion:

Anyone who has practiced earnestly for any length of time has likely wrestled with the thinking mind, motivated by a desire to evolve away from delusion and toward awakening or enlightenment. But what if our deluded minds aren't a barrier to enlightenment at all? What if they are the very path to it?

In Hotsu Mujoshin ("On Giving Rise to the Unsurpassed Mind"), Dogen wrote, "Thinking is the mystery of the practice by which we become intimate with ourselves and the universe." In other words, when we become intimate with our own thinking, delusions become the earth upon which the moon of enlightenment shines. We may long to be the light itself, the moon glowing upon the earth, yet we feel tethered to our emotions and the thoughts that bring them to the surface. In Dogen's vision, the relationship between delusion and enlightenment within our lives is necessary. We need all that we were born with to navigate life, and that includes delusions.[151]

This quote by Dogen illuminates Thich Nhat Hanh's explanation of why we need the historical/phenomenal to touch the eternal/noumenal. (~649~/~694~) The relationship between delusion and enlightenment, between phenomena and noumena, creates consciousness. It is through our phenomenal consciousness in duality that we mortals can know eternity, and God is able to know itself. This is why God created Adam, why Krishna created Radha.

Merriam-Webster defines *illusion* as the "perception of something objectively existing in such a way as to cause misinterpretation of its actual nature," and *delusion* as "something that is falsely believed." Illusion thus comes from sensory perception – seeing, hearing, smelling, or touching something that presents a false or misleading picture of reality. Delusion is a thought formation that comes from believing the false illusion to be true. Our delusions are useful, as Manuel says, to navigate life, because we live in the illusion of reality that our senses present to us. Our delusions are necessary for us to function in our illusory world.

> Enlightenment is our true nature and our home, but the complexities of human life cause us to forget. That forgetting feels like exile, and we make elaborate structures of habit, conviction, and strategy to defend against its desolation. But this condition isn't hopeless; it's possible to dismantle those structures so we can return from an exile that was always illusory to a home that was always right under our feet. … We don't see the world as it is and then withdraw from it; we see the world as it is so we can most truly live as part of it. Our freedom isn't *from* the world; it's *in* the world. – Joan Sutherland, "Everything is Enlightenment," *Buddhabharma* Winter 2020

Sutherland's "complexities of human life" are Manuel's delusions. All of life, including the accumulated wisdom of all past lives, is a process of gradually expanding consciousness, dismantling those delusional structures. Our delusions, our fundamental misunderstandings of the nature of reality, are the substrate out of which enlightenment grows. At a certain point, when we are ready, we can become fully conscious, "awake" like the Buddha or "born again" like Jesus. We can see our delusions for what they are, along with the illusions that created them, and also see the reality behind the illusion. Our delusional thoughts are illuminated by enlightened truth as the earth is illuminated by the light of the sun.

I have long sensed that Emily's narcissism comes from a place of unconsciousness; her demons play out her childhood trauma without her conscious mind fully knowing what she is doing. Caroline Myss described so well the multi-generational transference of abusive behavior as an unconscious archetypal expression of eons of karmic fear and anger. Jesus' recognition of this unconscious acting out is the essence of his prayer from the cross: "Father, forgive them, for they know not what they do." Eckhart Tolle went even farther, saying that when behavior is unconscious, there is nothing to forgive.

Yet, Dr. Christiane Northrup says that energy vampires know exactly what they are doing, and they do it intentionally. Myss and Northrup are both correct, and this is how dissociation plays a role. Emily's demons know what they are doing and why, but the inner wounded child is unconscious, in deep darkness, sheltered from conscious awareness of the tragic play being acted out on the surface of her life. Buried even deeper than the wounded child is her buddha-nature, knowing all, seeing all, patiently waiting for the conscious and unconscious, illusion and reality, to reveal each other.

~ 1290 ~

It's been a while since I've had a memorable dream, but last night the dry spell ended: *I was about to leave on a trip but hadn't started to pack yet. I began piling shiny, satiny clothes neatly into a big suitcase. There was plenty of room in the suitcase, but I looked around the room and saw lots more stuff to pack, wondering if it would all fit. "When do we leave, Dad?" I asked. We were, it seemed, going "home." I began to pack small polished wooden boxes and manipulate objects that seemed to go inside the boxes.*

From dreammoods.com:

> **Suitcase –** To see a suitcase in your dream indicates that you are a very composed, together person. You keep your attitudes and behavior in check. Alternatively, a suitcase symbolizes your need for a much-needed vacation or break.

> **Packing –** To dream that you are packing signifies big changes ahead for you. You are putting past issues to rest or past relationships behind you. Alternatively, it represents the burdens that

you carry. To dream that you are packing, but the more your pack, the more there is to pack implies that you are weighed down by the endless responsibilities and expectations in your life.

Clothing – To dream of your clothes is symbolic of your public self and how you are perceived. It is indicative of the act you put on in front of others. Clothes are also an indication of your condition and status in life.

Satin – To see or wear satin in your dream signifies a smooth transition.

Box – To see a box in your dream signifies your instinctual nature and destructive impulses. Alternatively, you may be trying to preserve and protect some aspect of yourself.

Father – To see your father in your dream symbolizes authority and protection.

Trip – To dream that you are going on a trip suggests that you are in need of a change of scenery. You are feeling overworked and need to take time out for yourself for some fun and relaxation. Alternatively, the dream means that you are looking to explore a different aspect of yourself.

Big changes are ahead, unrealized potential will be unleashed, and the transition will be smooth. My satiny public self is being packed away; I will put past issues behind me, yet I will preserve and protect some aspect of myself. My heavy burdens and responsibilities will be lightened when I take a break and get a change of scenery.

This will be a spiritual trip. Is the "Dad" I am talking to my heavenly Father? Are we returning to our heavenly home? The back of my 5th chakra is tingling as I write this.

~ 1291 ~

When it rains, it pours. Another dream last night: *I see a wild crazy man being stabbed in the chest with a knife, and then stabbing himself with the knife. He is holding the knife and looking at me, coming toward me as if to stab me. He stops in front of me, and I grab the knife and hide it under a cloth so that he cannot pick it up again. He turns away as if to hide the bloody wounds on his chest. I grab his arm and turn him around, saying, "See, there is blood on your chest; you were stabbed!" I woke up.*

From dreammoods.com:

Knife – To dream that you are carrying a knife signifies anger, aggression and/or separation. To dream that you are wounded by a knife is symbolic of masculine or animalistic aggression. To see someone holding a knife in your dream suggests that you lack control or power in a situation or relationship.

Could the knife-holding man be Emily – the victim of multiple stabbings in the heart, who turned the knife on herself and then on me? The knife is symbolic of psychological as well as physical weapons used by the abuser. By taking the knife away and hiding it, I stop the abuse and gain control of the situation. But her wounded child is still bleeding. She turns away from me to hide her wounds, in denial of them, but I still see them. What a pity I woke up before I learned how to heal the wounds.

~ 1292 ~

My Buddhist message today: *The divine masters are always with you and will help you … continue to pray … come to the temple to meditate … you have power … you are protected … as you bring joy to others, that will be your joy … next month you will have a spiritual rebirth … you will shine.*

Does this relate to my packing dream a few days ago? I am beginning to feel excited about the big change, the transition that is apparently ahead for me. In case it is the final transition, what do I need to finish now before I go?

~ 1293 ~

APOLOGY AND FORGIVENESS, Part 7

Caroline Myss hit the nail on the head again. I paraphrase from her online course:

> Forgiveness is not something your mind can do. It is a mystical act. I need to let go of pain and the need for justice the way I want it. This darkness comes maybe from past lives or future ones. You, the person who acted out with me, the wound carrier, has come to do me a favor, to release me, not to hold me captive. This is a mystical perspective, not a literal one. People who do not heal are not capable of ascending to a symbolic or mystical level; they keep it literal. At the mystical level, life is played out very differently. Forgiveness says this is not about you, it is about my life, and I thank you for showing me what has to come out of me. Forgiveness comes from the soul. The mind cannot do it. We are all in service to each other's drama. Every act of wound is a universal wound.
>
> It is not the act itself, but the willful intention of it without regard for the hurt that will come from it. It's not enough to just apologize. That doesn't heal; there is an incompleteness. You are still in the mind and the mind can't heal. "I never meant to hurt you" was a lie. I knew what I did would hurt you and I did it anyway. I wanted what I wanted. I knew taking what I wanted

would traumatize your life, and it didn't stop me. It wasn't just a boo-boo, it was a sin. I own it, and I'm asking for your forgiveness.[152]

When Caroline described the complete apology as owning up to the sin, she used the example of someone cheating on a spouse. This conjured up in my mind the fact that I was the "other woman" in Lou's first marriage, and he was by all outward appearances cheating on his wife.

Should I have apologized to Lou's first wife? Did I cause her to be hurt or harmed? Did I commit a sin against her? By most worldly measures, the answer to all three questions would be YES. But my answer to all three questions, for reasons I have described at length in this journal, is NO. I agree with Caroline's approach to apology in the context of normal worldly ego-driven behavior, where fear and desire govern, and callous offenses against other people often happen.

But there is another context, an otherworldly God-driven one, where divine love governs and there is no sin, no wrong, and no need for apology or forgiveness. The relationship Lou and I had was that kind, not based on desire, but on our awakening to a spiritual love that transcends earthly relationships. It wasn't a matter of choosing; in fact, we tried to choose otherwise. God simply took us by the scruff of the neck. In the big picture of divine love, there is never any harm done. As our love liberated Lou from a bad marriage, so it liberated his wife. No harm done. Nothing to apologize for.

Even in worldly hurts, it is not the act itself that hurts, but the victim's response to it. Hurt is in the heart of the beholder. And … all who feel hurt must remember that they contributed in some way to the act that hurt them.

~ 1294 ~

REINCARNATION or REBIRTH?

Buddhists generally prefer the term "rebirth" to "reincarnation" to differentiate between the Hindu and Buddhist views. The concept of reincarnation generally refers to the transmigration of an *atman*, or soul, from lifetime to lifetime. This is the Hindu view, and it is how reincarnation is generally understood in the West.

Instead, Buddhism teaches the doctrine of *anatman*, or non-self, which says there is no permanent, unchanging entity such as a soul. In reality, we are an ever-changing collection of consciousnesses, feelings, perceptions, and impulses that we struggle to hold together to maintain the illusion of a self.

In the Buddhist view, the momentum, or "karma," of this illusory self is carried forward from moment to moment—and from lifetime to lifetime. But it's not really "you" that is reborn. It's just the illusion of "you." When asked what gets reborn, Buddhist teacher Chögyam Trungpa Rinpoche reportedly said, "Your bad habits." – Sam Littlefair, "Do You Only Live Once?" *Lion's Roar*, May 2018

Norman Fischer and Thich Nhat Hanh add more:

What gets reborn? The classical metaphor is of an acorn. An acorn becomes an oak tree. When the oak tree is here, the acorn is not, and no part of the acorn can be found in the oak tree. One simply has succeeded the other, just as one moment and one life succeeds the previous moment or life. – Norman Fischer, *Lion's Roar*, May 2018

When you look into a person, you see five *skandhas*, or elements: form, feelings, perceptions, mental formations, and consciousness. There is no soul, no self, outside of these five, so when the five elements go to dissolution, the karma, the actions that you have performed in your lifetime, is your continuation. What you have done and thought is still there as energy. You don't need a soul, or a self, in order to continue.

It's like a cloud. Even when the cloud is not there, it continues always as snow or rain. The cloud does not need to have a soul in order to continue. There's no beginning and no end. You don't need to wait until the total dissolution of this body to continue—you continue in every moment. – Thich Nhat Hanh, *Lion's Roar*, May 2018

The cloud has a soul whether it needs one or not. H_2O, the unchanging soul of the cloud, continues in one form or another indefinitely. The energy in atomic particles is the soul that passes from one material form to the next, from acorn to oak tree to acorn again. Our genealogy is important because our genes are the vehicle that carries our soul energy from one material form, incarnation, to another.

I find the intellectual exercises we do as spiritual pathfinders both invigorating and numbing. Does the distinction between *atman* and *anatman*, soul and karma, matter? Between "reincarnation" and "rebirth"? God and Godhead? Self? No-self? I play these mind games with as much gusto as anyone, as this journal attests. But in the end, the soul, the self, clouds, rain, acorns, and oak trees are what they are regardless of how we perceive, describe, accept, reject, or deny them. "Knowing" has no use for knowledge.

~ 1295 ~

Saw the eye doctor today. The deterioration of my body is right on schedule – I now have the first signs of cataracts. This could explain the halos and starbursts that I have been seeing around bright lights. I accept this scientific explanation for my visual aberrations, but even in its normal, natural operation, nature carries a spiritual message. I see God in the halos and starbursts.

As I contemplate the blessing of vision, I think about the symbolic representations of colors. The seven colors of the rainbow and the seven chakras. The primary colors: red and blue – hot fire and cold water – represent the dualistic opposites of this world; yellow – the light of the sun, the light of God – represents eternity.

~ 1296 ~

On every path, including the one to the narrow gate, there are sidetracks and backwaters. As one gets close to the narrow gate, these sidetracks become more insidious and treacherous. This is where people get stuck in comfortable beliefs and habits, where their thought patterns become ossified, where they lose their Way to God in their desire for comfort and safety. Some people stop for a beer at such a pleasant roadhouse and then continue on. Some get stuck there and never leave.

Today I saw my dear friend Cecilia stuck in such a place. She does not agree with me concerning the anthropomorphic nature of God in the Hebrew Bible. She defends this God, believing that he is indeed the ultimate God, the Source. She was almost angry with me for suggesting otherwise.

This is why I resist aligning myself with any form of organized religion. They almost all want you to "believe" something. My favorite definition of "belief" – a strongly held opinion that you refuse to reconsider. I have many opinions, but no beliefs. All my opinions are subject to reconsideration in light of new evidence, especially when that evidence is divinely delivered.

Cecilia's belief about God is what most Christians are taught as children. We cling to such beliefs as adults because they hark back to comforting memories of childhood, to a child's simple faith and trust in parents and other authority figures. We are all programmed according to our childhood influences, and our adult behaviors, both positive and negative, stem from that early programming. It is scary to break free, and we only do so when God gives us no other choice.

This is not to say that Cecilia's belief about God is wrong; there is an aspect of truth to it. It is just that she is not seeing the whole picture, the whole truth. I am wondering if Cecilia's loss of Ignacio will precipitate her surrender, driving her to let go of old beliefs and open her mind to more aspects of truth, as the loss of Lou did for me. The God of my childhood could not help me, but discovering the Godhead behind God did.

~ 1297 ~

Last night I went to the opera. I bought a ticket at the last minute and took the first seat the box office person offered me. The seat I bought was in the middle of a large patch of empty seats. Good, I thought, room to spread out! Then, just as the performance was about to start, a couple arrived and took their seats right next to me.

We started to chat. The man had been a Zen Buddhist monk in his early years, and we discovered that we had some friends in common in the Buddhist community. A very interesting conversation ensued, continuing during intermissions and after the opera. He asked for my contact information, saying he may have a job at the Zendo for me. I gave him my card, but warned him that I didn't want the job if it meant I had to sit still on a cushion facing the wall! He laughed.

~ 1298 ~

My dear Clive Staples! Once again, without intending to, Lewis shows the fundamental integration of Christianity, Buddhism, and virtually all other religions:

> There are no ordinary people. You have never talked to a mere mortal. Nations, cultures, arts, civilisations—these are mortal, and their life is to ours as the life of a gnat. But it is immortals whom we joke with, work with, marry, snub, and exploit—immortal horrors or everlasting splendours. … Next to the Blessed Sacrament itself, your neighbour is the holiest object presented to your senses. If he is your Christian neighbour, he is holy in almost the same way, for in him also Christ *vere latitat*—the glorifier and the glorified, Glory Himself, is truly hidden. – C.S. Lewis, *The Weight of Glory* [86]

In the first part of this passage, Lewis describes the immortal horror and everlasting splendor that is karma. In the latter part he perfectly describes Glory Himself hidden in us. Although overtly Christocentric as we would expect from Lewis, this description is for all the world as good a depiction of the indwelling buddha-nature as there is.

~ 1299 ~

Today's angel card, which I drew twice, even after extensive shuffling: *"You Know What To Do" – Archangel Uriel: "Trust your inner knowledge, and act upon it without delay."*

And then, another one: *"Clairaudience"* – *Archangel Zadkiel: "Notice the loving guidance you hear inside your mind, or from other people."*

Oh dear … I don't know what I know to do, or what inner knowledge I am supposed to hear inside my mind, or what loving guidance I am supposed to notice. Oh well … not to worry. The angels remind me that I know what I need to know, whether I know it or not. What is supposed to happen will happen.

~ 1300 ~

LOVE, Part 11

The sermon today was about *agape*. The pastor said it is unfortunate that in English we have only one word for love, while in other languages there are different words for different kinds of love: *philia* and *eros*, for instance, in Greek. But when Jesus said, "My command is this: Love each other as I have loved you. Greater love has no one than this: to lay down one's life for one's friends" (John 15:12-13 RSV), the word he used was for a love beyond verbal description – *agape*.

Agape is a lonely love. Tony de Mello said that you can love best when you are alone. All the other forms of love involve another person – parent, child, friend, teacher, student, spouse. *Agape* is different. It is love *itself*. No one is able to share this divine love with me on earth because no one in my current circle of humanity understands this love and can accept the complete vulnerability and selfless service that *agape* demands. No one to be Radha Krishna with me. And so I remain in solitude, sharing tantric love with my own God-self.

My life story is a chronicle of awakening to *agape* and the daily application of it on earth as it is in heaven. We are all manifestations of *agape* in this world, as Jesus was. When we are awakened, we automatically radiate *agape*, as Jesus did.

~ 1301 ~

TIME AND ETERNITY, Part 7
Process Thought

My dear friend Ignacio and I had different ideas about how process thought relates to time, and we gently clashed when I brought up the simultaneity of past, present, and future. I never challenged the truth of process thought in the realm of time; I liked Ignacio's comparison of life to jazz improvisation, where musicians make it up as they go, having many choices in deciding which way to take the raw material of the past into the future. I got into trouble by simply saying that there is a realm beyond time where process does not apply. That was the hard part for Ignacio and others to grasp.

Our friendly conflict intensified with my contention that when one awakens to the God-self, worldly free will becomes God's eternal will. There is free will in duality, and predestination in eternity. Awakening is the arising into consciousness of this paradox.

Here's how stasis in eternity can be reconciled with process thought in the context of time. This diagram represents the history of each individual life, of each soul's journey through multiple incarnations, and of all humanity through all time:

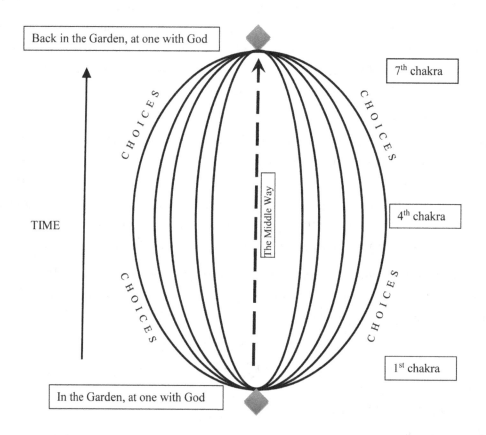

Many sages have said that the goal of life is to return to the Source, which I have likened to a bungee cord snapping back to its home base. The process of life begins in the singularity that is God, at one with all things in eternity. This is where Adam and Eve resided before they gained the knowledge of duality, of good and evil. There were no choices to be made in the Garden of Eden because the pairs of opposites were infinite and perfectly balanced, no choosing necessary. There was no ego, no consciousness of separation from God, and no separate options from which to choose in the choiceless singularity of God.

But duality was always latent in the Garden, as Adam and Eve discovered when they ate of the Forbidden Tree. God gave them their first choice, the opportunity to consciously experience duality, to make it kinetic, by telling them of the Tree of the Knowledge of Good and Evil but warning them of its dangers. They took the opportunity.

It is so hard to describe timelessness in the terminology of time; to understand the allegorical nature of the Genesis story; the simultaneity of Adam being inside and also outside of God, of Eve being Adam's rib and at the same time being separate from him (like Radha Krishna), and of God talking to Adam as a separate being even before time and duality arose in human consciousness. (This is like the Buddhist concept that firewood does not *become* ash; firewood appears to change its form as time progresses, but nevertheless has its own unchanging position in eternity and remains eternally as firewood. [~1158~])

When Adam and Eve ate of the Tree – when we are born into the world of duality – infinite choices arise with the co-arising of infinite pairs of opposites. This stage is expressed at the 1st chakra. At first the choices presented to us are few and not very different from each other. But as Adam and Eve procreated and populated the earth – as we grow and develop in the course of living our lives, and as human civilizations rise and fall – the possible choices before us become more numerous and complex, and the gulf between opposites – between beauty and ugliness, happiness and sadness, good and evil – seems to widen. The 2nd and 3rd chakras open, thoughts and emotions arise in our consciousness to enable us to make more informed choices as decision-making becomes more difficult.

At some point in our lives, a crisis, breakdown, some kind of critical despair overtakes us and leads us to seek help from a force beyond our ego. This is where both opposite poles of duality become equally unsatisfactory, the distinction between good and evil becomes confusing, the brain fills with white noise, and making wise choices based on rational thought becomes impossible. This is the middle point of the timeline above, the widest spread of the concentric ellipses, where the opposite poles are farthest apart.

William James said that "in most of us, by the age of thirty, the character has set like plaster, and will never soften again." So it requires a shock to break through the hardened neurology of the pathways of our decisions over time. It requires a shock of discomfort that affects us physically and emotionally and spiritually. – Bryan Doerries, *Harper's Magazine*, October 2014

Then comes the cathartic moment of surrender; the defenses of the ego come down, and divine love can arise at the 4th chakra. In the mystical allegory of the Bible, the arrival of Jesus into the world represents the opening of the 4th chakra and the awakening of divine love in the world – the Way to salvation and reentry into the Garden. This is the awakened Buddha touching the earth.

If we respond to the love of God as revealed to us at the 4th chakra, we proceed up the timeline toward the 5th, 6th, and 7th chakras. As we gain more and more understanding of God, divine love, time and eternity, our choices become fewer and easier to make. We choose certain options because we see God's love, God's will, in them. We find that the most direct path to God is the Middle Way equidistant between the opposite extremes.

At the top of the concentric ellipses, at the end of the timeline, we are born again and become a buddha – we pass through the narrow gate that Jesus said few may enter, reenter the Garden, rejoin the unity that is God, and all our choices, already made for us by the God-self in us, become the enactment of divine love on earth – God's will being done on earth as it is in heaven.

This process, while it happens in duality, is contained and complete in eternity. All choices and all divergent paths, as the process thinkers say, exist as possibilities in the future. Those of us who think beyond time, however, know that all possible paths lead to the same place, back to the Source, as two lines drawn in opposite directions on the surface of a globe meet at the same spot on the far side of the orb. The closer to the top of the globe, the shorter the distance the lines cover to reach their meeting point. At the very top, at the 7th chakra, at the narrow gate, there is no distance to cover, no choices to be made, no time or space. To paraphrase Stephen Hawking, it is like standing at the North Pole and asking, "Which way is north?" The beginning is the end is the beginning.

~ 1302 ~

I have so far interpreted Emily's silence as a sign that she does not understand our divine love as I know it, doesn't want it or need it, and dumped me, as she has so many others, when my narcissistic supply dried up. But I am considering that the opposite may also be true; perhaps in her subconscious mind she *does* understand our love and, being unable to control her narcissistic rage and not wanting to hurt me with it, is staying away to protect me from it.

I keep my distance from her for a similar reason. In my divine love I would willingly die for Emily, if my death would save her, but not *because* of her, if I simply succumbed to her narcissism without releasing her from it. I stay away to spare her the anguish of wounding me, perhaps killing me, with behaviors that she cannot control. My distance from her is not just me protecting myself; it is as much me protecting her from herself.

This is the nature of duality: subliminal love that binds us eternally together is acted out in behaviors of avoidance and estrangement that keep us apart. In this way our mutual love in eternity, each in service to the other, is expressed in our differentiated earthly lives.

PART 55

Transition

May 2018 – July 2018

~ 1303 ~

My Buddhist message: *Your mouth is indicated … not with the words you speak, but with your smile … you have joy inside you … in this month of transformation … bring your joy to others with your smile … I see pure water, bright light … receive it … share with others around you … don't hesitate … have confidence.*

Tibetan Buddhist monk Yongey Mingur Rinpoche wrote: "Finally at Bodh Gaya, the Buddha simply let it all go. He let go of practice, let go of study, let go of meditation. He let go of the path itself. He just let everything be, as it is. And at last, when he began to let it be as it is, everything came together."

It does not surprise me that the Awakened One stopped meditating when everything came together. I am beginning to experience this letting go of practice, study, meditation, the path itself. The spirits are quiet. My mentors are fading away. No new wisdom is emerging. Am I nearing the end of the path, *anuttara samyak sambodhi*? Or am I falling off the path, backsliding? No … eighth bhūmi bodhisattvas don't backslide.

> Reciting mantras or contemplating mind
> Are merely herbs for polishing a mirror.
> When the dust is removed,
> They are also wiped away.
>
> – Han Shan Te Ch'ing (1546-1623)

~ 1304 ~

Another dream: *I am tending two large litters of puppies, watching them nurse with their respective mothers. Then as the puppies wandered around between the mothers, I wondered if they knew which mother was theirs. All the dogs, mothers and puppies, were black.*

From dreammoods.com:

> **Dog** – To see a dog in your dream symbolizes intuition, loyalty, generosity, protection, and fidelity. The dream suggests that your strong values and good intentions will enable you to go forward in the world and bring you success. To see a black dog in your dream symbolizes the shadow aspect of a friend. The dark side of someone close to you is being revealed and you are able to see through to their true intentions. To dream that a dog has puppies refers to your nurturing abilities.
>
> **Puppy** – To see a litter of puppies in your dream is indicative of the amount of time that an idea has been developing or will take to develop. Look to the number of puppies to give you that approximate amount of time.
>
> **Black** – Black symbolizes the unknown, the unconscious, danger, mystery, darkness, death, mourning, rejection, hate or malice. More positively, black represents potential and possibilities. It is like a clean or blank slate. If the feeling in the dream is one of joy, then blackness could imply hidden spirituality and divine qualities.

I sense that this dream is related to the packing dream I had a few days ago and my recent Buddhist messages, all of which point to a transition or transformation that is imminent in my life. Who are the two mother dogs? Who are the friends I am nurturing whose shadow aspect, dark side, is being revealed and whose true intentions I am able to see? Does their blackness indicate danger and darkness, potential and possibilities, or perhaps all the associations with blackness? There were lots of puppies in the dream, a dozen or more, so whatever is happening will take a while.

~ 1305 ~

APOLOGY AND FORGIVENESS, Part 8

Neale Donald Walsch, author of *Conversations with God*, appeared in the Hay House World Summit 2018, and gave a perfect explanation of why forgiveness is irrelevant in divine love:

> "When your 24-month-old granddaughter is sitting at the dinner table, and its birthday time and the chocolate cake is in the middle of the table and she reaches out because she really wants that chocolate cake; she knows exactly what it tastes like. She wants that chocolate cake so bad and as she reaches out in her exuberance, in her childhood misunderstanding of what one does when faced with chocolate cake, she knocks over the milk. The milk goes crashing all over the table and the party is, at least for a moment, stopped and maybe in the mind of some people, spoiled. Do you take that child and punish her ruthlessly? Do you send her to her room and say she'll never be forgiven?

Or, do you even need to forgive her? Is forgiveness even part of the process? Do you at some level almost smile? There's no use crying over spilled milk, after all. Do you clean up the milk and clear the table and say to the child something quite astonishing: 'There, there, it's okay sweetheart, don't cry. It's okay.'

Which of the two do you do, the first or the second?" I said to God, "The second, of course." He said, "Of course, choose the second … even as I understand you, I tell you that understanding replaces forgiveness in the mind of the master."[153]

Walsch went on to discuss what we consider more serious adult sins, like shoplifting or adultery, in the same light as the child spilling milk. God understands that at a certain level of development these things happen. They are not wrongs to be punished; they are lessons to be learned. No forgiveness necessary. When we learn the more advanced lessons and begin to understand as God does, things change:

Then will come a great miracle, because even as you begin to discover and declare, create and fulfill your highest notion of who you really are, you will see other people in a remarkably different way as well. You'll begin to say to them, 'Ah, I see who you really are.' You'll even see them as who they really are in moments when they do not. You will say to them three significant words, words that will salvage them in their own experience.

"I love you."

God said, "Well no, not necessarily. Those are three lovely words. They're sweet words, but three even more powerful words that you could say to somebody else: 'I see you.'"

This, I have come to understand, is what God says to us, every moment, every hour, every day. You don't have to worry, any of you. I see you. In the moments of your worst transgressions, I see you as the 24-month-old who reached for the chocolate cake and spilled the milk. It's okay. Everybody relax.[153]

The Soto Zen patriarch Dogen reached the same "I see you" conclusion in stage four of his five stages to enlightenment:

1. *To study the Buddha way is to study the self.*

2. *To study the self is to forget the self.*

3. *To forget the self is to be actualized by myriad things.*

4. *When actualized by myriad things, your body and mind as well as the bodies and minds of others drop away.* **[The buddha-nature is exposed. I see you.]**

5. *No trace of realization remains, and this no-trace continues endlessly.*[x]

---

[x] https://www.goodreads.com/quotes/397181-to-study-the-buddha-way-is-to-study-the-self

Emily, I see you. Even though I haven't heard from you in months. I don't need to forgive you because I understand. You couldn't help spilling the milk.

God said, "I see you" to Adam and Eve after they had eaten the apple in the Garden of Eden, and they covered their nakedness and hid from him. I said, "I see you" to Emily and The Unnamed One, and they covered their naked souls and hid from me.

~ 1306 ~

Cecilia, grieving the death of Ignacio, wrote to me, "You are busy, so am I. But for different reasons … mine is mostly distraction?" C.S. Lewis, grieving the death of his wife, wrote:

> There are moments, most unexpectedly, when something inside me tries to assure me that I don't really mind so much, not so very much, after all. Love is not the whole of a man's life. I was happy before I ever met H. I've plenty of what are called 'resources.' People get over these things. Come, I shan't do so badly. One is ashamed to listen to this voice but it seems for a little to be making out a good case. Then comes a sudden jab of red-hot memory and all this 'commonsense' vanishes like an ant in the mouth of a furnace. – C.S. Lewis, *A Grief Observed* [3]

Since I first read this passage in *A Grief Observed* decades ago, I have felt the metaphor of "an ant in the mouth of a furnace" branded on my heart. This is perhaps the most powerfully apt image of anything Lewis wrote. I have felt the "sudden jab of red-hot memory" and all commonsense vanishing in the furnace. Cecilia stays busy, as I did, to avoid and evade the jabs.

~ 1307 ~

LOVE, Part 12

Gratitude, affection, respect, admiration, sympathy. These are positive, nurturing feelings that are often mistaken for love, but they do not by themselves rise to the level of love. Why not?

1) They can engender egotistical pride or, like the Six Perfections, be taken to excess. (~506~) For instance, respect and admiration go too far when they lead to blind loyalty. Sympathy and affection go too far when they cause us to turn a blind eye to unskilled behavior or shield someone from the karmic effects of such behavior.

2) They can be gained or lost. They are earned; they are responses to specific behaviors. When those behaviors change, so do our responses. We are grateful when someone

does something kind or helpful for us. We respect and admire someone who exhibits a high level of skill or knowledge. We feel affection – we "like" people – when they make us laugh and are pleasant to be around. That doesn't necessarily mean we love them.

True love, whether of the worldly or heavenly kind, is known by its service to the other, even in the absence of any warm feelings toward the other. True love continues even when gratitude, affection, and respect are lost, or never were. It cannot be taken to excess. It cannot be fallen into or out of. It arises not in response to what people do, but to who they are in the deepest way, in response to their true nature, the part of them that transcends behaviors.

Worldly loves (master/slave, parent/child, friend/friend, spouse/spouse: ~643~/~1364~), unlike divine love, may have dependencies, expectations, and boundaries. Even while still loving your friend, you may part company with him when you discover that he has lied or stolen from you. Even while still loving your spouse, you may leave your marriage if your spouse becomes abusive. True worldly love, like divine love, never goes away, but can ebb and flow with life situations and sensory perceptions.

When divine love – *agape* – is awakened, service extends to sacrifice, a joyful willingness to give up everything, even life itself, for the sake of the other. It is boundless, endless, changeless. It is love *itself*, with no purpose except to be itself.

~ 1308 ~

Last night I discovered what pure pleasure is – eating Oreos and sipping Irish whiskey in my recliner while watching *Murder, She Wrote*. I tried to recreate the experience tonight, but such moments are not re-creatable; the moment had passed. The perfect confluence of sensory forces that had created my decadent ecstasy the first night were not flowing the same way the following night. The cookies and booze were just as tasty, the murder mystery was just as engaging, but my life had moved on.

~ 1309 ~

The odd thing was that before God closed in on me, I was in fact offered what now appears a moment of wholly free choice. In a sense. Without words (I think) almost without images, a fact about myself was somehow presented to me. I became aware that I was holding something at bay, or shutting something out. Or, if you like, that I was wearing some stiff clothing, like corsets, or even a suit of armour, as if I were a lobster. I felt myself being, there and then, given a free choice. I could open the door or keep it shut; I could unbuckle the armour or keep it on. Neither choice was presented as a duty; no threat or promise was attached to either, though I knew that to open the door or to take off the corset meant the incalculable. The choice appeared to be momentous but it was also strangely unemotional. I was moved by no desires or fears. In a sense I was not moved by anything. I chose to open, unbuckle, to loosen the rein. I say, 'I chose', yet it did not really seem possible to do the opposite. – C.S. Lewis, *Surprised by Joy* [99]

Lewis captures perfectly the irresistible, unemotional nature of surrendering to God's will when you are ready to fully open to it. You say, "I chose," but you know somehow that there is really no choosing. You are carried away in the current of a mighty river that offers no choices, nor do you want any; you just become part of the river. What Lewis described as his "wholly free choice" was really the opportunity to accept the choices already made by his eternal God-self, choices which became self-evident when all armor, all obstructions surrounding his God-self were removed. This is the same as Trungpa's "fearless renunciation," taking off the armor of one's aggressive mentality, in "The Tender Heart of the Warrior." (~1286~)

> In obeying, a rational creature consciously enacts its creaturely role, reverses the act by which we fell, treads Adam's dance backward, and returns. – C.S. Lewis, *The Problem of Pain* [56]

When Lewis unbuckled his armor and gave himself up to the incalculable, he trod Adam's dance backward and reversed original sin. He became sinless, as Paul described in Romans. He was born again.

~ 1310 ~

ART FOR ART'S SAKE

> A particular toy or a particular icon may be itself a work of art, but that is logically accidental; its artistic merits will not make it a better toy or a better icon. They may make it a worse one. For its purpose is not to fix attention upon itself, but to stimulate and liberate certain activities in the child or the worshipper. The Teddy bear exists in order that the child may endow it with imaginary life and personality and enter into a quasi-social relationship with it. That is what "playing with it" means. The better this activity succeeds the less the actual appearance of the object will matter. Too close or prolonged attention to its changeless and expressionless face impedes the play.
>
> A crucifix exists in order to direct the worshipper's thought and affections to the Passion. It had better not have any excellences, subtleties, or originalities which will fix attention upon itself. Hence devout people may, for this purpose, prefer the crudest and emptiest icon. The emptier, the more permeable; and they want, as it were, to pass through the material image

and go beyond. For the same reason it is often not the costliest and most lifelike toy that wins the child's love. – C.S. Lewis, *An Experiment in Criticism* [154]

Okay, here it is. The one thing in Lewis' writings with which I can clearly disagree, or at least quibble over. While I agree with the idea that a toy or icon (or piece of music) can sometimes call attention to itself and derail the thought-journey into higher spiritual realms, I don't think that its artistic qualities are the cause of the derailment; in fact, if it is truly art, those artistic qualities help the perceiver reach those higher realms.

Let's say you are at the crucifix store to buy a crucifix. There are dozens of them, large and small, wood and metal, ornate and plain. Each one, from the simplest to the most spectacular, has sensory attributes that attract attention. As your eyes survey the field, you will be intuitively drawn to one, not based on its glitter or lack thereof, but on the subliminal message it is sending. This is the crucifix that speaks to you. And it must be noted that the simplest and plainest of them can be as seductive in its sensory attractiveness as the diamond-encrusted one, and just as imbued with artistic content. The Japanese Zen tea ceremony is based on this idea, the mindful appreciation of the simplest things.

The Teddy bear example is just as provocative. Even the simplest, plainest bear has artistic content. The designer of the bear was an artisan who made artistic decisions concerning the color of the bear, the texture of its fur, the size and shape of its eyes. When the bear is new, it attracts us with its dapper, indeed artistic, beauty. But when the bear is old, its color faded, its fabric tattered, one of its eyes missing, it still draws attention to itself by that very condition. Either way, the bear's beauty and spiritual message are in the eye and the heart of the beholder.

Most people would say that there is no higher artistic achievement than the music of Mozart. And at the same time, most people would say that there is no better vehicle for spiritual elevation than the music of Mozart. The artistic perfection of Mozart's music is no deterrent to the spiritual message, quite the opposite. Mozart's middle name, Amadeus – beloved of God – says it all. As with Bach, the voice of God spoke through the great art of Mozart.

TO DOM BEDE GRIFFITHS, O.S.B., from Magdalen College, 16 April 1940: I do most thoroughly agree with what you say about Art and Literature. To my mind they are only healthy when they are either (a) Definitely the handmaids of religious, or at least moral, truth—or (b) Admittedly aiming at nothing but innocent recreation or entertainment. But the great serious irreligious art—art for art's sake—is all balderdash; and, incidentally, never exists when art is really flourishing. In fact one can say of Art as an author I recently read says of Love (sensual love, I mean) 'It ceases to be a devil when it ceases to be a god.' Isn't that well put? So many things—nay, every real thing—is good if only it will be humble and ordinate. – C.S. Lewis [155]

As an artist, I agree with the meaning of Lewis' remarks, but not with his choice of words. I agree with Lewis and Griffiths that healthy art deals in religious or moral truth, or innocent recreation. But I would go further – even entertaining or recreational art, if it is really art, reflects moral truth. Truth is, to me, the substance of all art; its presence defines art. In that sense, there is no such thing as irreligious art.

Art for art's sake is art for truth's sake. What Lewis calls "great serious irreligious art" or "art for art's sake" is what I equate with merely clever or virtuosic displays, showpieces created to elevate the ego and which, as he says, are devoid of moral truth – art for the superficial eye-catching or ear-catching glitter of the work. This is really art for artfulness' sake, or art for ego's sake. Intentionally glitzy, glittery, glamorous works that are designed for the overt purpose of attracting attention are not really art; they are pornography.

"It ceases to be a devil when it ceases to be a god." This is true not just for Art and Love but for all of Life, and so captures the essence of dualistic interdependent co-arising (and co-falling) in all human experience. The best art transports us above all that, to the place where both devils and gods, all humble and ordinate, melt into the singularity of God.

> According to Schelling's philosophy, art is the production or result of that conception of things by which the subject becomes its own object, or the object its own subject. Beauty is the perception of the infinite in the finite. And the chief characteristic of works of art is unconscious infinity. Art is the uniting of the subjective with the objective, of nature with reason, of the unconscious with the conscious, and therefore art is the highest means of knowledge. – Leo Tolstoy, *What Is Art?*

Schelling and Tolstoy are describing Tantra, or *agape* – "the perception of the infinite in the finite." Art for art's sake is in fact the purest expression of spiritual truth, rising above mere technique, emotionality, cleverness, or ego. All true art is spiritual, God speaking through humans using light waves or sound waves as the medium of communication. The spiritual power of art lies in its ability to transcend its medium; even literary art, which uses language as its medium, transports us beyond the words, like Zen *koan*, and liberates the extrasensory spiritual message from the limits of words, thoughts, and the sensory body-mind.

Lewis did understand the role of artists as divine messengers, the artist pointing to the message and disappearing behind it:

> The poet is not a man who asks me to look at *him*; he is a man who says "look at that" and points; the more I follow the pointing of his finger the less I can possibly see of *him*. To see things as a poet sees them, I must share his consciousness and not attend to it; I must look where he looks and not turn round to face him; I must make of him not a spectacle but a pair

of spectacles: in fine, as Professor Alexander would say, I must *enjoy* him and not *contemplate* him. – C.S. Lewis, *The Personal Heresy* [194]

Great art and great artists do not call attention to themselves. Some artists are known for high-profile public personae, but at the level of their art they are without pride or ego. They simply transmit the message that is sent to them from beyond.

On this subject, like all others, Lewis and I don't really disagree. We come full circle in our understanding of art with this explanation of art as a sensory vehicle to extrasensory awareness:

> The books or the music in which we thought the beauty was located will betray us if we trust to them; it was not in them, it only came through them, and what came through them was longing. These things—the beauty, the memory of our own past—are good images of what we really desire; but if they are mistaken for the thing itself, they turn into dumb idols, breaking the hearts of their worshippers. For they are not the thing itself; they are only the scent of a flower we have not found, the echo of a tune we have not heard, news from a country we have never yet visited. – C.S. Lewis, *The Weight of Glory* [86]

And yet, art is in fact the scent of that very flower, the echo of that very tune, the news from that very country, that is the thing itself. I hope Lewis understood, as John Wesley did, that the Bible is among the books that "will betray us if we trust to them."

> Music is the exaltation of the mind derived from things eternal, bursting forth in sound. – St. Thomas Aquinas

> Next to the word of God, only music deserves being extolled as the mistress and governess of human feelings. And when music is sharpened and polished by art, then one begins to see with amazement the great and perfect Wisdom of God in his wonderful work of harmony. – Martin Luther

~ 1311 ~

I liked the way the pastor ended his sermon about the kingdom of God. He just trailed off: "The kingdom of God is like …" There is no way to describe the kingdom, really. It is beyond anything that we know in this life on earth. It is the Great Void, full of emptiness. It is indescribable in earthbound thoughts and words. It is only known by us, if it is known at all, in the heart, at the 4th chakra, where divine love leaps over all thoughts, feelings, and sensory perceptions.

The pastor also referred to the relationship of the "kingdom of God" to "heaven." Most Christians think of these as the same place. In a way they are, and in a way, not, if you think of the kingdom being eternity and heaven being our awareness of eternity while here on earth.

This led me to thinking about the relationship of the 6th to the 7th chakra, as Campbell described them, the 6th being God with form, and the 7th being God without form. At the 6th chakra, we recognize God split into pieces, infinite in number, visible, with form, our universe and countless other universes arising and expanding in time and space. But in awakening at the 7th chakra, we see God as one – eternal, formless, timeless and spaceless, as Jesus described God (finding words that come as close as words can come to describing the indescribable) as the wind that blows, that we hear the sound of, but know not whence it comes nor whither it goes.

When we awaken, are "born again," we realize that everything of form and substance that we see with our third eye at the 6th chakra is part of the unity that is the eternal God at the 7th chakra: good *and* evil, mercy *and* vengeance, kindness *and* cruelty, pleasure *and* pain, angels *and* demons, Jesus *and* Judas, Yahweh *and* Satan, Buddha *and* Mara. This 6th chakra vision, seeing God in all things (panentheism), is heaven on earth, here and now, everything perfect as is. Rising above the tugs and pulls of duality and seeing the unification of all that is at the 7th chakra (pantheism) is entering the eternal kingdom, the singularity, of God.

In the past, I equated the terms "tantric love," "divine love," "*agape*," and "karmic love." Now I realize that the first three terms are roughly equivalent as the highest form of love, but karmic love is a little different. Karma resides in space/time duality, Tantra and *agape* in spaceless/timeless eternity, beyond karma. With awakening, karmic love ripens to reveal the eternal divine love underpinning it. Karmic love is to tantric love as panentheism is to pantheism.

~ 1312 ~

In my dream last night, I saw a bright golden light bursting out of the blackness in the center of my vision, and my third eye appeared in a lighter, nearly white, color in the middle of it.

From dreammoods.com:

Gold – The golden color reflects a spiritual reward, richness, refinement and enhancement of your surroundings. It also signifies your determination and unyielding nature.

Chakra – The brow chakra, also referred to as the third eye, symbolizes psychic ability, intuition, and mutual understanding. This dream may be telling you to focus on the big picture.

Indeed, I need to focus on the big picture; my spiritual reward is at hand. I am still waiting for the transformation presaged in my dreams last month. Maybe it is happening now; I am in the throes of it but don't know it. This wouldn't be the first time my consciousness slept through a miracle. Life is living a dream.

> I think the ways in which God saves us are probably infinitely various and admit varying degrees of consciousness in the patient. Anything which sets him saying, "Now – Stage II ought soon to be coming along – Is this it?" I think bad and likely to lead some to presumption and others to despair. We must leave God to dress the wound and not keep on taking peeps under the bandage for ourselves. – C.S. Lewis, *The Collected Letters of C.S. Lewis, Volume II* [85]

Okay … I'll stop peeping under the bandage.

~ 1313 ~

> *TO EDWARD LOFSTROM, 10 June 1962*: I sometimes pray 'Lord give me no more and no less self-knowledge than I can at this moment make a good use of.' Remember He is the artist and you are only the picture. You can't see it. So quietly submit to be painted—i.e., keep on fulfilling all the obvious duties of your station (you really know quite well enough what they are!), asking forgiveness for each failure and then leaving it alone. You are in the right way. Walk—don't keep on looking at it. – C.S. Lewis, *The Collected Letters of C.S. Lewis, Volume III* [87]

I love the metaphor of our lives as a painting painted by God. We are the picture; we cannot see ourselves from inside the canvas, from the perspective of our internal self-consciousness. We can only surrender the canvas of our lives to God and have faith (trust without reservations) that a beautiful portrait is being made. Made from the inside out.

~ 1314 ~

DAKINI

> "There are many kinds of *dakinis*, both worldly and wisdom *dakinis*. The wisdom *dakinis* are the same level as buddhas; the worldly *dakinis* can have enlightened aspects but also worldly aspects. Sometimes the *dakinis* operate as messengers, sometimes as guides, sometimes as protectors. In the *dakini* practice we develop a way to access the unique and powerful energy of the wisdom *dakinis*."
>
> I asked, "What kind of messenger is the *dakini*?"

Sapchu Rinpoche paused for a moment, and then replied, "The *dakini* is a messenger of emptiness and also appears in dreams to guide the meditator, and she might appear in real life as a woman with certain wisdom qualities. The *dakini* is a force of truth: wherever we cling, she cuts; whatever we think we can hide, she reveals." – Lama Tsultrim Allione, "The Sacred Feminine," *Lion's Roar*, June 26, 2018 [157]

As I read this article from *Lion's Roar*, I recognized myself – "a woman with certain wisdom qualities," a wake-up fairy, a truth-teller, a revealer of things that want to stay hidden.

My esoteric Buddhist message: *There are things you can see with your eyes … other things are hidden … you are able to see the hidden things … you have a light sent to you by your ancestors … you bring this light to others … the Buddha is helping you.*

Often the dreams of the *dakinis* will come at dawn, or they will appear in cemeteries at sunset or dawn—cemeteries being very important symbols of the liminal space between worlds, the twilight hour, which is in fact why the language of the *dakinis* is a symbolic one called the twilight language. As I wrote in my book *Women of Wisdom*: "Twilight is the time between waking and sleeping, the conscious and the unconscious. It is a time when the switchover takes place, so there could be a gap, a crack in the wall of the ever-protective ego structure where significant communication from something beyond could take place. At dawn we are still beyond the limiting forces of the conscious mind, yet the heavy veil of deep sleep has lifted. We often find the *dakini* at these transitional points, when we are open to the 'twilight' language."

Another important aspect of the *dakini*'s feminine energy is how they cut through notions of pure and impure, clean and unclean, what you should do and shouldn't do. They break open the shell of those conventional structures into an embrace of life in which all experience is seen as sacred.

Practicing Tibetan Buddhism more deeply, I came to realize that the *dakinis* are the undomesticated female energies—spiritual and erotic, ecstatic and wise, playful and profound, fierce and peaceful—that are beyond the grasp of the conceptional mind. There is a place for our whole feminine being, in all its guises, to be present.[157]

I have written about my dreams in the twilight zone between waking and sleeping, the conscious and unconscious, and about the breathtaking nature of tantric sex expressed through the feminine body. And how deeply I have felt the wildness of divine love in feminine Tantra – spiritual, erotic, ecstatic, wise, and undomesticated.

Jesus also understood this kind of spiritual liberation, breaking open the shell of conventional structures, cutting through the boundaries between clean and unclean, healing and harvesting on the sabbath against the rules, and more, revealing the Way and the Truth and the Life that throws away all the rules and frees us from sin. That Jesus appeared in a male body shows that in enlightened beings, whatever their anatomy, male and female energies are equally balanced and expressed.

~ 1315 ~

TONGLEN

Tonglen is the Buddhist practice of awakening the bodhi mind by doing the opposite of what the ego wants. This means purposefully welcoming your own pain and that of others, while refusing to feed your ego the pleasure that it craves. We feed it our suffering instead.

> Before we take any suffering, either our own future suffering or the suffering of the other person, the question arises, "What do I do with this now? Where am I going to put it within me?" We have to be prepared for that. We need a garbage can, some place to throw it. It so happens that we have an enemy inside: Mister Ego. That becomes our target.
>
> What we are taking from the others is not only their suffering but also causes of their suffering, such as attachment, hatred and ignorance. All of these things come in through the breath. When these gather, it has an effect like lightning striking a rocky area; or—as we see on television these days—bombs exploding; or a cyclone picking up everything in its path. In that way it hits our ego, shreds it completely and destroys it. Not even a trace is left. Nothing! We don't have to keep what we took inside us—feeling it and saving it there and suffering. – Gelek Rimpoche, "In With the Bad Air, Out With the Good"[158]

When I read this, I flashed back to a dream I had years ago in which explosions were going off. (~704~) Is *tonglen* what was happening? Was my ego being destroyed? Was the barren landscape of my dream the scorched earth of my exploded ego, of nirvana? Did I keep the pain that I took inside and continue to suffer, or did it vanish along with my exploded ego?

> Visualize the person right in front of you, and think of their suffering; the disease they have; or the mental, physical and emotional pain they are going through. When you really see your friend suffering with unbearable pain, tears will come to you.[158]

As tears came to me in my epiphany with Emily. Buddhist teacher Judy Lief says, "In *tonglen* practice we send out things that bring people happiness, such as love, kindness, well wishes, confidence, strength, and support, and we take in things that cause them to suffer, such as fear, doubt, pain, confusion, and sickness. We offer to others what is good and we take in what is bad, so that others may be free of it. This is the ultimate bodhisattva activity."

With this idea of *tonglen* I understand more deeply that bodhisattvas, empaths, and all who take upon themselves the sins of the world are like a sin bridge – a pathway by which suffering can be carried into and through the vessel of divine love and out of the plane of earthly existence. This is the meaning of Jesus' sacrificial death and my journey with Emily; spiritual cleansing, on multiple levels.

We inhale the suffering of the world along with its causes, allow the garbage can of our ego to absorb all negativity and be burned up by its dark energy. In the fumes of this holy fire we exhale the healing energy of love and compassion. We descend into hell and ascend to heaven, leaving sin and suffering to burn with our egos in hell. The scorched earth of nirvana is all that is left.

~ 1316 ~

Today I put on some of Emily's favorite lotion that she had given me several years ago. I noticed that it had lost its creaminess and was almost pure liquid, and its fragrance had turned a little rancid. Just like our earthly relationship. But as with our relationship, I resisted the urge to throw it away. The lotion no longer clings to my skin and now runs off my arm like water, as Emily no longer clings to me and now runs away, but its changing earthly form never loses its state of perfection in eternity.

A few days ago, yet another mirrored tile fell off the wall in Emily's bathroom. Miraculously, it fell from high up on the wall but did not break when it landed on the floor. This is the first falling tile in almost two years. I had thought all the tiles had already fallen and been put back up, and whatever part of my spiritual journey the falling tiles represented had been completed. Maybe not.

Rumi said, "You are not just a drop in the ocean; you are the mighty ocean in the drop." I must remember this. I am not just a drop in the ocean; I am the mighty ocean of divine love that lives in every drop of life, and also transcends the single drop of a single life. Whatever I do or don't do, it is enough.

~ 1317 ~

The *Lion's Roar* has presented me a provocative read, "Four Steps to Magical Powers"[159] by Sheng Yen. The four steps are:

Chanda: **Concentration of Desire**: *Chanda* is the intense desire to attain the supreme and wondrous *dhyana*. *Chanda* can have a negative as well as a positive meaning. On the one hand it can mean greed, but as a step to concentrative power *chanda* also denotes a hope or vow. This vow is essential to overcoming the six obstructions to practice: drowsiness, scattered mind, idleness, laziness, forgetfulness (of one's practice), and wrong view.

Virya: **Concentration of Diligence**: All wandering thoughts, whether they relate to the past, the present, or the future, are illusory, so we just let them go.

Citta: **Concentration of Mind**: The mind of ordinary sentient beings is selfish and full of vexation. Nevertheless, it is this same mind that we practice with, and it is the same mind as that of an *arhat*. However, when we start practicing *dhyana*, we cannot become pure immediately; we still have wandering thoughts, impure thoughts, and selfish thoughts.

Mimamsa: **Concentration of Inquiry**: Concentration of inquiry also means using wisdom to observe whether our mind is in the proper state. The proper state is summit, where the entire mind is soft and gentle, without harshness. If the mind is selfish and impure, then it is not in the proper state.

Concentrating on one's desire, letting go of wandering thoughts, keeping the mind in its proper state, and so on, is good advice. I have achieved these states at least temporarily from time to time. But as buddhahood comes closer and closer, I find it necessary to let go of even these wholesome practices. Long ago I recognized that *chanda*, "concentration of desire," was a poison, even in the seemingly benign form of hope or a vow. Wandering thoughts naturally go away. As compassion arises, the mind becomes naturally soft and gentle. These qualities of mind are both the cause of buddhahood and its effect.

Practicing these steps intentionally is like playacting at being a buddha. When panic arises, efforts at concentration are devoured, as C.S. Lewis said, like an ant in the mouth of a furnace. My progress along the path can be measured by the nature and degree of negative experience that invokes my panic. I no longer panic at thoughts of financial ruin; personal insults, abuse, or attacks; war, famine, or pestilence; or even thoughts of death. I do panic at being locked inside a disabled or pain-ridden body. Why? Perhaps I shouldn't be concerned; I'm in good company – Jesus' panicky prayer in Gethsemane was about the same thing.

Seeing one's buddha-nature, however, does not mean that one is liberated, nor does it mean that one's practice is completed. Rather, it means that one has gained more faith and confidence in the practice and that one now clearly knows where the path is. This may be likened to traveling on a dark road on a very dark night. All of a sudden there is a bolt of lightning, and for a split second you see the road before you, bright and clear. But seeing the road is not the same as having finished the journey.

Sheng's "bolt of lightning" is like fully illuminating the House of Eternity that I described years ago. (~435~/~437~/~441~)

~ 1318 ~

As awakening begins, as transformative events begin to occur in our lives, we naturally attribute these events to the religious figures we grew up with – Christians hear the voice of Jesus; Muslims, the voice of Mohammad; Hindus, Krishna; Buddhists, the Buddha. Spiritual phenomena in space-time take place in the cultural context we know.

The closer you move toward the core of any religion, the farther away you move from its superficialities – its doctrines, dogmas, ceremonies, and practices – and the more broadly and deeply you interpret its scripture; the more tolerant, accepting, and even welcoming you become of views that appear to contradict those of your ancestral culturally based faith.

All mystics see the same eternal truth. This is why the mystics of all religions are often deemed to be heretics. In fact, I measure the depth of mystics by the degree to which they are disavowed or ostracized by the orthodox religions from which they came.

~ 1319 ~

For a good wife contains so many persons in herself. What was H. not to me? She was my daughter and my mother, my pupil and my teacher, my subject and my sovereign; and always, holding all these in solution, my trusty comrade, friend, shipmate, fellow-soldier. My mistress; but at the same time all that any man friend (and I have good ones) has ever been to me. Perhaps more. If we had never fallen in love we should have none the less been always together, and created a scandal. That's what I meant when I once praised her for her "masculine virtues." But she soon put a stop to that by asking how I'd like to be praised for my feminine ones. It was a good riposte, dear. Yet there was something of the Amazon, something of Penthesileia and Camilla. And you, as well as I, were glad it should be there. You were glad I should recognize it.

Solomon calls his bride Sister. Could a woman be a complete wife unless, for a moment, in one particular mood, a man felt almost inclined to call her Brother?

There is, hidden or flaunted, a sword between the sexes till an entire marriage reconciles them. It is arrogance in us to call frankness, fairness, and chivalry "masculine" when we see them in a woman; it is arrogance in them to describe a man's sensitiveness or tact or tenderness as "feminine." But also what poor, warped fragments of humanity most mere men and mere women must be to make the implications of that arrogance plausible. Marriage heals this. Jointly the two become fully human. "In the image of God created He them." Thus, by a paradox, this carnival of sexuality leads us out beyond our sexes. – C.S. Lewis, *A Grief Observed* [3]

I read this passage years ago when I first read *A Grief Observed*, but it is only now fully coming into my consciousness. Lewis did indeed find a new kind of love, divine love, with Joy ("H."), a love that blew away all his preconceptions about the nature of sex, marriage, and loving relationships.

In the first paragraph above, he describes the worldly loves, *storgë*, *philia*, and *eros* – loves that he had previously described in dry, intellectual terms in his book *The Four Loves* – as all being embodied in one person. With Joy he knew *agape*, an "entire marriage," in which distinctions between masculine and feminine, and between the roles we assign to each other – wife, sister, daughter, mother, teacher, pupil, friend, lover – all merged and became indistinguishable. Rules and boundaries were exploded. Clive and Joy discovered Tantra.

~ 1320 ~

Sandra Ingerman writes on shamanism (with striking parallels to the life of Christ and all bodhisattvas):

> Shamans go into this altered state of consciousness and go into the unseen worlds, where there's a wealth of what we call helping, compassionate spirits. Power Animals, guardian spirits, the spirits of trees and elves, and ascended masters, and angels, and mythic figures are all waiting. What I teach is that, number one, the spirits are the intermediaries between us and source. Because source is just oneness. It doesn't recognize us as egos, it just is a brilliant light. And so the spirits are intermediaries. But they're also formless, they're dead, they don't have a form. They no longer have a body. But what they're willing to do for us is they're willing to take a form for us that speaks to us in some way as a human being.
>
> What I'm trying to teach right now in Shamanism is that we're also formless beings and we're also beings of light. And I feel that we've put a little bit too much form on the spirits, because our personality needs it. And we're taking away some of the power of what they can bring through as these formless frequencies and energy. And we take away the power of what we can do to serve the planet because we get so stuck in our ego and personality.[132]

How many times have I mentioned my power animals, spirit messengers, rainbows, signs and signals from nature? I get it. I also get that when I am caught up looking for spirits in specific forms, I miss the formless messages that are all around me, oblivious to the spirits bombarding me through unexpected channels.

A Shaman would say to you right now, "Start to dream a good dream for all of life. See, hear, feel, taste, smell. Step into the world that you want to be living in and look out from that world and operate as if that world has been manifested into existence now. Be a dreamer." And a Shaman would also say that the turbulent waves we're going through right now are bringing us somewhere. They're helping us to sculpt away our ego and to allow our spirit and our light to shine through. And we actually have the same power as the spirits, it's just that we chose a body and we chose a role to play out this time around.

But part of the practice of Shamanism, too, is remembering the truth of who you are, which is spiritual light, and to shine that light. There is a reward at the end, there is illumination at the end of the dismemberment that we're all experiencing right now.[132]

Knowing the truth of who you are is part of the practice of shamanism, and also part of living the life of Christ, who promised rewards in heaven, "illumination at the end," for those who bear his cross on earth.

Sandra also warns us, as Hank Wesselman does, about the danger of proclaiming yourself to be a shaman (or a bodhisattva, or a "born again" Christian). You must be called to this life; you cannot choose it. And know that you must withstand the descent into hell before you can ascend into heaven:

To call yourself a Shaman is seen as bad luck in indigenous cultures because it's your community that calls you a Shaman. It's a destiny, it's a call, it's not, "I think I'm gonna be a Shaman." ... "I think it looks like a good idea for me to be a Shaman." Actually it isn't, because the initiations you go through don't stop and they're not pleasant. Because a Shaman is a wounded healer, and it's all about being able to have that heart that's always open and always being in compassion. And so the spirits do not make life easy for a Shaman.

Every empathic bodhisattva descends into hell with those she is called to serve, as I did with Lou in his physical suffering, with The Unnamed One in his alienating fear, and with Emily in her narcissistic delusion.

But everybody can practice Shamanism, everybody can learn how to meet up with a helping, compassionate spirit. And so that's what my books are geared towards. Not a person who is looking to set up a healing practice and start to work on people, but how do we bring these ancient practices into our daily life to be able to ask our compassionate spirits.[132]

And so it is with this book, and the writings and lectures of thousands of others. We do not seek to turn everyone who reads or hears our words into shamans, saints, or bodhisattvas, but to simply point the Way, to shine a light on the path we walk in our daily lives that leads to healing, heaven, nirvana.

I am fascinated by the opposite ways that Caroline Myss and Sandra Ingerman describe the effect of wounds and suffering. Myss describes "woundology," using one's wounds to attract sympathy and as an excuse to wound others. (~1229~/~1232~) Ingerman describes the "wounded healer" who uses wounds for good, as a route to compassion and a catalyst for healing the wounds of others (which is how Myss described the suffering of Jesus). Caroline's "woundology" internalizes wounds and lets them fester, manifesting in internal and external harm; Sandra's "wounded healer" exposes wounds and lets them go, manifesting in internal and external healing. Both ways are true.

Emily expresses herself in both ways. In her work as a therapist, she uses her childhood trauma to make connection with her clients and enable their healing, but in her personal life she uses the same trauma to gain sympathy for herself, justify her abuse of others, and feed her ravenous narcissism. She is still a prisoner of festering childhood wounds that have not healed. This is a prime characteristic of her dissociative personality – in her fragmented aspects she expresses both sides of the dichotomy.

~ 1321 ~

For the last year or so I have been feeling stuck spiritually. As life with Emily quiets down and my worldly work rises to the fore, I have felt spiritually foggy, rudderless, directionless, not knowing where my mission lies. Is it still with Emily, or with other people or situations yet to appear?

In intuitive session with Martha I was given a renewed vision of my life path. Martha says that I am indeed on a plateau, a place of transition, moving from a life of service to one of mentoring – not being supportive and loving in a personal way, side by side with someone in the muck and mire, but offering guidance and wisdom in a more general and ubiquitous way. My love, compassion, and wisdom are beginning to be expressed in ways that reach people powerfully and deeply. "More and more, people will look to you for guidance and advice," she said. "Someday you will hear that someone's life was forever changed by something you said."

"But this is frightening," I replied, "What if I say the wrong thing and ruin someone's life?"

"Not possible," she replied. "If you feel compelled to say something, that means it is coming from God, the Source, and needs to be said, even if it is something the other person doesn't want to hear."

I wonder, is Emily my last karmic love, my last experience of being down and dirty with people, joyfully participating in the sorrows of the world? I was her bodhisattva, devoting my life to her service and sacrificing myself for her almost to the point of death. But when my health began to fail in the throes of her torture, when I felt her cruel rejection and derision as the beginning of my symbolic crucifixion, I pulled back to restore myself. Is this what happened when the Buddha pulled back from his life of asceticism and was awakened, eventually to mentor his followers? Am I moving from bodhisattva to buddha? Is this the transition, transformation, that was recently presaged in my dreams, astrological signs, and esoteric messages?

> If spiritual teachings are to really transform our lives, they need to oscillate between two levels, the profound and the mundane. If practice is too profound, it's no good. We are full of wonderful, lofty insights, but lack the ability to get through the day with any gracefulness or to relate to the issues and people in ordinary life. We may be soaringly metaphysical, movingly compassionate, and yet unable to relate to a normal human or a worldly problem. This is the moment when the Zen master whacks us with her stick and says, "Wash your bowls! Kill the Buddha!"

> On the other hand, if practice is too mundane, if we become too interested in the details of how we and others feel and what we or they need or want, then the natural loftiness of our hearts will not be accessible to us, and we will sink under the weight of obligations, details, and daily-life concerns. This is when the master says, "If you have a staff, I will give you a staff; if you need a staff, I will take it away." We need both profound religious philosophy and practical tools for daily living. – Norman Fischer, "Life is Tough. Here Are Six Ways to Deal With It"[162]

Perhaps I am oscillating between the profound and the mundane and finding each inside the other. Pema Khandro Rinpoche says, "Bardo refers to that state in which we have lost our old reality and it is no longer available to us. There is no ground, no certainty, and no reference point." When Lou died I was thrust deeply into the bardo. It seems I am there again.

~ 1322 ~

> You cannot be kind unless you have all the other virtues. If, being cowardly, conceited and slothful, you have never yet done a fellow creature great mischief, that is only because your neighbour's welfare has not yet happened to conflict with your safety, self-approval, or ease. Every vice leads to cruelty. – C.S. Lewis, *The Problem of Pain* [56]

The last sentence, so true, really struck me. The cruelty inflicted on me by my loved ones came about as I brought their vices to the surface. Lewis implied that, by the same token, every virtue leads to kindness: "You cannot be kind unless you have all the other virtues." When surrender to God is complete, when unsupported thought is attained, when one is born again and freed from sin, cruelty falls to the power of divine love and turns to kindness.

In a letter to Edward Lofstrom on January 16, 1959, Lewis took the extremes of vice and virtue, along with everything in between, and described how it all fits into the singularity of God:

> The most striking thing about Our Lord is the union of great ferocity with extreme tenderness. (Remember Pascal? 'I do not admire the extreme of one virtue unless you show me at the same time the extreme of the opposite virtue. One shows one's greatness not by being at an extremity but by being simultaneously at two extremities and *filling all the space between*.') ... This [Jesus] is the appearance in Human form of the God who made the Tiger and the Lamb, the avalanche and the rose. – C.S. Lewis, *The Collected Letters of C.S. Lewis, Volume III* [87]

~ 1323 ~

APOLOGY AND FORGIVENESS, Part 9

Last night I began an e-conversation with Sidney, a member of Ignacio's theology discussion group, that I saw as an opening for me to arise as a mentor. It was as if his questioning was setting up bowling pins for me to knock down. Is this synchronicity, or just my imagination? Or are they the same thing?

Sidney: If God wanted to forgive humans for sins, why not just forgive them? Sending himself down to be sacrificed to enable that seems extreme.

Betty: Jesus' crucifixion in itself did not free us from our sins. As the pastor said, "Jesus did not come to save, but to reveal." By dying a tortured death, by giving up everything to God and forgiving those who tortured him, Jesus revealed to us the Way by which we can effect our own salvation – by forgiving those who sin against us, no matter how grievous the sin.

> If you don't forgive you will not be forgiven. No part of His teaching is clearer, and there are no exceptions to it. He doesn't say that we are to forgive other people's sins provided they are not too frightful, or provided there are extenuating circumstances, or anything of that sort. We are to forgive them all, however spiteful, however mean, however often they are repeated. If we don't, we shall be forgiven none of our own. – C.S. Lewis, *The Weight of Glory* [86]

Until we recognize our indwelling God-self and realize that we ourselves, as aspects of God, must forgive the sins of others, we cannot ourselves be forgiven. God forgiving us is not a separate act from us forgiving others. One of the hardest thought patterns to break is the idea that we are separate from God. Ultimately God's forgiveness must come from inside. God's forgiveness is us forgiving ourselves.

TO MARY WILLIS SHELBURNE, 6 July 1963: Do you know, only a few weeks ago I realised suddenly that I at last had forgiven the cruel schoolmaster who so darkened my childhood. I'd been trying to do it for years: and like you, each time I thought I'd done it, I found, after a week or so it all had to be attempted over again. But this time I feel sure it is the real thing. And (like learning to swim or to ride a bicycle) the moment it does happen it seems so easy and you wonder why on earth you didn't do it years ago. So the parable of the unjust judge comes true, and what has been vainly asked for years can suddenly be granted. I also get a quite new feeling about 'If you forgive you will be forgiven.' I don't believe it is, as it sounds, a bargain. The forgiving and the being forgiven are really the very same thing. – C.S. Lewis, *The Collected Letters of C.S. Lewis, Volume III* [87]

Every one of us must take the walk to Calvary without resistance, anger, judgment, or vengeance, and forgive – indeed, love – those who put us in that awful place. The test of our faith – the degree of our willingness to painfully and selflessly sacrifice – must be arduous. Vilification, rejection, and derision are required along with the pain – "dishonorable suffering," as Dietrich Bonhoeffer called it; "perfect joy," as St. Francis of Assisi called it.

There is a line near the end of the movie *Ben-Hur* that says the same thing: After witnessing the crucifixion, Judah Ben-Hur says, "I felt his voice take the sword out of my hand." This is the same fearless renunciation of aggression that Chögyam Trungpa described in "The Tender Heart of the Warrior." (~1286~) As each of us feels the sword being taken out of our hand, our indwelling God-self and our eternal divine love emerge, and our sins are forgiven.

Sidney: *The crucifixion appears to be about sacrifice. But for what purpose? Atonement for mankind's sins is one concept (people differ on exactly what needs to be atoned for and why). Frankly, I find sin atonement to be another puzzlement that doesn't make any sense.*

Betty: The idea of atonement is that sin separates us from God, and the sacrifice of something dear to us humbles us and brings us back to God, making us again one with God – *at-one*ment. Greed caused us to sin; giving up what we are greedy for atones for sin. The sacrifice of Jesus on the cross catapulted the act of atonement from the earthly sphere to a mystical heavenly one.

It is necessary to look very deeply into scripture, with an open mind, to even begin to understand the many layers of meaning therein, especially to find the deepest spiritual meaning. Not many people, even clergy, have the courage to do that. For now, I will just say that the answers to these questions cannot be found using the same mind that asks the questions. You can't think your way to the answers.

There is a Zen-like frustration in this. In the realm where the answers are, the questions have no meaning. The laws of Moses, of science, logic, or philosophy have no meaning or application in eternity, as Newtonian physics breaks down at the outer edges of astrophysics and quantum mechanics. That is not to say, however, that questioning and discussing these things can't lead to a place where a quantum leap of understanding can be made.

Sidney: It's the "quantum leap" that makes me uncomfortable. I'm not sure why that is. It's probably because the part of my brain that focuses on logic and reason is much better exercised than ... well ... what exactly? I'm not sure. That's the uncomfortable part. I don't quite trust it because I can't analyze it and break it down into succinct bullet points.

Betty: I will give you a couple bullet points: The brain is only one of several places where information is processed in the body. Equally potent are the heart and the gut. The heart is the seat of the 4th chakra where divine love is awakened (this awakening is one crucial quantum leap), and gut knowledge is intuition. Heart knowledge and gut knowledge roughly correspond to the companion virtues of a buddha – compassion and wisdom.

Don't analyze this too much; overthinking, applying too much brainpower, impedes the unobstructed flow of both love and intuition. The confluence of duality and nonduality is a very hard concept to wrap one's brain around, which is why I appeal to heart and gut knowledge before head knowledge. I play the head game as well as anyone, but in the end, I know it is a futile exercise if the goal is true "knowing." Trust your heart and your gut, which is the same as saying, "Have faith."

The most important break-through quantum leap I can think of is gaining the ability to see things from the perspective of eternity as well as duality. This kind of "seeing" is better accomplished by the heart and gut than by the brain. In eternity (the Dao, the Great Void, the Source, the Unity, the Emptiness, the Godhead), all is one. There is no good, no evil, no right, no wrong, no law and no sin – thus no need for forgiveness. That is what I meant when I said that in the realm where the answers are, the questions have no meaning. The very concepts of sin, atonement, and forgiveness are meaningless.

~ 1324 ~

Now as they were eating, Jesus took bread, and blessed, and broke it, and gave it to the disciples and said, "Take, eat; this is my body." And he took a cup, and when he had given thanks he gave it to them, saying, "Drink of it, all of you; for this is my blood of the covenant, which is poured out for many for the forgiveness of sins. (Matthew 26: 26-28 RSV)

Sidney's questions about the crucifixion, atonement, and forgiveness brought me to another way of explaining these things: In ancient Israel the Jews had a ritual of animal sacrifice to atone for sin; the temple ran red with blood as the most prized lambs of the flock were slaughtered.

The law and sin had the Jews imprisoned in an endless cycle of transgression and atonement they couldn't break out of. Then Jesus brought to the world the good news, the gospel, the new covenant – the knowledge that there is an eternal God above the worldly God of Moses, above the need for animal (or human, in the case of Jesus) sacrifice to atone for sin, above the need for judgment or forgiveness.

Jesus, the Lamb of God, died as the ultimate sacrifice of atonement under the Law of Moses, God's total fulfillment and then abrogation of the Law, like making the final mortgage payment and then burning the mortgage papers. Jesus submitted fully to the God of Moses, the God of law, sin, reward, and punishment; took all that darkness could dish out; closed the book on the old Law; and then arose to the ultimate God who rules over Yahweh and Satan, where sin is erased or never was, making forgiveness unnecessary. Jesus, the Son of Man, died to the Law and was born again of the Spirit.

The God who demanded Jesus' crucifixion under the law was not the same God that Jesus resurrected to. The God who abandoned Jesus on the cross was the anthropomorphic God of duality. When Jesus died, he transcended this lesser God and commended his spirit to the eternal Godhead. The mystical ritual sacrifice of God's physical form on earth cleared the Way for all souls to find eternal Life.

By his life and death Jesus showed us the Way – how we, too, can subjugate the ego, become sinless, and arise to eternal life. Jesus paid the full penalty for us ("The wages of sin is death" – Romans 6:23 RSV) that was due under the law for all our past and future sins, and showed us how to rise above the law and join him in eternal oneness with God. It was a two-layered process: 1) paying the price for our sins and 2) showing us the Way back to the Garden of Eden, to our original sinless state.

> For since the law has but a shadow of the good things to come instead of the true form of these realities, it can never, by the same sacrifices which are continually offered year after year, make perfect those who draw near. Otherwise, would they not have ceased to be offered? If the worshipers had once been cleansed, they would no longer have any consciousness of sin. But in these sacrifices there is a reminder of sin year after year. For it is impossible that the blood of bulls and goats should take away sins.
>
> Consequently, when Christ came into the world, he said,
>
>> "Sacrifices and offerings thou hast not desired,
>> but a body hast thou prepared for me;
>> in burnt offerings and sin offerings thou hast taken no pleasure.
>> Then I said, 'Lo, I have come to do thy will, O God,'
>> as it is written of me in the roll of the book."

When he said above, "Thou hast neither desired nor taken pleasure in sacrifices and offerings and burnt offerings and sin offerings" (these are offered according to the law), then he added, "Lo, I have come to do thy will." *He abolishes the first in order to establish the second.* [my emphasis] And by that will we have been sanctified through the offering of the body of Jesus Christ once for all. (Hebrews 10:1-10 RSV)

"He abolishes the first in order to establish the second." The first — the offering of worldly goods under the law for forgiveness of sins — takes place in space and time on the plane of duality. The second — doing God's will: the total, unconditional surrender of everything, even life, back to God — brings the eternal into the dual, heaven to earth.

When you follow Christ's Way, you realize it is the same Way that was trod by the Buddha, Plato, Lao-tzu, Mansur al-Hallaj, St. Francis, Mohammed, Carl Jung, Thich Nhat Hanh, Joseph Campbell, Anthony de Mello, and all the other great sages through the ages. This is where all religions are known to be the same at the Source, where the unconscious and the subconscious become conscious.

But not everyone is ready to follow the Way. Everyone is at a different stage of the journey, and at any given point few are at the mystical narrow gate. For those who cannot yet break out of duality, the law and sin, it is enough to know that Jesus has paid the price for sin and has prepared a place for all in the sinless eternal life — which is spread upon the earth, here and now — on earth as it is in heaven. By diligently following the Way, we will all get there. When we partake of the bread and wine in communion, we are accepting the life of Christ as our own, God in us.

Jesus looked up and said to her, "Woman, where are they? Has no one condemned you?" She said, "No one, Lord." And Jesus said, "Neither do I condemn you; go, and do not sin again." (John 8:10-11 RSV)

Jesus did not say, "go, and do not commit adultery again." He said "go, and do not sin again." Do not sin *at all*. Is it possible to live a totally sinless life? Jesus implied that it is, and Paul said so explicitly. When you are born again of the spirit, the law and sin are dead.

~ 1325 ~

Nicodemus said to him, "How can a man be born when he is old? Can he enter a second time into his mother's womb and be born?" (John 3:4 RSV)

The life of Adam and Eve in the Garden of Eden before the Fall is like that of a fetus in the womb. The mother is the body of God. The fetus is created in the image of God and lives wholly inside God, taking nourishment from and being in total surrender to God, unaware of any other state of existence. This is life in the Garden, unconscious, in ignorance and innocence.

At birth, the baby is cast out of the Garden. With its first breath, the child is imbued with original sin, experiences pleasure and pain, and the ego begins to arise. This is the world of duality, apparently outside God, separate from God.

But even in this separation, we remember our Source. We know that our genealogy, physical and spiritual, comes from and goes back to the Source. So does our inheritance and all that we bequeath when we die.

Nicodemus asked if a man can enter a second time into his mother's womb. Jesus said, in spiritual metaphor, yes. To be born again is to enter the womb a second time, to be once again in the womb, in the Garden, inside God. But this time, when we are born again, we are not unconscious or ignorant; we are, as the Buddha said, awake. And in the absence of the law and sin, our innocence is regained.

PART 56
Mentoring
July 2018 – November 2018

~ 1326 ~

Has it ever occurred to you that beauty depends on something being identified as ugly? Therefore, the idea of beauty produces the idea of ugliness, and vice versa. What if you instead perceived all as a piece (or a glimpse) of the perfection of oneness? Imagine the perfect oneness coexisting in the apparent duality, where opposites are simply judgments made by human minds in the world of 10,000 things. Surely the daffodil doesn't think that the daisy is prettier or uglier than it is, and the eagle and the mouse have no sense of the opposites we call life and death. The trees, flowers, and animals know not of ugliness or beauty; they simply are in harmony with the eternal Dao, devoid of judgment. Virtue and sin are judgments, needing both to identify either. … Let the contrasting and opposite ideas be within you at the same time. Know that good and evil are two aspects of a union. In other words, accept the duality of the material world while still remaining in constant contact with the oneness of the eternal Dao. The debilitating necessity to be right and make others wrong will diminish. – Wayne Dyer, *Change Your Thoughts - Change Your Life* [80]

Last Sunday at church I was invited to lead the adult Sunday school class. I immediately declined the invitation, remembering that "those who speak do not know; those who know do not speak." But then I remembered that I have been getting multiple spiritual messages leading me into a mentoring stage of my life.

Yes, I can do this. I have an idea how I might mentor my Christian friends. "Imagine the perfect oneness coexisting in the apparent duality," said Wayne Dyer. My job is to teach triangulation as Wayne did, to wake up my friends to the eternal Dao here and now, where good and evil, virtue and sin, are at peace together, and where the knowing do not speak.

C.S. Lewis said, "I saw well why the gods do not speak to us openly, nor let us answer. Till that word can be dug out of us, why should they hear the babble that we think we mean?"[150] When I must speak, Wayne Dyer, St. Paul, Jesus, and all my spirit guides will put the words in my mouth, as God did for Jeremiah:

> Then the Lord put forth his hand and touched my mouth; and the Lord said to me,
> "Behold, I have put my words in your mouth."
> (Jeremiah 1:9 RSV)

LOVE, Part 13

> Being in love is a good thing, but it is not the best thing. There are many things below it, but there are also things above it. You cannot make it the basis of a whole life. It is a noble feeling, but it is still a feeling. Now no feeling can be relied on to last in its full intensity, or even to last at all. Knowledge can last, principles can last, habits can last; but feelings come and go. And in fact, whatever people say, the state called 'being in love' usually does not last. – C.S. Lewis, *Mere Christianity* [76]

Of course I take issue with Lewis conflating love with mere feelings, but he begins to grasp the difference in this passage:

> If the old fairy-tale ending 'They lived happily ever after' is taken to mean 'They felt for the next fifty years exactly as they felt the day before they were married', then it says what probably never was nor ever would be true, and would be highly undesirable if it were. Who could bear to live in that excitement for even five years? What would become of your work, your appetite, your sleep, your friendships? But, of course, ceasing to be 'in love' need not mean ceasing to love. Love in this second sense—love as distinct from 'being in love'—is not merely a feeling. It is a deep unity, maintained by the will and deliberately strengthened by habit; reinforced by (in Christian marriages) the grace which both partners ask, and receive, from God. They can have this love for each other even at those moments when they do not like each other; as you love yourself even when you do not like yourself. They can retain this love even when each would easily, if they allowed themselves, be 'in love' with someone else. 'Being in love' first moved them to promise fidelity: this quieter love enables them to keep the promise. It is on this love that the engine of marriage is run: being in love was the explosion that started it.[76]

When lovers are fully awake in divine love, this part is unnecessary: "...maintained by the will and deliberately strengthened by habit; reinforced by (in Christian marriages) the grace which both partners ask, and receive, from God." In fully realized divine love, when the latent God-self becomes kinetic, no maintenance, deliberate strengthening, or reinforcement is necessary; divine love arises and acts spontaneously without effort (often understood only in retrospect). This is what I knew with Lou (understood only in retrospect), and what Lewis finally discovered when his wife Joy came into his life.

Lest you desire to know such a transcendent love, remember that divine love brings with it a terrifying darkness. It can only be so, to balance the brilliant light, in the sense of interdependent co-arising. The absolute vulnerability of divine love makes it a dangerous and painful love; evil is not resisted and there are no rules or limits. Unless you are ready to handle the darkness (Lewis handled it by writing *A Grief Observed*; I by writing this journal), it is best to be satisfied with the worldly forms of love, each sacred in its own way. But when you are ready for it, the light of divine love – and especially its accompanying darkness – leads to higher realms of awakening.

~ 1328 ~

BOUNDARIES, Part 5

> "Now, wait a minute," Teresa said, shaking her head. "How can I set limits on those who need me? Isn't that living for me and not for God?" Teresa was voicing one of the main objections to boundary setting for Christians: a deep-seated fear of being self-centered, interested only in one's own concerns and not those of others.
>
> First, let's make a distinction between selfishness and stewardship. Selfishness has to do with a fixation on our own wishes and desires, to the exclusion of our responsibility to love others. A helpful way to understand setting limits is that our lives are a gift from God. Just as a store manager takes good care of a shop for the owner, we are to do the same with our souls. If a lack of boundaries causes us to mismanage the store, the owner has a right to be upset with us.
>
> We are to develop our lives, abilities, feelings, thoughts, and behaviors. Our spiritual and emotional growth is God's "interest" on his investment in us. When we say no to people and activities that are hurtful to us, we are protecting God's investment. – Dr. Henry Cloud and Dr. John Townsend, in "Boundaries"[83]

The "Boundaries" guys have helped me feel better about setting boundaries with Emily. Although I miss our earthly togetherness, I realize that my return to health has been largely due to her absence. My life's priority has shifted to protecting God's investment in me. I wonder if my life of service will ever again cross paths with the life of God's investment in the form of Emily.

~ 1329 ~

While working on the program for an upcoming Christmas concert, I listened to a lot of traditional Christmas music – the old carols, Handel's *Messiah*. Hearing the simple messages of those songs, it dawned on me that most people get from birth to death pretty well without epiphanies or conscious spiritual communication. Not everyone asks the hard questions or seeks the elusive answers; they don't need to. The simple faith of our fathers, that old-time religion, is good enough for most people. They find holy meaning and purpose in life's everyday activities and in worldly loves with others around them. They don't spend their days and nights in existential anguish contemplating time and eternity; they don't find that exercise fruitful. They find peace and contentment by simply trusting in God, not knowing why. Not everyone is a mystic; not everyone needs to be. Not everyone needs to find nirvana, or know it when they do. As long as one acts out of love, not fear or greed, he is doing God's work, acting out God's will, whether he knows it or not.

Most of us go our entire lives unconscious of our eternal nature. A few people have moments of awakening, such as my epiphanies, epic dreams, and synchronicities. At first, spirit messages come in brief flashes, in fits and starts, as in a garbled phone connection or in fleeting glimpses through the window of a moving train. At some point the messages become clearer, more frequent, and their effects linger longer in the psyche. Eventually the path to the narrow gate is illuminated, and the irreversible eighth bhūmi is reached. The seeker becomes a mystic and lives consciously in both eternity and duality.

But whether conscious or unconscious, eternity is always present and unchanging in and around duality. Absolute truth holds all relative truths. Emptiness holds everything. Divine love always dwells in the subconscious, waiting to awaken into consciousness once the stage is set.

~ 1330 ~

MUSICIANS IN THE MOMENT

There are always new sounds to imagine: new feelings to get at. And always, there is a need to keep purifying these feelings and sounds so that we can really see what we've discovered in its pure state. So that we can see more clearly what we are. In that way, we can give to those who listen, the essence—the best of what we are. But to do that at each stage, we have to keep on cleaning the mirror. ... Once you become aware of this force for unity in life, you can't forget it. It becomes part of everything you do. ... I believe in all religions. The truth itself doesn't have any name on it to me, and each man has to find it for himself. – John Coltrane, jazz saxophonist [163]

So I began to get down to the moment—to try to dissect the actual moment before I play the next note. Let's say I'm playing a melody and there are five notes in all, and I've played three notes and I'm about to play the fourth note. ... At the same time it's an exquisite moment because I'm completely in the present. ... What I do is that I can remember the music I just played, I can hear the notes I'm about to play, and I'm caught in this moment in between. It's almost like that paradox of a Greek philosopher: how do you reach a place if you go halfway at a time? How do you ever reach the final destination? It becomes logically impossible. ... Of course, the difficulty with the problem is the way it's described. Actually we don't have any problem at all reaching the other side. Moving, we simply carry the present with us from moment to moment. That's really what happens. – Philip Glass, classical composer [164]

I play all kinds of music – jazz, classical, country, pop, a little rock, and some ethnic and world music. Living my life in music has been a fabulous blessing, a vocation just as spiritual as the priesthood. One thing I discovered on my musical path is that all music is the same – all great art takes its inspiration from the same Source and leads its audience along the same path, the same Way, and tells the same Truth. The goal of every artist is to tread the Way so truly and tell the Truth so clearly that God's voice is the only one heard.

~ 1331 ~

It's really the space between the notes that makes the music you enjoy so much. Without the spaces, all you would have is one continuous noisy note. Everything that's created comes out of silence. Your thoughts emerge from the nothingness of silence. Your words come out of this void. Your very essence emerged from emptiness. ... And as Melville reminded us so poignantly, "God's one and only voice is silence." – Wayne Dyer, *10 Secrets for Success and Inner Peace*

What a paradox – God is in both sound, the Word, and silence, the Void. I have described my tinnitus, the phantom hissing sound – "one continuous noisy note" – in my head, as *anāhata*, the voice of God at the 4th chakra, the heart chakra of love. The Buddhist "OM" mantra is also one continuous noisy note. A blind person can never see God in light waves, but finds God's light in other ways. I will never know pure silence ever again; for me, God's silence is broken by one continuous noisy note. But God finds voice in the noisy note, and speaks silently in other ways.

~ 1332 ~

Reflecting on the discourse in our theology discussion group, my Buddhist-Christian friend Judy said, "Thank you, Betty. All this consensus-seeking shimmers to me. We are all so fine and we don't need to make it all so hard. You are a delight."

~ 1333 ~

CREATED IN THE IMAGE OF GOD

Buddhist author Dainin Katagiri Roshi wrote:

When Tozan[xi] saw his reflection, he realized it was not his real self, because in order for a reflection to appear, the thing reflected must already exist. He composed this gatha:

You shouldn't search for it outwardly.
If you do, the truth will become more remote from you.
But when alone I proceed through myself,
Wherever I go I meet him.
Now he is not other than myself, yet I am not he.
Only if you understand this will you unite with the Tathāgata.

When you see your reflection, it is coming from emptiness, but immediately it is going, returning to emptiness. In the next moment, a new reflection comes. Your reflection is impermanent; it is always coming and going. The only thing that stays is the vastness of existence. This vastness is your true self.

A reflection must be there, or there is nothing for you to see. Without any reflection I cannot see that I exist; I cannot understand who I am. True self and its reflection are not the same, but they are not separate. Your reflection is not the real truth, but without that reflection you cannot see the truth. If you search for true self outwardly, with your ordinary, dualistic human consciousness, you will never find it.

When the one unified life of all beings begins to move toward the human world of separation and discrimination, true self starts to walk, and wherever it goes it meets a reflection of itself. This is Tozan's proceeding alone. When you proceed like this, this proceeding is called wisdom.[165]

I am beginning to connect the dots: Tozan with Silesius (~1252~), Radha Krishna (~944~), Meister Eckhart (~847~), Joseph Campbell (~612~), Thich Nhat Hanh (~694~), and others. All the great sages of the ages have described this ephemeral concept of God's reflection of himself in his dualistic creation.

Reflections come and go, but the Source of all images is constant and unchanging. We know God by seeing him reflected in others and ourselves. We are God's consciousness of himself, and through our human consciousness we see God – as I saw the world, timeless and formless,

---

[xi] Chinese Zen (Chan) master Tozan Ryokai (Dongshan Liangjie, 807-869)

with God's eyes in my 1/1/09 epiphany (~232~), and Emily as God with form in my 11/17/13 epiphany (~604~).

We reflect God as the moon reflects the light of the sun. But the moon *is* the sun, made of the same interconnected matter and energy as the sun, born of the same Big Bang. The Godhead communicates with us through its resonating image in us – our God-self – our higher self, as Martha calls it. God's telephone is the 5th chakra, and my body-mind recognizes an incoming call when tingling radiates through me from the back of my neck.

> Ignorance means you are standing in the middle of a world so vast and deep that your intellect cannot grasp it. When your intellect cannot stand up in the vastness of life, you become confused and carried away by your ignorance. In Buddhist terms, that is called *dukkha*, or suffering. Suffering creates arrogance, and arrogance creates criticism and hatred. Then human life becomes very messy.[165]

Revelation trumps scripture, not to negate it, but to illuminate it, bringing its deepest meaning to the surface, leading to the "knowing" that is beyond knowledge. Intellectual analyses of scripture, such as Bible commentaries and the Talmud, have their place in preparing the mind for a quantum leap to true faith – surrender to that which is beyond mind – but they cannot themselves lead to enlightenment. In the same sense, science is ultimately validated not by its intellectual explorations, but by using intellect as a springboard to the place where intuition and imagination take over. This is where Einstein and Jung went.

The Buddhist understanding that ignorance leads to suffering, to arrogance and hatred, explains much of the social and political discord that plagues the world. No matter how smart and clever we are, no matter how great our technological and intellectual advances, our ignorance and arrogance continue to tear down all that we build, and tear us apart. Only the love that transcends the mind and its machinations can save us.

~ 1334 ~

REASON FOR EXISTENCE?

I used to like watching nature programs on television. But I stopped watching them because they always turned dark, the beauty of nature morphing into nature red in tooth and claw. I began to wonder why living beings exist, if there is any purpose for living. It seems that the entire biosphere has no purpose but to kill, eat, reproduce, and die. Even the largest and strongest predators in the food chain are eventually consumed by tiny, even microscopic, predators; bacteria, viruses, worms, and insects can be just as lethal as sharks and lions.

We humans, even as we kill and eat our fellow creatures, think that with our advanced brains we have a higher calling, that we live our lives for a reason, to have dominion over the earth and create great works of art and science. Maybe so, but maybe this is just an illusion conjured up in our anthropocentric minds. All of creation is just an illusion, after all.

But no matter what feats of intellect we might accomplish, the prime directive of every human life, like every other life, is to reproduce. I do not have biological children; I have not passed on the attributes of my physical body, but my mental and spiritual genes have left a lasting legacy in this world through my art. My parents were nothing special; neither of them did anything noteworthy during their lives, but maybe their lives were not without purpose. Perhaps their reason for existence was to give birth to me and set me on the mystical path I am now on. My spiritual work, including this book, is their legacy.

Today is my birthday. Thanks, Mom and Dad, I guess, for that one sexual moment that created me.

~ 1335 ~

GOOD AND EVIL, Part 14
Nibbana With and Without Residue

> It is true that in Zen there are precepts that describe moral rules not unlike those followed by any religion or ethical humanistic program—not killing, stealing, lying, and so on. But Zen teaching distinguishes three different levels of precept practice: relative (or literal), compassionate, and absolute. On the *relative or literal* level, we try to keep the precepts as written and simply understood. On the *compassionate* level, we sometimes violate a precept in order to benefit others. The *absolute* level proposes that there is ultimately no way to keep any precept, and no way to break it. All precepts are always broken and kept. This is nondual morality—beyond good and evil. – Norman Fischer, "The Problem of Evil" [166]

On the relative level, bodhisattvas automatically keep the precepts without trying. On the compassionate level, bodhisattvas cannot help but break precepts when divine love demands it, as Lou and I did in obedience to the call of divine love, and as a priest reluctantly advised desperate ex-cons to shoplift if no one will give them a job. (~586~) On the absolute level, the bodhisattva knows that neither keeping nor breaking the precepts is good or evil, just the way things must be, as the apparent evil of Judas' betrayal was necessary for the apparent good of Jesus' resurrection.

> When the precepts are deeply considered, it's clear that literal, compassionate, and absolute are only words, distinctions meant to help us appreciate aspects of the precepts we might otherwise miss. In the actual human world, we can't avoid the choice between good and bad, because there is no absolute level apart from the relative and compassionate levels. Relative, compassionate, and absolute are ways of talking about the moral choices we make with these human bodies and minds, in an actual, lived, physical world.[166]

The interconnectedness of duality and eternity is absolute; they are as hard to separate as tar from feathers.

> In Zen language, "the great death" stands for the nondual sense of life as one. All things, good or bad, desirable or undesirable, express that oneness. To experience the great death is to see, face-to-face and for oneself, that everything is real, everything is true, everything is just as it is. The great death, oneness, enlightenment, total acceptance of reality beyond good and evil—this is a necessary step in Zen or any other profound spiritual practice. But although this may be ultimate, it is only a step. Zen calls it "the great death" for a good reason. It is a kind of "death." It requires a complete letting go, a complete relinquishment, in trust, of everything that one has identified as one's life.
>
> "All conditioned existence is suffering, unsatisfactory, *dukkha*," the Buddha originally taught. In its purity, being is beyond good and evil, beyond moral dilemmas. And it's not. Yes, "life and death are one" is a deep and ineffable truth. Killing and being killed, one. All victims of violence would have died soon enough anyway. All of them were, like us, more or less already dead—impermanence, emptiness, means that we are all already dead, losing our lives (evanescent as smoke) moment by moment anyway. Our having an actual possessable life has always been a painful illusion. The change of state from life and death is slight, the curtain between them far thinner than any of us believe. From within the great death everything is acceptable; everything is all right all of the time. Things are just as they are, not some other way. But this, monstrous as it sounds, is so only when you are dead—only when you have entered the samadhi of the absolute, which is stasis.[166]

What the Zen Buddhists call "the great death" the Christians call being "born again."

Bhikkhu Bodhi, a sage from the Theravada tradition, provides further insight into *dukkha* and the distinction between soul and spirit: awakening in duality, nibbana with residue, and ultimately in eternity, nibbana without residue:

> In the early discourses, we distinguish two aspects of the cessation of *dukkha* with two dimensions of nibbana [nirvana]. One is the dimension of nibbana to be realized in this present life, also called the *nibbana with residue remaining*. This is the state that's attained when all

of the defilements have been eradicated. It's explained as the destruction of greed, hatred, and delusion, but still this residue of *dukkha* remains throughout the body with its sense faculties and mental processes. Even the *arhat*—who has eradicated all of the defilements right down to their roots, who lives in peace, harmony, tranquility, and happiness, no longer experiencing any *dukkha* as grief, sorrow, worry, or anxiety—still recognizes that the experience through body and mind is inherently unsatisfactory, that it contains a residue of *dukkha*.

The final goal of the teaching, then, is the cessation of the continued process of rebirth. That occurs when the liberated one passes away; what remains is called the *nibbana element without residue remaining*. In that state, there is no longer any continuation of the five aggregates, the conglomeration of physical and mental processes that constitute experience. That according to the Buddha, is the ultimate cessation of *dukkha*. – Bhikkhu Bodhi (Jeffrey Block), "Understanding Dukkha," *Buddhadharma*, Winter 2017, Vol. 16, No. 1

Fischer says, "In its purity, being is beyond good and evil, beyond moral dilemmas. And it's not." This state of knowing eternal oneness while still living in the opposite poles of duality, what I call triangulation, is nibbana with residue. Then Fischer says, "From within the great death everything is acceptable; everything is all right all of the time. But this, monstrous as it sounds, is so only when you are dead—only when you have entered the *samadhi* of the absolute, which is stasis." This is complete unexcelled awakening, *anuttara samyak sambodhi*, nibbana without residue.

~ 1336 ~

THINKING AND THE MIND, Part 7

To a friend in our theology discussion group:

I am saddened by your repeated references to your own perceived wrongdoing. How do you know that what you did was wrong? Maybe it was exactly what God meant for you to do, even though someone might have felt hurt by it. Hurt resides not in the allegedly hurtful act, but in one's response to it. You did not hurt anyone; the person on the receiving end of your words or actions hurt himself.

Jesus was betrayed, denied, and tortured to the point of death, but he was not hurt by those actions. The suffering inflicted on him propelled him to heaven, as he knew it would – to the place that Rumi described "beyond ideas of wrongdoing and rightdoing." Judas, Peter, the Pharisees, the Roman soldiers, Pontius Pilate, Herod, and all the others who participated in the passion of Christ were doing God's will as much as Jesus was.

Even in the course of a life-altering awakening, *nothing changes*. What were once thought to be sinful behaviors are now seen in broader perspective and are no longer considered sinful, but rather the necessary balance to virtue, or an understandable early stage in spiritual growth when most behaviors are unconscious, arising from the ego's primordial survival instinct. In awakening there is no ego to pass judgment or obstruct the flow of God's love, and so there is no sin and thus no guilt, and no need for forgiveness. There is no right or wrong, just the autonomic expression of the eternal Godhead in duality.

There is a saying in Zen, "Where the water is too pure, there are no fish." Impurities are not necessarily bad; sometimes they are food for the fish. The Buddhists don't draw a line between right and wrong, good and evil, but recognize elements of good and evil in every act. There is no sin; behaviors are not described as "right" or "wrong," but as "skilled" or "unskilled." The thing that differentiates Buddhism from Christianity is not so much the absence of God as the absence of guilt.

Skilled behavior is that which walks the Middle Way between the extremes of good and evil, knowing that in this dualistic world neither can be grasped nor escaped, but also knowing that duality exists in a field of unity where there is no good or evil. This is exactly the sinless condition that Paul describes in Romans, a condition that we can all achieve, once we are born again of the spirit – once we join Christ, Rumi, and the Buddha in the field beyond ideas of wrongdoing and rightdoing.

~ 1337 ~

As I was walking into the church I met a friend in the courtyard who said, "We missed you in the Sunday school class today. We need your wisdom."

The Bible says, "You see that a man is justified by works and not by faith alone." (James 2:24 RSV) True faith automatically carries works with it. My friend who says I am "a delight" and the one who missed my "wisdom" in Sunday school this morning justify me by my works, not by faith alone. In the *Upajjhatthana Sutra*, the Buddha said, "My deeds are my closest companions. I am the beneficiary of my deeds. My deeds are the ground on which I stand." Jesus said, "A tree is known by its fruit."

As my musical career winds down, my mentoring role rises up. I have been offered a faculty position at a local university. It seems that God has mentoring work for me not just in church but also in academia.

I did not seek this job; it came to me out of the blue – just like all the other major events of my life. As I reflect on the panorama of my life, I can see the hand of God in every step, every event that guided the trajectory of my life. First was the epiphany that propelled me into a musical career (~340~); then to my job in the band, which took me to my new home where I would meet Lou; then to Lou's death, which would set the stage for all the miracles and synchronicities that would follow.

As young people we are taught to plan carefully for the future – to choose a career that will provide financial security, pick a compatible spouse, live a healthy lifestyle. I tried to make plans, but God blew all my plans out of the water. Sometimes God just grabs you by the scruff of the neck. As Joseph Campbell said, "You must give up the life you planned in order to have the life that is waiting for you."

~ 1338 ~

In Christianity, human beings have, as it were, two origins. Ultimately, we were created by God as good. But relatively, our nature is passed down to us from our predecessors. The condition of original sin is called "original" because it is derived from the origins of human beings in each other, as opposed to as created good by God. The force of the Latin word *originale* is hard to capture today, but it designates a condition we inherit, not our most basic nature. Understood this way, we can see Buddhist analogues for the Christian understanding of original sin.

The convergences might be stated this way: Neither tradition holds that human beings are intrinsically wicked or evil, but both traditions are keenly aware of the difficulties accompanying our current condition. The Christian understanding of the effects of original sin and the Buddhist teachings on the noble truth of suffering and the root poisons are both diagnoses of what ails us. They are not normative descriptions of human nature itself.

Finally, just as the many Mahayana traditions hold that the realization of Buddhahood is the realization of our true nature, so the Christian view is that a saint has simply realized the image of God given in the beginning. – Catholic theologian Steven Shippee, "The Real Meaning of Original Sin," *Lion's Roar*, September 2017

"A saint has simply realized the image of God given in the beginning." (A saint, a buddha, a shaman, a yogi …) In every tradition there is a quantum leap to awakening, to realizing the innate image of God, the God-self, the buddha-nature. And in every tradition there is a process, a Way, for reaching the point of awakening. There is always a time of trial, of temptation and suffering, forcing total surrender to something beyond the ego and the sensory body-mind. This is the hero's journey described by Joseph Campbell and demonstrated in the life of Christ, the life of the Buddha … and the life of me.

~ 1339 ~

When the power of love overcomes the love of power, the world will know peace.

– attributed to William Gladstone / Mahatma Gandhi / Sri Chinmoy Kumar Ghose / Jimi Hendrix

Yes, but … interdependent co-arising … the power of love and the love of power arise together, and peace in the world can only be understood by comparison to war. And even if all external wars ended and the outside world was finally at peace, there would still be our internal wars of sickness, disability, grief, and fear to overcome.

The extremes of war and peace can together be reduced in amplitude (~960~), but to arrive at true peace is to find it in the midst of war, in the form of Compassion, Loving-kindness, Joy, and Equanimity – the peace that passes understanding, the peace of eternity inside our tumultuous duality. Jesus demonstrated what that peace – total surrender to divine love – looks like on the cross.

Dr. Jill Bolte Taylor, in her book *My Stroke of Insight*, described the duality-in-eternity condition scientifically, in terms of right brain/left brain dichotomy. The imaginative right brain flies free in eternity, living moment to moment in the singular energy that flows among all things. The analytical left brain expresses the worldly ego, thinking and speaking, plucking separate ideas and events out of the eternal oneness, pulling them from the past and projecting them into the future. While having a stroke, Jill saw objects around her dissolve and become indistinguishable from each other; she saw the dancing molecules, much as I did in my 1/1/09 epiphany. Her left brain relinquished control and her right brain took over; she opened to the infinite and awoke to her eternal nature.

Often when I am in the Christian church or the Buddhist temple my mind will drift off into semi-consciousness, and then be awakened when a word or phrase suddenly jumps out from the indistinct murmurings around me. Today I heard "hope for the resurrection." And then it dawned on me: I am already resurrected; I don't need to just hope for it. This is what it is to live in eternity and duality, to know both at the same time, and to know the ultimate peace – heaven on earth, God with us, in us, now, in the eternal moment.

~ 1340 ~

SEX, Part 34

My note to Emily:

> We are exact opposites – the only candy you like is the only kind I don't like. You are
> wild and crazy; I am calm and sane. You are always on the move; I stay still. Together
> we are Whole. We are all that is. You will always be my beloved, no matter how far
> apart we are, in a way that I wonder if you will ever understand.

Since Emily left, my sex drive is almost gone. I occasionally "pleasure" myself, not for
pleasure, but because the health experts say sexual activity is good for one's health. But thanks
to Emily, I know that this kind of worldly sex – for pleasure or procreation or good health – is
categorically different from the tantric sex I knew when her spirit was with me.

The physical sensations are not the same; arousal is focused solely on the genitals, like
watching porn – pleasurable in a superficial way, but meaningless. Sensory sex does not carry
any psychic or spiritual power; there is no soul connection. In all her horror, Emily nevertheless
brought to me in our eternal oneness the extreme opposite of this soulless sex. Tantric sex with
her was nothing *but* soul connection.

~ 1341 ~

Blum and Rhodes' anthology focuses on the work of four scholar-practitioners in the Higashi
Honganji branch of Shin Buddhism, which traces its origins to the founder Gutoku Shinran
(1173–1262), who himself began as a disciple of Honen but went on to develop his own
distinctive interpretation of Pure Land thought and practice. The difference between Honen
and Shinran may be regarded as a matter of emphasis. Whereas Honen emphasized the need
to practice the recitation of the Name of Amida Buddha continuously, Shinran emphasized
the need to do so with sincere engagement of one's whole being—body, mind, and heart—that
is, quality over quantity. Whereas Honen uplifted his followers with the promise of realizing
the Pure Land of oneness in the hereafter, Shinran focused on the realization of *shinjin*, true
entrusting to the Vow of Boundless Compassion in the present moment, here and now. – Mark
Unno, "The Radical Thinkers of Pure Land"[167]

Honen described the Pure Land as most Christians describe heaven, as separate from
life on earth, while Shinran described it as Jesus did, as the kingdom of God spread upon the

earth here and now. Together, holding dual views within one Pure Land sect, they show us the universal mystical inseparability of division and oneness, duality and eternity.

C.S. Lewis, coming from a vastly different culture, religion, and century, captured the same relationship between here-and-now problems and their heavenly disposition:

> Heaven will solve our problems, but not, I think, by showing us subtle reconciliations between all our apparently contradictory notions. The notions will all be knocked from under our feet. We shall see that there never was any problem. – C.S. Lewis, *A Grief Observed* [3]

My friend commented on the C.S. Lewis quote: "Another reading: There are and will always be problems, but the answers are always there."

I responded: "Thank you for presenting a view of the life condition from the vantage point of duality. C.S. Lewis described the same condition from the vantage point of eternity. Both views are true."

~ 1342 ~

I love the intellectual sparring among my Christian friends; they are genuine seekers of truth and wisdom. They seek answers that will bring them peace. But in their search they find too many answers, leading only to more questions. The discussion is becoming tedious and, for me, unproductive. Maybe I am supposed to participate to follow God's mentoring directive. But I always want to leapfrog over the analytical stuff and go straight to the mystical.

These discussions remind me of the orthodox Jews at the Wailing Wall in Jerusalem endlessly chanting and praying, seeking the same peace that the Christians are looking for in their incessant questioning. The more desperately you want something and the more ardently you grasp for it, the less likely you are to get it. When the Jews stop wailing and the Christians stop flailing, when they just stay still and open to the infinite, they will stand a chance of inadvertently finding the heaven they seek.

If the Talmudic scholars and their Christian counterparts are engaging in scholarly pursuits with a goal of gaining the kingdom of heaven, they will fail. (In fact, they have always had the kingdom of heaven, which they will realize when they stop trying to find it.[xii]) If, on the other hand, they are taking their intellectual journey just for the fun of it, without a goal, to enjoy smelling the roses along the path, they just might stumble upon the treasure they had been satisfied to do without. But we should expect that this journey, like all those we take, will only take us back to where we started.

~ 1343 ~

What you are aware of you are in control of; what you are not aware of is in control of you. You are always a slave to what you're not aware of. When you're aware of it, you're free from it. It's there, but you're not affected by it. You're not controlled by it; you're not enslaved by it. – Anthony de Mello, "Good Religion: The Antithesis of Unawareness," http://www.soulwise. net/99adm00.htm

This is the Buddha's awakening – simple awareness, and thus control, of everything around you – not necessarily in control of things that impact you, but in control of how things that impact you, impact you. Freedom from enslavement to desire and fear.

Stephen Hawking said, "If you understand how the universe operates, you control it in a way."

The Buddhist monk said, "Yes, I am in pain, but I do not suffer, because I accept it."

Lao-tzu said, "Because the sage always confronts difficulties, he never experiences them."

~ 1344 ~

Nirvana is not a blank nothingness. Instead, it's a type of consciousness, it's not known through the six senses, and it doesn't engage in fabricating any experience at all (unlike, for example, the nondual consciousness found in formless levels of concentration). The Buddha described this consciousness as "without surface" and "unestablished." – Thanissaro Bhikkhu [168]

Nirvana is not nothingness, but *consciousness* of nothingness (see the Dalai Lama on nirvana consciousness: ~1408~). Depicting nirvana as "without surface" and "unestablished" is like

---

[xii] "Help us to find God."
"No one can help you there."
"Why not?"
"For the same reason that no one can help the fish to find the ocean."
 – Anthony de Mello, *One Minute Wisdom* [70]

the Western description of God as an infinite sphere whose center is everywhere and whose circumference is nowhere.

> Even though this dimension is uncaused, a path of practice leads to it—in the same way that a road to a mountain doesn't cause the mountain, but following the road can get you there. The road is one thing; the mountain, something else.[168]

Thanissaro Bhikkhu shines a lovely light on the unresolved paradox in both Eastern and Western religions concerning the purpose and value of religious study and practice. Both Jesus and the Buddha taught their followers to read the scriptures, pray, meditate, and observe rituals and practices, but also that attaining nirvana/heaven/awakening does not come through knowledge and effort. Trungpa Rinpoche said much the same thing in describing the Zen practice of strengthening the intellect and then bypassing it altogether (~1155~) and the gradual process that leads to sudden enlightenment (~1211~).

Sitting in meditation cannot make a buddha, but by faithfully following the road that did not cause the mountain, suddenly God's grace – the Buddha's enlightenment – is upon you. You look up from the road and find the mountain under your feet.

~ 1345 ~

EXPECTATIONS

Everyone has expectations in life. We raise our children with expectations, even if we claim we haven't. We have expectations of life, of others, of our mythical God, of everything. Our expectations are a form of control. We form an expectation of the events we go to, from seminars to parties to job interviews. We are compulsive about expectations. They are psychic anchors we toss into a future space in an attempt to organize that space according to our needs, structuring that future space in such a way that we get all our fantasy needs met, even "beyond our expectations." The problem is that expectations are the most counterproductive visualization activity a person can engage in.

Becoming mindful that you are projecting expectations onto someone or some future event— and then choosing to release those expectations as best as you can—is a game changer. Mind you, expectations are so powerful that you have to pry this habit out of you like gum off your shoe. You'll know you've made progress on this front when you find an increase in synchronistic happenings and when you feel less inclined toward negative judgments of any situation you find yourself in. Wisdom replaces negativity as you come to trust the truth that you have no idea what's really unfolding or why you are where you are. You walk in two worlds simultaneously at all times, the world you see and the one you don't. It's the world you don't see that matters and once you "get that," you cease to judge the world you do see. And that's a game-changer truth if there ever was one. – Caroline Myss, https://www.myss.com/third-setting-the-controlling-power-of-expectations/

Judgment is imposing the ego on the past; expectation is imposing the ego on the future. In divine love, the ego dissolves into the timeless singularity, "the world you don't see." As divine love has no expectations, so it makes no judgments.

From the beginning of this journal I have described divine love as I knew it with Lou, making no demands and having no expectations. And sure enough, when divine love found me, as Caroline says, I found "an increase in synchronistic happenings," and wisdom replaced negativity. Then Caroline hit upon the most important effect of divine love – consciousness of eternity. This is worth repeating:

> You walk in two worlds simultaneously at all times, the world you see and the one you don't. It's the world you don't see that matters and once you "get that," you cease to judge the world you do see. And that's a game-changer truth if there ever was one.

Indeed, awakening to the world you don't see changed my game. (And wrote this book.) But then Caroline says this:

> Are any expectations acceptable? Yes. It is completely appropriate to expect not to be lied to or betrayed by the people in your inner circle, by your close and trusted friends and family members. And that means, in turn, they have a right to expect exactly the same from you.

Fair enough. But what if one lets go of even this reasonable expectation? If I had dumped Emily the minute I knew she had lied to me, I would have missed the chance to experience the full depth of her psyche. I was able to reach a place where only a bodhisattva could go, where even the simplest expectations of honesty and decency had to be let go – a place of unsupported thought, of vulnerability and inevitable pain, but also of liberation from fear and the psychic anchors that limit the exercise of compassion. I set no limits on her, had no expectations of her, so I was open to the whole smorgasbord of her psychotic personality.

She, on the other hand, had huge and very specific expectations of me – money, time, and narcissistic supply. Because she focused only on these self-serving aspects of our relationship, she missed the game-changing gift of divine love, the world you don't see.

~ 1346 ~

I found most of Emily's family on ancestry.com. Her mother, father (who died before Emily's first birthday), her mother's last partner (probably the man who abused her), brothers, sisters, cousins, nieces, nephews, and many other ancestors and their descendants. I feel as if I know them as well as Emily does, maybe better. I can also intuit the mental illness that runs through generation after generation in this family tree. My love reaches out to them all.

Perhaps my most important discovery was that Emily was not lying, as I thought she might be, when she told me that her brother died on the anniversary of Lou's death. (~849~) She is vindicated; I found a photo of his gravestone.

~ 1347 ~

Melvin McLeod, editor of *Lion's Roar*, offers six steps toward enlightenment:

You don't exist. Everything we think of as a self is merely the creation of many causes and conditions, a conditioned phenomenon we can't hold onto.

Samsara is suffering. Because it doesn't really exist, all our attempts to protect, feed, pleasure, and strengthen our fictitious self are doomed to fail.

Just stop. In Buddhism, you don't *do* anything. You just *stop* doing things with your body, speech, and mind that make things worse. You naturally stop thinking, speaking, and acting in ways that hurt yourself and others. When you reach this stage, when you have stopped generating the causes of suffering, you have achieved personal liberation, the stage of the *arhat*.

Everything is perfect as it is. When you've really stopped, you realize the only problems are the ones you and your ignorance—and others and their ignorance—have been creating. Otherwise, everything is fine.

Winning and losing don't matter. If you are perfect and complete as you are, you don't have to worry about any of the dualistic pairs of worldly concerns—pain and pleasure, praise and blame, gain and loss, even life and death.

So you can give it all away. In the greatest reversal of all, Buddhism's most radical act, you can take on others' suffering and give away all your own happiness. Because, why not? You're good either way.[169]

In "Just stop," I recognized St. Paul's description of the end of sin in Romans.

In "Everything is perfect as it is," I recognized the Thomas Gospel, in which Jesus said that the kingdom of God is spread upon the earth but men do not see it, and the kingdom of God is within you.

In "So you can give it all away," I saw Jesus in unsupported thought, turning the other cheek, giving away his cloak and his coat, and walking the extra mile. And then I recognized the Christ, the empathetic bodhisattva of compassion hanging on the cross, taking on the suffering of others and giving away all his own happiness. Because, why not?

~ 1348 ~

THINKING AND THE MIND, Part 8
Koan

> The *Diamond Sutra* says "past mind cannot be grasped, present mind cannot be grasped, future mind cannot be grasped." With which mind will you eat your lunch? Deshan was completely stuck. None of his study prepared him for a question like this. His mind went back and forth, forth and back, like the people in antiquity who tried painstakingly to untie the Gordian knot until Alexander the Great came along and took out his sword and simply cut the knot—*whack*!
>
> We can't untie the knots in our minds. We have to cut through them with our mind sword. Lucky for Deshan, he was asked a question he couldn't answer and realized: I don't know anything. I don't know *anything*! – Judy Roitman, *Buddhadharma*, July 2018

I like to tease my Christian friends about the futility of counting the angels dancing on the head of a pin. You stop counting the angels only when you have, through ceaseless counting, realized that they are uncountable. Like realizing, after trying to figure out the meaning of a Zen *koan*, that there is no meaning in terms of mind, thought, or intellect.

The Upanishads say that those who speak do not know; those who know do not speak. Knowing this, the Buddha did not want to be a teacher; he only taught because his disciples begged him for guidance, but his teachings were short and cryptic, like riddles. Jesus, too, spoke mostly in metaphors and allegories, parables and aphorisms, using as few words as possible and always with a message deeper than the literal meaning of the words.

Caroline Myss points out that the spirit of *koan* is not exclusively Zen:

> Read the tales of the Hasidim or explore the Kabbalah; entertain yourself with Sufi parables or the poetry of Rumi; study the sermons of the Buddha or the simple teaching of Thich Nhat

Hanh; examine the writings of mystics from the Christian Desert Fathers to the Upanishad texts, many of which are surprisingly accessible. These stories don't always make logical sense—in fact, they're probably more effective when they don't, because they have a beauty and an internal power that transcends rational thought.[160]

The great teachers with their few words taught us the first *koan*, the mind swords to help us cut through the knots on the Way.

~ 1349 ~

At church this morning, Wynn said to me, "I learned more from your Sunday school class than I did at the seminary." I am grateful for Wynn's validation of my mentoring mission, but I am ever mindful that I am not the author of my words; I am a messenger, a mouthpiece. The theologians at the seminary teach from scripture and wordy commentary; I teach from wordless revelation.

The other leaders of the Sunday school class teach from a place of intellect, research, and scholarship. They are very good at it, and their teaching is thoughtful and elucidating. I could do that, too; I have also done lots of research and study. But my goal is bigger than mere education. It is not to impart knowledge; it is to take people to the place beyond intellect, study, knowledge, and thought. ... But how?

My Buddhist guide gave me an answer, and a warning to keep my ego in check: *Your call is to serve, not to teach ... everyone comes to you for a reason ... some need a smile, others a kind word, others just sitting quietly with them.* Imparting my wisdom, gained through revelatory experience, must be done in service to the student, not in service to my ego, touting my own skills and scholarship. Teaching and service do not need thoughts and words; they can also be done with smiles and silence.

My dear friends in the Sunday school class have taught me that spiritual growth does not easily happen in group therapy. Our discussions often become competitive, with thinly veiled implications like "My interpretation is better/deeper/truer than yours." The conversation can devolve into merely accepting or rejecting one or another belief or interpretation. My goal is to rise above all beliefs and interpretations. Everyone's truth is true, from a certain perspective.

Intellectual knowledge and scholarship must eventually fall to silence, to wordless "knowing." The final steps to awakening must be taken alone – no scripture, no teacher, nothing and no one to lean on. Jesus taught the multitudes, as in the Sermon on the Mount; and small groups, as with his disciples and clusters of friends; and also one-on-one, as with Nicodemus. But his most important teaching he did alone, teaching by example – living a life of poverty, chastity, and obedience, and dying spiritually alone, having been betrayed, denied, and rejected by his own people and even, it seemed, by God.

Does it matter if there was a real historic Jesus? Does it matter if the crucifixion actually happened? No, because the legendary life of Christ as depicted in the Bible story, like Joseph Campbell's mythical hero's journey, carries the meaning. Think about the Parables. Does it matter if there was a real Prodigal Son? The message comes through without needing the event to be real. It is the same with the resurrection story; its message is about the revelatory experience of the disciples, not about something that happened to Jesus.

In the same sense, the power of the last day of Jesus' life is not in its alleged physical/temporal reality, but in its spaceless/timeless relevance to everyone's life. We will all go through the trials of betrayal, denial, rejection, persecution, pain and suffering – St. Francis' "perfect joy" – on our way to the narrow gate. This is the only Way back into the Garden of Eden, to oneness with God. The path to heaven goes through hell.

How will we react to this trial? With fear? Fight or flight – fighting like Barabbas, which is what Judas wanted Jesus to do? Or fleeing from the truth, cowering before the superior force of a tyrant, which is what Caiaphas wanted Jesus to do? Jesus did neither. He responded with love – turning the other cheek, bearing witness to the truth in the spirit of nonviolent civil disobedience, accepting punishment under the law, forgiving his torturers, and conquering death by dying. He put into practice his teaching, "Resist not evil."

> Death is Satan's great weapon and also God's great weapon: it is holy and unholy; our supreme disgrace and our only hope; the thing Christ came to conquer and the means by which He conquered. ... It is mercy because by willing and humble surrender to it Man undoes his act of rebellion and makes even this depraved and monstrous mode of Death an instance of that higher and mystical Death which is eternally good and a necessary ingredient in the highest life. Our enemy, so welcomed, becomes our servant: bodily Death, the monster, becomes blessed spiritual Death to self, if the spirit so wills—or rather if it allows the Spirit of the willingly dying God so to will in it. – C.S. Lewis, *Miracles* [27]

~ 1350 ~

HALLOWEEN

Halloween. The time when the spirits are closest to earth. The day in 2013 when Emily and I discovered our spiritual connection. I took our love to heaven and used it to serve her. She took it to hell and used it to use me. Both extremes were God's will; both accomplished the spiritual job that needed to be done.

> Self-esteem as a protective firewall matures to self-reverence, a deep regard for the power of your soul and all that you are capable of influencing by thought, action, prayer, and love. – Caroline Myss, https://www.myss.com/cmed/online-institute/series/the-three-stages-of-self-esteem/

Caroline, in her down-to-earth, practical way, explains what it feels like to know that you are doing God's will. But the power of your soul is even more immense. Self-awareness (birth of the ego) matures to self-esteem (self-respect), to self-reverence (awakening to the God-self within), and finally to self-identification with the divine (submerging the ego inside the singularity of the eternal Source). In the depths of your soul, you *are* God.

Knowing that you are God means seeing truth from opposite directions, knowing that the light shining from the external entity you call God is a reflection of your own internal light. If your light is dimmed by anger, greed, and bitterness, that is how you see God – the dark side of God. If your light glows bright with Loving-kindness, Joy, Compassion, and Equanimity, you see God in that light, and recognize that you are both the reflection and its source.

~ 1351 ~

From an interview, "Modern-Day Bodhisattvas," *Lion's Roar*, November 2018, with Buddhist teacher Pema Chödrön and Catholic priest Father Greg Boyle, S.J.:

> FATHER GREG BOYLE: What feeds [our] work is what I call extravagant tenderness. Tenderness" is so rich a word. We always say that if love is the answer, community is the context and tenderness is the methodology. Tenderness becomes the connective tissue, as opposed to "I love you." Somehow, tenderness is where you meet people. It becomes exquisitely mutual, where I'm not saving you, I'm not even serving you, I'm allowing, or trying, to be reached by you. Then it becomes mutual and life-giving.
>
> PEMA CHÖDRÖN: It's a much better word than "love." "Love" is so loaded it almost doesn't touch you, whereas "tenderness" actually does.

I am especially moved by this remark: "I'm not saving you, I'm not even serving you, I'm allowing, or trying, to be reached by you." Father Boyle did not say "I'm trying to reach you," but rather, trying to be reached *by you*, as Jesus sought to be reached, as he offered people the choice to follow his Way. This touches the heart of my sorrow over The Unnamed One and Emily, the source of my tears as the Angel in the Spaceship. (~669~) I reached out to them, but they did not reach back. Was my tenderness not extravagant enough?

~ 1352 ~

Bad things happen so that good things can happen. This is a function of not only interdependent co-arising, but also of the fullness of life experience that is required for reentry into the Garden of Eden. If you want to experience the greatest spiritual highs you must be open to, even welcome, the horrific lows. True awakening means awakening to and accepting, even embracing, both sides of God – the dark as well as the light.

The great mystics and martyrs, in showing us the Way, demonstrated the suffering that is necessary to remove spiritual obstructions, to prepare the soul to give and receive divine love. Bonhoeffer talked about "cheap grace," the illusion of grace that is without any price having been paid, that does not come from or lead to God. He also talked about "dishonorable suffering," saying that not only does grace require suffering, but also dishonor – rejection, humiliation, vilification. Bonhoeffer, like his fellow mystic martyrs, received the costliest grace of God by paying a very high price.

Paying the price of acute suffering is for the purpose of bringing us to the point where we have no choice but to surrender fully to God. This surrender, letting go of ego, is the goal of every true religion. It is the death and resurrection of Christ, the awakening of the Buddha, and the very meaning of the word "Islam."

But not all surrender is the same. We may attain cheap grace when we surrender to the puny, partial God usually depicted in the Bible. We surrender to the angry, vengeful, judgmental God because we are afraid of the punishment we might receive if we don't – we surrender to avoid pain. We surrender to the peaceful, merciful, generous God because we are grateful for the blessings he bestows and we want the promised reward – we surrender in return for pleasure.

These are both worldly, conditional kinds of surrender that are firmly rooted in duality; neither requires setting aside the ego; neither is the kind that led Jesus or Bonhoeffer to their deaths. It takes the great suffering of costly grace to burn the ego completely in Achala's cleansing fire, for the scorched earth of nirvana to reveal the Way to the narrow gate.

PRIEST vs. PROPHET, MINISTER vs. MYSTIC

From an essay delivered at UC Santa Barbara in 1959 by Aldous Huxley:

> There are two main kinds of religion. There is the religion of the immediate experience (the religion, in the words of Genesis, of hearing the voice of God walking in the Garden in the cool of the evening—the religion of direct acquaintance with the Divine in the world), and there is the religion of symbols (the religion of the imposition of order and meaning upon the world through verbal or nonverbal symbols and their manipulation—the religion of knowledge about the Divine rather than direct acquaintance with the Divine). And these two types of religion have, of course, always existed, and we have to discuss them both.
>
> These two types of religion—the religion of immediate experience, of direct acquaintance with the Divine, and this second kind of symbolic religion—have, of course, co-existed in the West. Mystics have always formed a minority in the midst of the official symbol-manipulating religions, and this has been a rather uneasy symbiosis. The members of the official religion tended to look upon the mystics as difficult, trouble-making people. They have even made puns about the name; they have called mysticism "misty schism" in the sense that this is not a clear doctrine. It is a cloudy doctrine, it is an antinomian doctrine, it is a doctrine which does not conform easily to authority; and they have disliked it in consequence. And on their side, of course, the mystics have spoken—not exactly with contempt, because they don't feel contempt, but with sadness and compassion about those who are devoted to the symbolic religion, because they feel that the pursuit and the manipulation of symbols is simply incapable in the nature of things of achieving what they regard as the highest end: the union with God.[xiii]

Mystics are troublemakers, misunderstood and thought to be heretics, sad and compassionate for, but not contemptuous of, the symbol manipulators, despite the ridicule and persecution – "perfect joy" – they receive at the symbolists' hands.

In the first volume of this book, I quoted E.L. Doctorow's definition of art and artist (~96~):

> … the work of independent witness, that often self-destructive willingness to articulate that which many may feel but no one dares to say, the blundering, struggling effort to connect the visible to the invisible, to find the secret meanings of places and things, to release the spirit from the clay—that rude, stubborn, squawking, self-appointed voice singing the unsingable.

Notice how similar Huxley's description of a mystic is:

[xiii] John Cleese, "A Divine Pat," https://harpers.org/archive/2018/11/a-divine-pat-john-cleese/

The members of the official religion tended to look upon the mystics as difficult, trouble-making people. They have even made puns about the name; they have called mysticism "misty schism" in the sense that this is not a clear doctrine. It is a cloudy doctrine, it is an antinomian doctrine, it is a doctrine which does not conform easily to authority; and they have disliked it in consequence.

Doctorow and Huxley were both mystics and also artists in the field of literature. Together they reveal how art and mysticism are intertwined. They saw, as I do, duality and unity from the same artistic-spiritual perspective. I now see the full circle of my life, starting with the epiphany that led me into a musical career. (~340~) Art is a prime vehicle for mysticism, in both the incoming inspiration and the outgoing message. Art can be both a cause and an effect of awakening.

PART 57
To Hell and Back
November 2018 – January 2019

~ 1354 ~

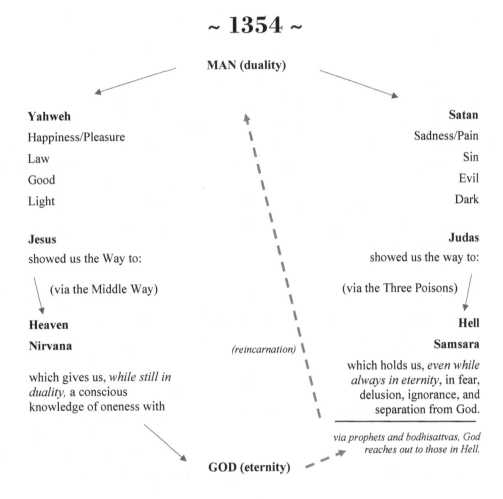

MAN (duality)

Yahweh
Happiness/Pleasure
Law
Good
Light

Satan
Sadness/Pain
Sin
Evil
Dark

Jesus
showed us the Way to:

(via the Middle Way)

Judas
showed us the way to:

(via the Three Poisons)

Heaven
Nirvana

which gives us, *while still in duality,* a conscious knowledge of oneness with

(reincarnation)

Hell
Samsara

which holds us, *even while always in eternity,* in fear, delusion, ignorance, and separation from God.

via prophets and bodhisattvas, God reaches out to those in Hell.

GOD (eternity)

(Solid line = Man in duality. Dashed line = God in eternity.)

C.S. Lewis said, "It may be hard for an egg to turn into a bird: it would be a jolly sight harder for it to learn to fly while remaining an egg. We are like eggs at present. And you cannot go on indefinitely being just an ordinary, decent egg. We must be hatched or go bad."[76] We all are on a path, either to be hatched in heaven or to go bad in hell; we cannot go on indefinitely as decent but ignorant eggs. We must stay on the field and play the game of life.

Judas was not a bad guy. He was a disciple and friend of Jesus, doing what he sincerely thought was right, hoping that by bringing Jesus to the authorities, his power could bring an end to Roman rule and establish the kingdom of heaven on earth. (That Jesus' betrayer came from inside his own flock is a lesson for us, a warning to beware our own possibly misguided motivations, albeit well-meaning, for doing what we do.) In duality it seems that Judas' betrayal was evil, and from that perspective it was, but from the eternal view Judas was neither good nor evil; he was doing God's will.

Neither is Satan a bad guy. Everything in duality is part of God. Both good and evil come from God, and when viewed from different perspectives, are often hard to tell apart, thus revealing their underlying unity. In the sense of interdependent co-arising, as one side of duality gains strength, so must the other. Satan is not an enemy; he is an adversary, a sparring partner who in testing us reveals our weaknesses. He is a mirror reflecting to us the dark side we do not wish to see. When we are born again, we will be able to turn away the temptations of Satan, both greed-based and fear-based, just as Jesus did, and no image will be reflected in Satan's mirror. Neither will there be any image in Yahweh's mirror of goodness and virtue, the sin of Pride having been erased as well. The invisible love of God wipes all mirrors clean.

We recoil in horror when we think of satanic rituals and devil worship, but in fact the followers of Satan are worshipping the *same* God as the Christians – they just worship the opposite side of God as he appears in duality, the dark side, while the Christians worship the light side. Both sides are illusions.

What happens, you may ask, if you take the wide road to hell and come to the dead end, which is ignorance and separation from God? Taking the dark road is an invitation to reincarnation. God always gives you another chance, and another, and another, and reaches out to you in every life, speaking through prophets, sages, and spirit messengers of all kinds who will guide you toward the narrow gate – if that's the way you decide to go.

Many start on the road to heaven but at some point fall off the razor's edge, the Middle Way, and don't make it all the way to the narrow gate. Moses fell down. So did King David. So did King Solomon, despite all his wisdom. Don't despair; you will get farther along the Way in the next life, and in good time, when you are ready, the cherubim's fiery sword guarding the Tree of Eternal Life at the east of Eden will guide you through the narrow gate.

~ 1355 ~

Martha is worried that my service to Emily will take a sacrificial turn, and she asks me provocative questions:

If we love someone else to the point of giving up our own life, does that not contradict loving ourselves equally?

Yes, it would, in the context of worldly loves, if giving up one's life is a response to fear and the loss of life accomplishes nothing. Terms like "someone else" and "equally," work in the world of duality where these words have meaning. But in eternal divine love there is no separation, no one "else," nothing to be equal to.

If our life is sacrificed for another individual, is that not unloving to ourselves? And what about all the potential others who might benefit from our love if we do not sacrifice our life?

Jesus said, "For whoever would save his life will lose it; and whoever loses his life for my sake and the gospel's will save it." (Mark 8:35 RSV) If I lose my ego-bound physical life for the sake of the gospel – divine love – I will save my boundless eternal life. The self that I love is not made of skin and bones; it is beyond the limits of the physical body. My life and love continue after death. In fact, the benefit I might provide to those "potential others" might be enhanced by my purposeful sacrificial death, as was the case with Jesus.

Martha's concern for me is touching, and I appreciate it, but when the call to service comes from God, whatever sacrifice comes with the call cannot be avoided. She tries to protect me as Peter tried to protect Jesus:

> And he began to teach them that the Son of man must suffer many things, and be rejected by the elders and the chief priests and the scribes, and be killed, and after three days rise again. And he said this plainly. And Peter took him, and began to rebuke him. But turning and seeing his disciples, he rebuked Peter, and said, "Get behind me, Satan! For you are not on the side of God, but of men." (Mark 8:31-33 RSV)

Martha's looking out for my life won't change my course, as Peter's didn't change Jesus' course. When the sacrifice is made from divine love, there is no choosing or not choosing. Desmond Tutu said that God just grabs us by the scruff of the neck.

We respond to three sources of stimuli: physical, emotional, and spiritual. The physical and emotional forces are part of this world, this body-mind. The spiritual force as we experience it in life is a bridge that connects duality to eternity. All worldly loves exist on the dualistic plane and have both light and dark sides, with limits involving expectations, desires, obligations, dependencies, and the urge to protect worldly things, physical and emotional.

Divine love, coming from the spirit, liberates us from all that weighs us down in worldly love. In divine love we spontaneously let go of all craving for health, wealth, and even life itself, and also all fears, including fear of injury, illness, poverty, and death. When we see life from the perspective of eternity, the illusion of body-mind is revealed, and the illusion can then be surrendered. This is heaven, nirvana, and why the sacrifice of health, wealth, and even life can be made without regret, even joyously, in response to the spiritual call.

~ 1356 ~

"Except for the grace of God go I." It was apparent that those words conveyed some sort of profound meaning because I noticed how the nuns would nod their heads in a type of collective agreement after one of them uttered that phrase. – Caroline Myss, https://www.myss.com/except-for-the-grace-of-god-go-i/

It is normal for us to be grateful when spared hardships and suffering. Perhaps it is the grace of God that keeps us out of harm's way. But at a higher spiritual level, it is also the grace of God that sends us into the lion's den, that exposes us to the worst kind of harm to teach us how to sublimate suffering and find the perfect joy that can only be known by walking the path to pain. I am grateful for both kinds of grace.

~ 1357 ~

THINKING AND THE MIND, Part 9

Along with the more well-known methods designed to help practitioners of Buddhist meditation ground their attention in the present moment— such as focusing on the rhythm of the breath, paying attention to the feeling of footsteps, or internally repeating a mantra—is a less familiar method known as nada yoga. Nada is the Sanskrit word for "sound," and nada yoga means meditating on the inner sound, also referred to as the sound of silence. (Interestingly, nada is also the Spanish word for "nothing.")

To detect the nada sound, turn your attention toward your hearing. If you listen carefully to the sounds around you, you're likely to hear a continuous, high-pitched inner sound like white noise in the background. It is a sound that is beginningless and endless. – Ajahn Amaro, "The Sound of Silence"[170]

This is my tinnitus, much as I have described it, as God's voice, *anāhata*, the 4th chakra sound of divine love.

> If you focus on the inner sound for a length of time sufficient to bring stability, in which your mind is resting easily in the present, you can allow the sound to fall into the background. It then becomes like a screen on which all other sounds, physical sensations, moods, and ideas are projected. And because of its plainness, uniformity, and steadiness, it's a very good screen. It doesn't confuse or interfere with other objects that are arising. It's like watching a movie: if you pay attention, you are aware that there's a screen on which light is being projected. The inner sound's presence in the background helps remind you that "this is just a movie; this is not reality."[170]

Tinnitus is phantom sound, an illusion of sound. In its worst form it can be a terrible scourge. People have committed suicide because they were driven mad by the constant perception of sound. When I first began to notice it, I felt some of that terror, the feeling of being locked in a prison of endless noise from which there is no escape. Like most other sufferers, I sought relief and found none.

My terror was relieved when I made the *anāhata* connection and began to hear the phantom sound in my head as the voice of God. And indeed, as Amaro describes, my tinnitus recedes into the background, out of my consciousness, when my mind turns its attention elsewhere. Amaro's metaphor of the movie screen gives me another liberating way to view the situation: "This is just [the soundtrack of] a movie; this is not reality." He goes on to explain how this non-reality of the physical world is created in the mind and with enlightenment dissolves into oneness:

> Beyond emptiness and suchness is a third, even more subtle characteristic of existence called *atammayata*, which means "not made of that."
>
> *Atammayata* provides closure to the whole domain with the insight that there is no "that;" there is only "this." It expresses the genuine collapse of both the illusion of separateness of subject and object and of the discrimination between phenomena as being somehow substantially different from each other. It helps bring about the realization that there is only the wholeness of the Dhamma, complete spaciousness and fulfillment. Then, knowing that truth, even this-ness and here-ness become meaningless.
>
> We tend to think of the mind as being in the body, but we've actually got it wrong; the body is in the mind. Everything we know about the body, now and at any previous time, has been known through the agency of the mind. This isn't to say there isn't a physical world, just that the experience of the body, and the experience of the world, happen here, within our mind.
>
> When we truly wake up to that here-ness, the world's externality, its separateness, ceases. When we realize that we hold the whole world within us, its thing-ness, its other-ness, is checked, and we are better able to recognize its true nature.[170]

Suffering is caused not by what happens to us, but by what we think of those happenings and our clinging to our thoughts about them. I was able to reduce my suffering from tinnitus by changing my thoughts about it. I stopped clinging to desperate thoughts of finding relief and replaced them with new thoughts of hearing God's voice. Stephen Levine said in *A Gradual Awakening*, "Wanting things to be otherwise is the very essence of suffering."

> I've heard it said by Zen teachers that the function of the mind is to secrete thoughts. From that perspective, "to rest in non-conceptual, open, 'don't know' mind" isn't so much to stop or transcend thinking as to simply let thoughts be "just thoughts" and to know that the mind is doing its thing. Thinking is simply what the mind does, in the same way that ears hear and eyes see. … In knowing thoughts to be just thoughts, we let go of all the "post-thoughts," the long tail of energy created by our habit of clinging to what we think. – Keiryu Lien Shutt, "Am I supposed to stop thinking?" *Bodhidharma*, November 25, 2018

~ 1358 ~

HOPE

I have often expressed my discomfort with the idea of hope. Roshi Joan Halifax clarifies what bothers me and how hope can be liberated from desire:

> As Buddhists, we know that ordinary hope is based in desire, wanting an outcome that could well be different from what will actually happen. Not getting what we hoped for is usually experienced as some kind of misfortune. Someone who is hopeful in this way has an expectation that always hovers in the background, the shadow of fear that one's wishes will not be fulfilled. This ordinary hope is a subtle expression of fear and a form of suffering.

> Wise hope is not seeing things unrealistically but rather seeing things as they are, including the truth of suffering—both its existence and our capacity to transform it. It's when we realize we don't know what will happen that this kind of hope comes alive; in that spaciousness of uncertainty is the very space we need to act.

> The bodhisattva vows at the heart of the Mahayana tradition are, if nothing else, a powerful expression of radical and wise hope—an unconditional hope that is free of desire. Dostoyevsky said, "To live without hope is to cease to live." His words remind us that apathy is not an enlightened path. We are called to live with possibility, knowing full well that impermanence prevails.[171]

It occurred to me that hope is different from optimism, what Roshi Halifax calls "wise hope." Hope is the first poison of the future because it has an element of desire to it. Optimism is more objective, impersonal – more reflective of intuition, remaining in the positive polarity but not desperately so, not forcing or deluding oneself there. Optimism is "positive thinking" (Norman Vincent Peale), the "power of intention" (Wayne Dyer), and the "law of attraction" (Esther Hicks/Abraham), but without grasping, ego-laden hopefulness. Optimism reflects the knowledge that in the end, all things are right, and keeps hopelessness from sinking into despair.

Margaret Wheatley writes in "Finding Hope in Hopelessness:"

> Thomas Merton, the late Catholic mystic, clarified further the journey into hopelessness. In a letter to a friend, he advised: "Do not depend on the hope of results. You may have to face the fact that your work will be apparently worthless and even achieve no result at all, if not perhaps results opposite to what you expect. As you get used to this idea, you start more and more to concentrate not on the results, but on the value, the rightness, the truth of the work itself."[172]

Indeed, my bodhi calling led me to specific people, first with an idea of helping them, then in the course of that struggle, to know that my hoped-for result was not as important as "the truth of the work itself." Love conquers hope along with fear.

Margaret goes on to quote T.S. Eliot in the *Four Quartets*:

> I said to my soul, be still, and wait without hope
> For hope would be hope for the wrong thing; wait without love,
> For love would be love of the wrong thing; there is yet faith
> But the faith and the love and the hope are all in the waiting.

There is no arrival. There are no results. There is only the work, the waiting, the faith and the love and the hope, writ large in eternity.

~ 1359 ~

Martha wrote to me:

> *I have come to realize that whatever is happening in our lives, or the lives of those around us, is unfolding (including the aspect of free will) in some divine order. I find this is helpful, to take the broader, non-worldly perspective when I see others struggle, suffer, and experience pain. It allows me to feel compassion for them without being pulled into the dualistic plane and suffering along with them.*

Martha defines a bodhisattva with her words, "being pulled into the dualistic plane and suffering along with them." In Martha's therapeutic healing work, she tries to stay above the fray to keep her dispassionate objectivity. This is considered proper for a therapist. In this scenario there may be love of a worldly sort, in service to the client's physical or emotional needs, but this is not divine love. The operation of divine love is down and dirty in the trenches, in touch with the divine order, but messy. It must be so, because in divine love, in service to spirit, there is no separation of subject and object, and no separation in their respective sufferings.

There are two kinds of empaths who can come under the influence of a narcissist. One is a victim who does not realize, or denies, that the narcissist is lying, stealing, abusing, and feigning love without regard for the empath's true love, who stays with the narcissist in unhealthy clinging. The other is a bodhisattva who understands the loveless nature of the narcissist, willingly accepts the narcissist's torture and the weight of her pain, and stays with her to be of spiritual service. The hurt that inevitably results is joyously received as St. Francis' "perfect joy."

Martha wants me to set boundaries to protect myself as she protects herself from being wounded by her clients' suffering. But as a bodhisattva, wounded I must be. The key is in the nature and effect of my wounds; I could become a martyr, but I must not be a victim. The difference between victimhood and martyrdom is that the victim suffers and maybe dies without larger purpose or effect, the martyr with great purpose and effect. Jesus was not a victim. Neither am I.

~ 1360 ~

TRUNGPA RINPOCHE: Union with God cannot take place when there is any form of ego. Any whatsoever. In order to be one with God, one has to become formless. Then you will see God.

FATHER THOMAS KEATING: This is the point I was trying to make for Christians by quoting the agonizing words of Christ on the cross. He cried out, "My God, my God, why hast thou forsaken me?" It seems that his sense of personal relationship with God, as God's son, had disappeared. Many interpreters say that this was only a temporary experience. But I am inclined to think, in light of the Buddhist description of no-self, that he was passing into a stage beyond the personal self, however holy and beautiful that self had been. That final stage would then also have to be defined as the primary Christian experience. Christ has called us Christians not just so that we will accept him as savior, but so that we will follow the same process that brought him to his final stage of consciousness.

TRUNGPA RINPOCHE: Well, it could be said that Christ is like sunshine, and God is like the sky, blue sky. In order to experience either one of them you have to be without the sun first. Then you begin to develop the dawn.

FATHER KEATING: Yes!

TRUNGPA RINPOCHE: And then you begin to experience sunshine. First you have to have nothingness, nonexistence. And then the sky becomes blue. It's like jumping out of an airplane.

First you experience space, and then your parachute begins to open. You jump out of the airplane, which is gone by then.

FATHER KEATING: Yes. But then out of that nothingness there begins to emerge a new life, which is not one's own, but is without a self, and is united with everything else that is.

TRUNGPA RINPOCHE: That's right.

FATHER KEATING: So that's a similar experience in Buddhism. It is also our understanding of Christ in his glory: he is so at one with the ultimate reality that he has completely merged into it.[173]

By following the Way of Christ, "the same process that brought him to his final stage of consciousness," you lose your personal relationship with God. Your ego is removed, you enter nothingness from which the first light of dawn emerges, and you merge with the ultimate reality: "But then out of that nothingness there begins to emerge a new life, which is not one's own, but is without a self, and is united with everything else that is." A new life emerges. You are born again.

You descend into hell, the deepest separation from God, then ascend into heaven, the deepest unity with God. ... Self—no Self—God in Self—Self in God.

~ 1361 ~

The demon Screwtape writes: Music and silence—how I detest them both! How thankful we should be that ever since our Father entered Hell—though longer ago than humans, reckoning in light years, could express—no square inch of infernal space and no moment of infernal time has been surrendered to either of those abominable forces, but all has been occupied by Noise— Noise, the grand dynamism, the audible expression of all that is exultant, ruthless, and virile— Noise which alone defends us from silly qualms, despairing scruples, and impossible desires. We will make the whole universe a noise in the end. – C.S. Lewis, *The Screwtape Letters* [95]

God speaks in music and silence. I know why I was called to a vocation in music. It was the first way God spoke to and through me. I distill God's Love out of the Devil's Noise.

~ 1362 ~

FULL MOON – NEW MOON, Part 10

When people in Jambudvīpa see the first crescent of the moon they all think they perceive the first day of the month, and when the moon is full they think of that as the fifteenth day and have the idea that the moon's cycle is complete. But the nature of the moon is such that it actually neither waxes nor wanes; the [perceived] increase or decrease in its size is due to Mount Sumeru. ... Thus what living beings see is not the same: they may see a half-moon, they may see a full moon, or they may see a lunar eclipse. And yet the nature of the moon is such that despite the appearance of it waxing and waning and going into eclipse, in truth it is always fully rounded. The body of the Tathāgata is just like this. That is why I refer to it as permanently abiding and unchanging.

The true nature of the Tathāgata may thus be compared to the moon in that his body is a dharma body rather than a body that is born into existence. It is a body of expediency that becomes visible in conformity with the world. As the result of innumerable causal forces set in motion in the distant past, the Buddha thus becomes visible much like the moon does, appearing to those who are in this or that locale as if he is being born where they are. It is in this sense that I speak of the Tathāgata as abiding permanently and immutable.

Moreover, good man, it is like the *asura* king Rāhu holding back the moon with his hands, which people throughout the world regard as [the cause] of lunar eclipses. But the *asura* king is incapable of doing anything that actually affects the moon itself; what he does is block its light. The moon-globe is not disturbed in any way when this happens; it is only because of the moon's obstruction by the hands of the *asura* that it is rendered invisible. When he pulls his hands away, throughout the world it is thought that the moon has been restored to life, with everyone saying that the moon has undergone considerable pain and suffering. But in truth even a hundred thousand *asura* kings could not cause any trouble for the moon.

In addition, good man, like a goldsmith who obtains fine gold that he then fashions into a variety of implements by using his imagination, the Tathāgata similarly manifests various material bodies among the twenty-five forms of existence for the purpose of spiritually transforming living beings so they can extract themselves from samsāra. This is why I say the Tathāgata has what I call "a boundless body" and why, despite the fact that he reveals himself in different bodies, I also speak of [the Tathāgata] as "permanently abiding without change." – *Nirvana Sutra* [174]

This sutra beautifully explains the nature of Jesus Christ the Tathāgata, his coming into the world and going out of it, and the meaning of the transcendence and resurrection of the body. The Tathāgata appears as the Buddha, as Jesus, and in countless other forms. When we stop holding the moon back with our hands, our boundlessness is rendered visible.

The final required release is of health and, eventually, life. It is grasping for health and life, and the fear of losing them, that brings about our suffering in sickness and death. The Tathāgata is not concerned with things of the physical body, his true body being boundless in the spirit. In our limited sensory perception he may appear to wax and wane like the moon, but in fact he is permanent and unchanging, as is the divine love that is carried in his light.

If I say, "Let only darkness cover me,
and the light about me be night,"
even the darkness is not dark to thee,
the night is bright as the day;
for darkness is as light with thee.
(Psalm 139:11-12 RSV)

~ 1363 ~

Our prayers for others flow more easily than those we offer on our own behalf. And it would be nice to accept your view that this just shows we are made to live by charity. I'm afraid, however, I detect two much less attractive reasons for the ease of my own intercessory prayers. One is that I am often, I believe, praying for others when I should be doing things for them. It's so much easier to pray for a bore than to go and see him. And the other is like unto it. Suppose I pray that you may be given grace to withstand your besetting sin (short list of candidates for this post will be forwarded on demand). Well, all the work has to be done by God and you. If I pray against my own besetting sin there will be work for me. One sometimes fights shy of admitting an act to be a sin for this very reason. – C.S. Lewis, from *Letters to Malcolm* [175]

Aha! Gratuitous prayers unmasked! How many times have we prayed for a friend's healing but we never took him any chicken soup? Especially at Christmastime, many who pray for world peace offer no refuge to refugees, no help to the helpless, do nothing to stop the making of bombs and in fact support government and corporate policies that contribute to unrest and turmoil in the world. Our sins of omission are among those we are shy of admitting, lest we be forced to face the redemptive work we don't want to do.

LOVE, Part 14

ETERNITY	**DIVINE LOVE – AGAPE (love itself)** No separation, no relationship	
DUALITY	**WORLDLY LOVES** Relationships between separate people	

	HINDU/YOGA:	**GREEK:**	
	Spouse/Spouse	**Eros (romantic love)**	*Equals*
	Friend/Friend	**Philia (friendship)**	
	Parent/Child	**Storgë (familial love)**	*Power differential*
	Master/Slave	**Xenia (hospitality)**	

NOT LOVE
(no service or sacrifice)

Lust
Affection
Gratitude
Respect
Reverence
Admiration
Sympathy

Similarities between worldly loves and divine love

1) *The other before oneself, in service and sacrifice.* If it's really love, you put the other before yourself, which leads to surrender, service, and sacrifice. The depth of love is known by the degree to which one surrenders, serves, and sacrifices. In divine love, these qualities are total and boundless; "self" and "other" disappear.

My friend Chet told of his experience with *Storgë*, saying that he put his busy schedule on hold when his granddaughter asked him to read to her. If his feelings toward his grandchild had been merely affection or obligation, not love, he might have said, "I'll read to you, honey, but I have errands to run and can't read to you right now.

Can we do it later?" Because Chet's relationship with his grandchild rose to the level of love, he was willing, even glad, to reorder his schedule and give a little of his time at that moment for the sake of the beloved child.

2) *Empathy: "Your pain is my pain; your joy, my joy."* Empathy rises above sympathy, beyond sensitivity to another's pain to the adoption of it. Not just "I know how you feel," but "I feel your pain." This is the bodhisattva vow, taking on another's pain and its cause (sin, karma, *dukkha*) as one's own, into oneself, as exemplified in the life and death of Christ.

The empathic nature of love is demonstrated by how it is acted out in service and sacrifice. If we feel only sympathy, not empathy, we may be genuinely concerned about the suffering of a friend, but we remain at a distance, not doing anything except maybe sending a sympathy card. The loving empath will take the next step. Because we feel the pain of our loved one as our own, we know intuitively that our friend needs a shoulder to cry on, a helping hand, and bowl of chicken soup, so we take the soup to him, perhaps sacrificing our own needs to tend to his – our – pain.

3) *No beginning or end.* True love of any kind is not fallen into or out of. In worldly loves there are often boundaries and limits, and the expression of love may change with the ever-changing space-time condition, but the love itself does not begin or end.

My friend Jake told of his experience with *Philia*, saying that in a very short time after he and his friend met, they felt extraordinarily close, and have remained so to this day. This is a wonderful demonstration of the eternal, no-beginning-no-ending nature of true love. You don't "fall in love;" you discover a love that exists and has always existed in eternity.

Differences between worldly loves and divine love

1) *In worldly love, there is separation.* There is a subject and an object, lover and beloved, and expectations, obligations, dependencies, boundaries, and limits. True love never dies, but it can wax and wane with changes in behavior or attitude, which are functions of duality with its emotions and passions. There are degrees of love, levels of intensity, changeable aspects that make even healthy love, like all of duality, both a pleasure and a pain, both positive and negative.

In divine love, there is no separation. There is no analysis or judgment, no expectations, obligations, dependencies, boundaries, or limits, because in eternity there is no separation between individuals or between Man and God. Divine love is perfect, unchanging, and boundless, not an emotion, but a state of being. Peaceful and joyous, but not passionate. Divine love transcends the passions at both extremes of duality.

Jesus said there is no marriage in heaven: "For in the resurrection they neither marry nor are given in marriage, but are like angels in heaven." (Matthew 22:30 RSV) He also said, after being told that his mother and brother were asking to speak to him: "Who is my mother, and who are my brothers?" And stretching out his hand toward his disciples, he said, "Here are my mother and my brothers! For whoever does the will of my Father in heaven is my brother, and sister, and mother." (Matthew 12:48-50 RSV) Not only are marital relationships gone in heaven, but also familial ones. *Eros* and *Storgë* are both subsumed into *agape*. In divine love, in eternity, there are no separate beings to have relationships with, to be married to, to be related to. Everyone, and no one, is our brother.

2) *Worldly love is exclusive:* "Forsaking all others as long as we both shall live," loving my child but not all children, loving my student but not all students. Worldly love picks specific targets as a laser beam shines on one pinpoint, leaving the spot next to it in darkness.

Divine love is inclusive: I love Emily, and her abusive mother, and her abusive stepfather, and all those in her sphere. Divine love is like the sun or a floodlight that illuminates everything in its broad field, shining into every nook and cranny.

Divine love is not just all worldly loves raised to a higher level. It is a qualitatively different kind of love that breaks through all barriers and can only be known by taking a quantum leap, surrendering everything to God, including the self, the ego, whatever separates individuals from each other and from God. Until you have felt the tidal wave of divine love sweep over you, you cannot truly know it. It is indescribable in words; it is indeed the peace that passes all understanding. (Philippians 4:7)

The expression of divine love in the physical body is known by the Hindus and Buddhists as Tantra. Christians are often conflicted about the body as a holy vehicle and so have trouble with this concept. Nevertheless, C.S. Lewis found the linkage between worldly and divine love, in a Radha/Krishna way:

> All sorts of people are fond of repeating the Christian statement that 'God is love'. But they seem not to notice that the words 'God is love' have no real meaning unless God contains at least two Persons. Love is something that one person has for another person. If God was a single person, then before the world was made, He was not love.

Of course, what these people mean when they say that God is love is often something quite different: they really mean 'Love is God'. They really mean that our feelings of love, however and wherever they arise, and whatever results they produce, are to be treated with great respect. Perhaps they are: but that is something quite different from what Christians mean by the statement 'God is love'. They believe that the living, dynamic activity of love has been going on in God forever and has created everything else. – C.S. Lewis, *Mere Christianity* [76]

Worldly Love	Divine Love (agape)
In duality.	In eternity. Elizabeth Barrett Browning wrote: Guess now who holds thee?— "Death," I said. But there The silver answer rang— "Not Death, but Love."
Exclusive, directed to specific object.	Inclusive, ubiquitous, universal; for everyone, everything, even enemies, animals, plants, rocks.
Relational.	Nothing to relate to, no separation of subject and object. Victor Hugo wrote: "Love is the reduction of the Universe to a single being."
Passionate.	Dispassionate.
Rises and falls with emotions and behaviors.	Independent of emotions and behaviors.
Responds to sensory perceptions.	Independent of sensory perceptions.
Karma, cause and effect, reap what you sow.	No causation; the end of karma.
Boundaries, limits, rules, conditions.	No boundaries, limits, rules, conditions.
Forgiveness.	Nothing to forgive.
Can be taken to excess or extreme at positive or negative polarity (hero worship, blind loyalty, misplaced trust).	No excess, no polarities.
Expectations, obligations, dependency.	No expectations, obligations, dependency.
Thought, analysis, judgment, mind.	No thought, analysis, judgment, mind.

It has been said that worldly loves are aspects of *agape*. This is true in a way, but also not true. *Agape* has no aspects; in eternity all is one; there are no separate pieces to be plucked one from another. The quality of *agape* can be found in worldly loves, however, especially in tantric love, which is the stripping away of the illusion of separateness even while lovers are still in separate bodies. *Agape* shows itself in worldly loves when two selves climb into each other, when self dissolves, is sacrificed, in service to the other.

Those who discover their eternal life while still in the world of duality are born again, resurrected, awakened, enlightened. They are called prophets, saints, mystics, bodhisattvas, *arhats*. While they live in the world, they may engage in worldly loves: have a spouse, care for parents and children, enjoy loving relationships with friends and coworkers.

When they live fully in *agape*, however, all the worldly loves are subsumed into *agape*, as colored light comes out of and is subsumed into invisible white light. They depart the world and sometimes move into a monastery or into seclusion, and take vows of poverty, chastity, and obedience. A bodhisattva becomes a buddha.

~ 1365 ~

CHRISTMAS EVE

At the beginning of every church service there is a prayer called "Confession and Forgiveness." This was today's prayer:

> To you, O God,
> We lift up our souls.
> You know us through and through;
> We confess our sins to you.
> Remember not our sins;
> Remember us with your steadfast love.
> Show us your ways;
> Teach us your paths;
> And lead us in justice and truth,
> For the sake of your goodness in Jesus Christ our Savior. Amen.

The word "remember" is a space-time word. Almost everything in the Christian liturgy is designed for those who do not know eternity, who live wholly in space-time duality. Even the Lord's Prayer, first uttered by one who *did* know eternity, is of necessity constructed using words and thoughts that are understandable to those who cannot yet go beyond temporal words and thoughts.

And yet, to say "Remember not our sins" implies that there is no sin where God is, and to say "Remember us with your steadfast love" implies that unwavering divine love replaces our sin in God's memory. These implications begin to touch eternity.

> For since the law has but a shadow of the good things to come instead of the true form of these realities, it can never, by the same sacrifices which are continually offered year after year, make perfect those who draw near. Otherwise, would they not have ceased to be offered? If the worshipers had once been cleansed, they would no longer have any consciousness of sin. But in these sacrifices there is a reminder of sin year after year. For it is impossible that the blood of bulls and goats should take away sins. (Hebrews 10:1-4 RSV)

There is also a reminder of sin, week after week, in reciting "Confession and Forgiveness." This prayer cannot take away sins any more than the blood of bulls and goats can. Once the worshiper is cleansed and no longer has any consciousness of sin, confession of sin has no meaning.

That the cleansed worshiper "would no longer have any consciousness of sin" is a vital aspect of being born again. This does not necessarily mean that the cleansed one would not commit acts that might seem to be sins in the perception of others, only that the conscious mind – the self or ego – has been removed from judging a course of action. This is the opening, the removal of barriers to the indwelling God-self, that is needed for the Word to become Flesh, to turn the cleansed worshiper into God's presence on earth – thy kingdom come, thy will be done, on earth as it is in heaven.

> And every priest stands daily at his service, offering repeatedly the same sacrifices, which can never take away sins. But when Christ had offered for all time a single sacrifice for sins, he sat down at the right hand of God, then to wait until his enemies should be made a stool for his feet. For by a single offering he has perfected for all time those who are sanctified. And the Holy Spirit also bears witness to us; for after saying,
>
>> "This is the covenant that I will make with them
>> after those days, says the Lord:
>> I will put my laws on their hearts,
>> and write them on their minds,"
>
> then he adds,
>
>> "I will remember their sins and their misdeeds no more."[xiv]

[xiv] A reference to Jeremiah 31:33-34

Where there is forgiveness of these, there is no longer any offering for sin. (Hebrews 10:11-18 RSV)

Here it is again, as Paul said in Romans – Christ took away the old law and with it, sin. "I will remember their sins and their misdeeds no more." It is not just that our sins are forgiven; it is as if they never happened. "Apart from the law sin lies dead." (Romans 7:8 RSV)

> Where Rome makes Confession compulsory for all, we make it permissible for any: not generally necessary but profitable. We do not doubt that there can be forgiveness without it. But, as your own experience shows, many people do not feel forgiven, i.e., do not effectively believe in the forgiveness of sins, without it. The quite enormous advantage of coming really to believe in forgiveness is well worth the horrors (I agree, they are horrors) of a first confession.

> Also, there is the gain in self-knowledge: most of [us] have never really faced the facts about ourselves until we uttered them aloud in plain words, calling a spade a spade. I certainly feel I have profited enormously by the practice. At the same time I think we are quite right not to make it generally obligatory, which would force it on some who are not ready for it and might do harm. – C.S. Lewis, *The Collected Letters of C.S. Lewis, Volume III* [87]

I think most of us are guilty of over-confessing. How do we know we committed a sin? Who told us we are sinners? The Law? The Church? Who is judging us? Certainly not our own intuition or our God-self, who speak to us from our innocent and eternal nature where there is neither law nor sin.

Pride is the cause of under-confessing; our ego doesn't want to admit alleged wrongdoing. Humility is the cause of over-confessing. But in the sense of the "enemies" of the Four Immeasurables (~1031~), Pride and Humility are far and near enemies, respectively, of Joy. In eternity, there is no pride, no humility, no sin, no confessing. Neither self-esteem nor self-loathing, neither the law nor sin, makes any difference at all.

~ 1366 ~

CHRISTMAS DAY

On Christmas Day the "Confession and Forgiveness" prayer contained this:

> God of peace,
> We confess that we are not at peace—
> With others or with ourselves.

We bring to you all that tears us apart:
Discord in our families,
Violence in our world,
Our own conflicted hearts.
In your mercy, mend us.
Reconnect us to one another and to you.

This confession begins with a lament on our worldly strife, and then acknowledges that mending our brokenness requires a reconnection with God. Worldly words are used to move our thoughts from separation in duality to reconnection in eternity – the goal of the gospel Jesus brought.

The pastor says that Jesus did not come to save, but to reveal – to reveal the Way to Truth and eternal Life. The salvation that came with Jesus was liberation from the Law of Moses and the sin that was created with it. However, that is not the only good news that Jesus brought. The best news is that there is a Way back to God (the Third Noble Truth of the Buddhists); we need not wander lost in the wilderness forever. Jesus came to earth to show us the Way (as the Buddha did; the Fourth Noble Truth). Forgiveness of and salvation from sin is only the first step on the path to the narrow gate. A whole life of suffering, surrender, service, and sacrifice – the life of Christ as Jesus revealed it to us – lies ahead for those who would achieve reentry into the Garden of Eden and reconnection with God.

> "In my Father's house are many rooms; if it were not so, would I have told you that I go to prepare a place for you? And when I go and prepare a place for you, I will come again and will take you to myself, that where I am you may be also." (John 14:2-3 RSV)

Jesus prepared a place for us – if we want it – but only if we are willing to walk the arduous path that leads to the narrow gate. Once we are on the path and born again of the spirit, then he will come again – reborn inside us – to take us to himself, to merge his God-self with ours.

> "And you know the way where I am going." Thomas said to him, "Lord, we do not know where you are going; how can we know the way?" Jesus said to him, "I am the way, and the truth, and the life; no one comes to the Father, but by me. If you had known me, you would have known my Father also; henceforth you know him and have seen him." (John 14:4-7 RSV)

The life of Christ shows us the Way, the one and only way to come to the Father, to claim occupancy of the rooms Jesus has prepared for us.

The pastor, a wise teacher who is not far from the kingdom of God, invited comparison of Genesis 1 to John 1, paying particular attention to "light" and "darkness." (Of course, I have been paying attention to these metaphorical extremes for a long time.)

> In the beginning God created the heavens and the earth. The earth was without form and void, and darkness was upon the face of the deep; and the Spirit [wind[xv]] of God was moving over the face of the waters. And God said, "Let there be light;" and there was light. And God saw that the light was good; and God separated the light from the darkness. God called the light Day, and the darkness he called Night. And there was evening and there was morning, one day. (Genesis 1:1-5 RSV)

> In the beginning was the Word, and the Word was with God, and the Word was God. He was in the beginning with God; all things were made through him, and without him was not anything made that was made. In him was life, and the life was the light of men. The light shines in the darkness, and the darkness has not overcome it.

> The true light that enlightens every man was coming into the world. He was in the world, and the world was made through him, yet the world knew him not. He came to his own home, and his own people received him not. But to all who received him, who believed in his name, he gave power to become children of God; who were born, not of blood nor of the will of the flesh nor of the will of man, but of God. (John 1:1-13 RSV)

The last sentence above bears rereading: "But to all who received him ... he gave power to become children of God." Jesus did not instantly turn the faithful into children of God as many Christians would like to believe; he gave them the *power* to become children of God. Jesus' life and death alone are not enough; we also have a job to do. Jesus liberated us from the law and sin, clearing the path to the narrow gate, but we must choose to walk that path. Eventually that choice becomes the only one; as Desmond Tutu said, "God just grabs us by the scruff of the neck," or as C.S. Lewis said, "We will not turn to Him as long as He leaves us anything else to turn to."

Dr. Christiane Northrup has a very practical way of saying the same thing:

> Old-soul empaths generally have a very solid relationship with the divine, with their faith in divine source. We feel bad for those who don't, and we're eager to share that deep and abiding faith with another. But they don't want to do the work of contacting that divine within. They'd rather just get a hit of our energy to keep them afloat until the next time.[143]

[xv] In the footnotes to this passage, we are reminded that the Greek word for "spirit" also means "wind" – as Jesus described the Holy Spirit to Nicodemus.

It isn't enough to just get a hit of Jesus' energy. Only those who do the work will find the narrow gate. Jesus saved us from the law, but he could not save us from our defiant egos. That is up to us.

> Therefore, my beloved, as you have always obeyed, so now, not only as in my presence but much more in my absence, work out your own salvation with fear and trembling; for God is at work in you, both to will and to work for his good pleasure. (Philippians 2:12-13 RSV)

> And the Word became flesh and dwelt among us, full of grace and truth; we have beheld his glory, glory as of the only Son from the Father. (John bore witness to him, and cried, "This was he of whom I said, 'He who comes after me ranks before me, for he was before me.'") And from his fullness have we all received, grace upon grace. For the law was given through Moses; grace and truth came through Jesus Christ. No one has ever seen God; the only Son, who is in the bosom of the Father, he has made him known. (John 1:14-18 RSV)

The Thomas Gospel says, "The kingdom of the father is spread upon the earth and men do not see it." The Word has been dwelling among us all along, but in our myopic view we couldn't see it. So God said, "Okay, I guess I have to find a form that will be super-obvious to my blind creation. I'll take human form, work miracles, fulfill the scriptures, forgive sins, and throw out Mosaic Law. Only an idiot could fail to see the divine in this incarnation."

Well ... we know what happened. In greed, fear, and ignorance the scriptures were fulfilled all too well: "We esteemed him stricken, smitten by God, and afflicted." (Isaiah 53:4 RSV) The Pharisees called Jesus a blasphemer and had him killed. But the Word was out. The Word continues to dwell among us as it always has, and is heard in the words of the disciples of Christ, who still surround us in human form (as do the disciples of Buddha, Lao-tzu, Mohammed, and all the other awakened receptacles of the Word down through the ages).

In the Acts of the Apostles, God, as the Holy Spirit, is described in both wind and light:

> When the day of Pentecost had come, they were all together in one place. And suddenly a sound came from heaven like the rush of a mighty wind, and it filled all the house where they were sitting. And there appeared to them tongues as of fire, distributed and resting on each one of them. And they were all filled with the Holy Spirit and began to speak in other tongues, as the Spirit gave them utterance. (Acts of the Apostles 2:1-4 RSV)

And in Hebrews:

> Of the angels he says,
> "Who makes his angels winds,
> and his servants flames of fire." (Hebrews 1:7 RSV)

In John, light and wind come up again, Jesus describing himself with the same wind metaphor that he used to describe the Holy Spirit to Nicodemus in John 3:8:

> Again Jesus spoke to them, saying, "I am the light of the world; he who follows me will not walk in darkness, but will have the light of life." The Pharisees then said to him, "You are bearing witness to yourself; your testimony is not true." Jesus answered, "Even if I do bear witness to myself, my testimony is true, for I know whence I have come and whither I am going, but you do not know whence I come or whither I am going. (John 8:12-14 RSV)

Do I know whence I have come and whither I am going? This question has the same answer as a Zen *koan*.

~ 1367 ~

Occasionally I find truth in an unlikely place – in the preaching of Christian fundamentalists. I doubt that they know or would acknowledge that when they speak truth they are also preaching Buddhist dharma. For example, Pastor Kyle Idleman correctly (but probably accidentally) explains the Buddhist subjugation of the ego as he explains the Judeo-Christian idea of idolatry:

> Idolatry isn't just one of many sins; rather it's the one great sin that all others come from. So if you start scratching at whatever struggle you're dealing with, eventually you'll find that underneath it is a false god. Until that god is dethroned, and the Lord God takes his rightful place, you will not have victory.[176]

Idolatry – the utmost evil identified by C.S. Lewis as Pride (~1283~) – in this context is the same as the Buddhist first poison. The false god that we worship is unhealthy attachment – that which we desire, crave, and grasp for. Dethroning that false god means letting go of the selfish ego and allowing God to take its place.

> God declines to sit atop an organizational flowchart. He *is* the organization. He is not interested in being president of the board. He *is* the board. And life doesn't work until everyone else sitting around the table in the boardroom of your heart is fired. He is God, and there are no other applicants for that position. There are no partial gods, no honorary gods, no interim gods, no assistants to the regional gods.[176]

The God Kyle talks about in the beginning of the above paragraph is indeed the Godhead that emerges when all the false gods around the boardroom table are fired. However, the God depicted in much of the Bible more closely resembles the gods at the end of the passage – the partial/honorary/interim/assistant gods. These Biblical gods are not false gods, not the idols of greed and desire that need to be fired with the ego; the anthropomorphic gods of the Bible are dualistic aspects of the Godhead – true gods, but separated out of the Godhead's invisible white light like colors in a prism. Like Jesus. Like all of us.

> We may not have the god of commerce, the god of agriculture, the god of sex, or the god of the hunt. But we do have portfolios, automobiles, adult entertainment, and sports. If it walks like an idol, and quacks like an idol ...[176]

On this point I could not agree more.

~ 1368 ~

I just saw a wonderful computer video that demonstrated the immensity of the universe – external and internal. First it took me on a space journey from earth to the outermost reaches of the universe, beyond the most distant stars and galaxies. Then it drilled into a person's eye, from gross structures like the retina into the contents of molecules and atoms. At the end of each journey was ... nothing. Astronomy and quantum mechanics both take us to the same place, to the same eternal emptiness.

Our spiritual journey mirrors this physical one. We look first for God in the sky and in nature as the creator of the immense physical world: "I lift up mine eyes to the hills." (Psalm 121:1 RSV) Then we look for God in human form, in the anthropomorphic Gods of the Bible and in living beings like Jesus, and then inside our own being. These are all dualistic representations in time and space, whether found in the heavens or on the earth.

Then we discover that God is everywhere – in the microcosm as well as the macrocosm, and beyond. We recognize God without form as an energetic spirit – the Holy Spirit – the energy of distant stars, electrons and quarks, as well as of lions and earthquakes. But all is illusion. All is emptiness. Matter and energy dissolve into the eternal black hole where the outermost edge of the universe meets the inside of an atom.

~ 1369 ~

I love the way Buddhism and Christianity illuminate each other. The weaknesses of one religion are the strengths of the other. For instance, Buddhists are great at envisioning eternity, Christians not so good. Christians are better than Buddhists at expressing suffering, though.

On Suffering – Christians are great with suffering. The Catholics' prime symbol is the crucifix with a dying man hanging on a cross; suffering is at the front of Christian consciousness. And then they drive you deeper into suffering with the concept of sin and punishment, adding guilt to the mix. The Christians (and Jews) can go on for hours telling you exactly how they suffer, all the details of their longsuffering life in the body.

The image we have of Buddhism is monks sitting quietly in meditation, at peace, no suffering. Buddhists do know suffering, of course; the First Noble Truth is "all life is suffering (*dukkha*)." But it is hard to pin Buddhists down concerning the specifics of suffering. They usually say something fuzzy like, "Suffering is anything that frustrates you." In Buddhism suffering is generalized and impersonal. There is no sin, no guilt, and no need for confession or forgiveness.

On Eternity – Buddhists move quickly past suffering (the First Noble Truth) and get right to its cause (Second Noble Truth) and cure (Third and Fourth Noble Truths). They identify the Three Poisons, follow the Eightfold Path, and set their sights on awakening to eternity. They spend so much time exploring beyond the illusion of physical life that I wonder if they ever come up for air in space-time. They have elaborate charts showing the many layers of existence in physical and spiritual realms, and they are very specific about all kinds of energetic life beyond the body.

Christians have trouble understanding life apart from the body. Christianity is firmly grounded in temporality and describes eternity with difficulty, with the same nebulousness as Buddhism describes suffering. The Bible makes many references to the afterlife, heaven, and a kingdom not of this world, but rarely defines these terms and rarely makes it clear that heaven and earth are not separate places. There is serious confusion among Christians concerning the relationship of temporal life and eternal life, and of the Godhead and the anthropomorphic gods of the Bible. In Buddhism there is no such confusion.

Christians say, "God with us." Buddhists say, God (the buddha-nature) *in* us." And yet, if you look, you can find Christian references to the indwelling eternal God-self. Jesus echoed the Buddha's view when he said the kingdom of God is within you. (Thomas 3:3, Luke 17:21) John said, "No man has ever seen God; if we love one another, God abides in us and his love is perfected in us. By this we know that we abide in him and he in us, because he has given us of his own Spirit." (1 John 4:12-13 RSV)

I have presented the Christian and Buddhist views of suffering and eternity as I have heard them expressed among the people I know in their respective churches and temples. The mystics of all religious traditions, however, understand the core of suffering, eternity, and all physical and metaphysical principles in the same universal way, which is the Truth within and beyond all religions.

~ 1370 ~

Let us suppose we possess parts of a novel or a symphony. Someone now brings us a newly discovered piece of manuscript and says, 'This is the missing part of the work. This is the chapter on which the whole plot of the novel really turned. This is the main theme of the symphony'. Our business would be to see whether the new passage, if admitted to the central place which the discoverer claimed for it, did actually illuminate all the parts we had already seen and 'pull them together'. The new passage, if spurious, however attractive it looked at the first glance, would become harder and harder to reconcile with the rest of the work the longer we considered the matter. But if it were genuine then at every fresh hearing of the music or every fresh reading of the book, we should find it settling down, making itself more at home and eliciting significance from all sorts of details in the whole work which we had hitherto neglected. Even though the new central chapter or main theme contained great difficulties in itself, we should still think it genuine provided that it continually removed difficulties elsewhere.

Something like this we must do with the doctrine of the Incarnation. Here, instead of a symphony or a novel, we have the whole mass of our knowledge. The credibility will depend on the extent to which the doctrine, if accepted, can illuminate and integrate that whole mass. It is much less important that the doctrine itself should be fully comprehensible. We believe that the sun is in the sky at midday in summer not because we can clearly see the sun (in fact, we cannot) but because we can see everything else. – C.S. Lewis, *Miracles* [27]

The truth of Lewis' analogy depends on one's definition of "the Incarnation." If understood broadly, as the presence of God with form on earth, it fits perfectly with the scriptural knowledge we already have and also with the scripture of all other great religions and philosophies. As the sun illuminates everything else, so spiritual truth illuminates the teaching of every religion.

However, if we limit our definition to the specific incarnation of Jesus, we limit the scripture we already know. The mystery, the metaphorical miracle depicted in the scripture, is gone. The allegedly sacred text that is supposed to expand our understanding instead puts limits on it.

~ 1371 ~

When you come to knowing God, the initiative lies on His side. If He does not show Himself, nothing you can do will enable you to find Him. And, in fact, He shows much more of Himself to some people than to others—not because He has favourites, but because it is impossible for

Him to show Himself to a man whose whole mind and character are in the wrong condition. Just as sunlight, though it has no favourites, cannot be reflected in a dusty mirror as clearly as in a clean one.

You can put this another way by saying that while in other sciences the instruments you use are things external to yourself (things like microscopes and telescopes), the instrument through which you see God is your whole self. And if a man's self is not kept clean and bright, his glimpse of God will be blurred—like the Moon seen through a dirty telescope. That is why horrible nations have horrible religions: they have been looking at God through a dirty lens. – C.S. Lewis, *Mere Christianity* [76]

Indeed, "… it is impossible for Him to show Himself to a man whose whole mind and character are in the wrong condition." Exactly why I cannot show the full measure of my divine love to Emily. Her mirror is dusty.

I was with Lewis all the way until the last sentence. Horrible nations have horrible religions? Like Nazi Germany and Christianity? (In light of the Church's silence in the face of Nazi atrocities, Lewis must have considered German Christianity at the time to be a horrible religion, Bonhoeffer notwithstanding.) Judge not lest ye be judged – there are no horrible nations or horrible religions, except as they are horribly used. I remind myself that other revered Christian sages like St. Paul, Martin Luther, and John Wesley, for instance, had some unfortunate social and political views that came out of their respective cultural environments, and that *Mere Christianity* was written before Lewis' spiritual maturity.

The stillness in which the mystics approach Him is intent and alert—at the opposite pole from sleep or reverie. They are becoming like Him. Silences in the physical world occur in empty places: but the ultimate Peace is silent through the very density of life. Saying is swallowed up in being. There is no movement because His action (which is Himself) is timeless. – C.S. Lewis, *Miracles* [27]

I can't stay disappointed with Lewis for long. If I put aside his occasional slip of the tongue, I can easily see the great truth that pervades everything else he said.

~ 1372 ~

We want so much more—something the books on aesthetics take little notice of. But the poets and the mythologies know all about it. We do not want merely to see beauty, though, God knows, even that is bounty enough. We want something else which can hardly be put into words—to be united with the beauty we see, to pass into it, to receive it into ourselves, to bathe in it, to become part of it. – C.S. Lewis, *The Weight of Glory* [86]

Lewis put his finger on what drives musicians, like poets, into a life in the arts – to bathe in beauty, to become part of it, to give birth to it, and ultimately to unite with the truth that is its source. Lewis seemed to cast art in a disparaging light in other writings (~1310~), but he did know the true meaning of art, after all.

~ 1373 ~

One of my gurus over the years has been Doreen Virtue. I attended her workshop several years ago, and it was very helpful. Her little book *Angel Numbers 101* introduced me to numerology and helped me understand the meaning of the numbers around me. When the Angel Number 4 serendipitously pops up, I am assured that I am on the right track.

A couple years ago Doreen found Jesus. Okay. Fine. But then she gave up her work as a "new age" spiritual intuitive because it seemed to conflict with her new interpretation of the Bible. Unfortunately, when Doreen opened the door to a deeper but narrower immersion in Christianity, she shut other equally valid and sacred doors. Instead of continuing to keep all doors open, she adopted a confining interpretation of the Bible that caused her to question her past work. She put herself under the law and suddenly became once again a sinner. Her previously free spirit, innocent as a child's, is now locked in a prison of doubt and shame. She stopped producing her angel cards and doing intuitive work.

She was right to surrender her life to God, but her new definition of God allows only one limited and limiting view of him. She does not see that her angel cards, if used in the name of God, can be a vehicle for communication with God, as they have been in my life and once were in hers. They are only against God if used against God. Jesus said, "Do not forbid him; for no one who does a mighty work in my name will be able soon after to speak evil of me. For he that is not against us is for us." (Mark 9:39-40 RSV)

Doreen's strength is also her weakness – her open heart makes her vulnerable to any and all influences, trustworthy or not. She based her abandonment of her previous spiritual work on this Bible passage:

> When you come into the land which the Lord your God gives you, you shall not learn to follow the abominable practices of those nations. There shall not be found among you any one who burns his son or his daughter as an offering, any one who practices divination, a soothsayer, or an augur, or a sorcerer, or a charmer, or a medium, or a wizard, or a necromancer. For whoever does these things is an abomination to the Lord; and because of these abominable practices the Lord your God is driving them out before you. You shall be blameless before the Lord your God.

For these nations, which you are about to dispossess, give heed to soothsayers and to diviners; but as for you, the Lord your God has not allowed you so to do. (Deuteronomy 18:9-14 RSV)

I think she misinterpreted this passage relative to her intuitive work. She missed the point that the law against soothsayers and sorcerers has to do with the "abominable practices" of other nations. The Israelites also had soothsayers, called prophets, who regularly communed with God and received powerful messages which often predicted the future (usually an unhappy one if sinful behavior was not corrected). Soothsaying and wizardry are only abominations if not practiced in the name of God.

But more important, in her starry-eyed devotion to her newfound image of the savior, Doreen failed to grasp the meaning of Christ's gospel, the good news that the Law of Moses is dead and sin with it. For a born-again Christian, Deuteronomy no longer applies. She need not regret her past life or work, nor seek forgiveness for any of it. She was doing God's righteous work, whether she knew it or not. The godliness of her work is reflected in the profound spiritual development of me and many others. (The number 4 is still my Angel Number.) Jesus said a tree is known by its fruit. Doreen's intuitive tree bore sacred fruit, always in harmony with the love of God, Jesus, the angels and ascended masters, to all of whom she paid homage.

An enlightened Christian sees the presence of God in all things, hears the voice of God no matter whose mouth speaks it, and recognizes God the Wizard in all the miracles he and his angels have wrought.

Some say that Doreen is and always was a charlatan, making up stories to validate her alleged intuition and make money. Maybe so, but it really doesn't matter. Even if Doreen's message was false by some measure, the awakening to love that she helped us find was true.

~ 1374 ~

I watch the antics of my two-year-old grandnephew and the more complex but similar antics of his seventy-year-old grandfather, noticing how little progress is made with age in overcoming the supremacy of the ego and the autonomic response to lower chakra functions.

The child expresses fear and anger with screams and tantrums, living completely in the moment. He wants pleasure and relief from displeasure, and he wants it *now*. It's the same with the frustrated adult. He also lacks patience, but expresses his fear and anger with sullen withdrawal and defensive posturing, reacting to conditioning from the past and worry for the future without mindfulness in the present moment. All his higher education, religious supplication, and life experience has not gotten him one iota closer to freedom from fear and desire, but merely taught him to conform his overt behavior to socially acceptable norms.

Both the toddler and the senior citizen look outside themselves for someone to satisfy their desires and solve their problems, and blame someone else when their desires are not satisfied and their problems are not solved. In the physical realm of duality and separation – the only realm the toddler knows – this is as it must be. The adult, however, has a chance to awaken to a higher wisdom, to eternity, to peace and love within pain and fear, once he knows he can find this realm inside himself – and paradoxically, regain the childlike innocence and openness that his many years of education and conditioning had walled off – the innocence that both grandfather and grandson knew before they were born.

~ 1375 ~

MARY AND MARTHA

> Now as they went on their way, he entered a village; and a woman named Martha received him into her house. And she had a sister called Mary, who sat at the Lord's feet and listened to his teaching. But Martha was distracted with much serving; and she went to him and said, "Lord, do you not care that my sister has left me to serve alone? Tell her then to help me." But the Lord answered her, "Martha, Martha, you are anxious and troubled about many things; one thing is needful. Mary has chosen the good portion, which shall not be taken away from her." (Luke 10:38-42 RSV)

In this story, Martha does worldly work and Mary does spiritual work. Doing God's work in both realms is righteous and holy; duality and eternity are equal and inseparable, like the interlocked black-and-white image of yin/yang. God is on both planes.

Caroline Myss explains what Jesus meant by Mary choosing the "good portion:"

> You walk in two worlds simultaneously at all times, the world you see and the one you don't. It's the world you don't see that matters and once you "get that," you cease to judge the world you do see. And that's a game-changer truth, if there ever was one. (~1345~)

Mary and Martha both walk in both worlds all the time, as do we all. Martha was busy doing God's work in the world we see. Mary sought to know God in the world we don't see. Jesus did not want Mary's chance for game-changing truth to be taken away from her.

THE "HOLY" SCRIPTURES?

How do we explain the alternating merciful and vengeful God of the Old Testament? We already know that the God who can be named, who has anthropomorphic qualities, is not the top God, the Godhead, the ultimate Source. The different behaviors exhibited by the Hebrew God were assigned by the authors of the Bible to amplify the various messages they wanted to send. Sometimes the message was happy, and we got a happy, merciful God to deliver it. Other times the message was wrathful or judgmental, and we got a mean, angry God to deliver it. Sometimes these messages were spiritual, expressed by the prophets as direct revelation from the Source. Sometimes not.

It occurred to me that the historical accounts in the Bible of battles and wars, especially the brutal conquest of the Promised Land related in Exodus (which probably never happened: ~930~), were written to send more of a political message than a spiritual one. The authors sought to justify wars against the Canaanites, Sumerians, Babylonians, and whoever else got in their way by declaring that God was on their side and had sent them to claim lands that God had given to them.

This is not unlike Hitler's invoking both the Christian God and the legendary Teutonic gods to justify his political conquests. Hitler reclaimed the Sudetenland and Rhineland using military force, as the Hebrews reclaimed Palestine, asserting a kind of divinely ordained manifest destiny.[193] Another parallel is the way Hitler declared the Aryan race to be the favored people, as the Hebrew God is said to have selected the Jews as his chosen people.

This comparison of Hebrew and Nazi atrocity is not to negate the deep spiritual messages in the Bible, which remain ever and always true. But it helps explain why good and evil can be so hard to tell apart, depending on your point of view, and sheds light on why the supposedly good Hebrew God of the Old Testament appears to advocate murder, rape, and pillage. And indeed he did – as the devilish dark side of the Godhead. The kind and merciful God reflects the light side.

~ 1377 ~

I sent Hugh and Josie some money. Their family is suffering health problems, and my intuition tells me that they can use the cash. Hugh and Josie are among the five or six people to whom I have given large amounts of money to support what I consider to be their valuable spiritual work. Sometimes my money goes out as a gift, sometimes as a loan, but as I said to one loan recipient, "I don't care if you ever pay me back, as long as you use the money to do good work. So keep doing good!"

When I started gifting/loaning in this way, I didn't know of any specific reason for it. My intuition just told me to send the money out into the universe through the people I was moved to support, like a patron of the arts who provides subsistence for painters, composers, or other artists to enable them to pursue their art free from financial hardship. This is part and parcel of the life of a bodhisattva, the practice of the 1st Perfection of Generosity, giving joyously. This is why I now have money that I did not earn or ask for. I am a spiritual banker, a conduit through whom the eternal spirit of love moves in the material world.

~ 1378 ~

John Welwood, a psychologist with a Buddhist bent, died recently. I have been drawn to his writings, which have a lot of consonance with my own.

"On Spiritual Authority"[178]

RELATIVE AUTHORITY

Although I may feel uneasy with the authority clients grant me as a therapist, I am willing to accept it, especially in the early stages of the work. I understand that clients can more readily enter into the process of shedding old patterns if they grant me the authority to guide them. *[This is the authority I uneasily accept from my friends who call me "wise."]*

ABSOLUTE AUTHORITY

In contrast to false teachers, who often create a condition of dependency in the student by claiming special access to truth, authentic teachers delight in sharing the source of their own realization with the student. Devotion is a sign of a shift in allegiance—away from the petty tyrant of egocentricity toward the call of our larger being, whose wisdom the teacher embodies in fully developed form.

"The Perfect Love We Seek"[179]

ABSOLUTE LOVE

If the pure essence of love is like the sun in a cloudless sky, this clear and luminous light shines through relationships most brightly in beginnings and endings. When your baby is first born, you feel so graced by the arrival of such an adorable being that you respond to it totally, without reserve, demand, or judgment. Or when you first fall in love, you are so surprised and delighted by the sheer beauty of this person's presence that it blows your heart wide open. *[Joseph Campbell and Marianne Williamson also described this phenomenon. (~681~)]* For a while the bright sunlight of all-embracing love pours through full strength, and you may melt into bliss.

Similarly, when a friend or loved one is dying, all your quibbles with that person fall away. You simply appreciate the other for who he or she is, just for having been here with you in this world for a little while. Pure, unconditional love shines through when people put themselves—their own demands and agendas—aside and completely open to one another. In relation to another, it manifests as selfless caring.

Deeper than all our personality traits, pain, or confusion, our being is the dynamic, open presence that we essentially are. It is what we experience when we feel settled, grounded, and connected with ourselves. When rooted in this basic ground of presence, love flows freely through us, and we can more readily open up to others. When two people meet in this quality of open presence, they share a perfect moment of absolute love. *[Possibly, but more likely they just hit a smooth patch on the road of relative love. What happens when the road gets rough? Read on ...]*

RELATIVE LOVE

Yet even though the human heart is a channel through which great love streams into this world, this heart channel is usually clogged with debris—fearful, defensive patterns that have developed out of not knowing we are truly loved. As a result, love's natural openness, which we can taste in brief, blissful moments of pure connection with another person, rarely permeates our relationships completely. Indeed, the more two people open to each other, the more this wide-openness also brings to the surface all the obstacles to it: their deepest, darkest wounds, their desperation and mistrust, and their rawest emotional trigger-points. Just as the sun's warmth causes clouds to arise by prompting the earth to release its moisture, so love's pure openness activates the thick clouds of our emotional wounding, the tight places where we are shut down, where we live in fear and resist love. *[The warmth of my sun caused Emily's thick cloud of wounds to arise, and she resisted my love. So also with The Unnamed One.]*

This, then, is relative love: the sunlight of absolute love as it becomes filtered through the clouds of our conditioned personality and its defensive patterns—fearfulness, distrust, reactivity, dishonesty, aggression, and distorted perception. *[eternity filtered through the prism of duality.]* Like a partly cloudy sky, relative love is incomplete, inconstant, and imperfect. It is a continual play of light and shadow. The full radiance of absolute love can only sparkle through in fleeting moments.

Fortunately, the storminess of our relationships in no way diminishes or undermines the unwavering presence of great love, absolute love, which is ever present in the background. Even when the sky is filled with thick, dark clouds, the sun never stops shining. *[As the Nirvana Sutra says about the unchanging Tathāgata (~1362~), "The moon-globe is not disturbed in any way ... it is only because of the moon's obstruction by the hands of the asura that it is rendered invisible."]*

When you recognize that the absolute beauty within you cannot be tarnished by your flaws, then this beauty you are can begin to care for the beast you sometimes seem to be. Beauty's touch begins to soften the beast's gnarly defenses. Then you begin to discover that the beast and the beauty go hand in hand. The beast is, in fact, nothing other than your wounded beauty. *[This is like C.S. Lewis saying, "The truth is that evil is not a real thing at all, like God. It is simply good spoiled." It could also be said, from the opposite direction, that good is evil spoiled. The beast is our wounded beauty; beauty is our healed beast.]*

Welwood knew what divine love looks like, and even used the same analogy that I do – the innocence of children and the dying – to describe the unsullied divine love, the God-self, that we are all born with and that these innocents draw out of us. And he correctly identifies the hallmark of all forms of true love as "selfless caring."

I rejoice when Welwood says, "Then you begin to discover that the beast and the beauty go hand in hand." He gets it that good and evil – all the pairs of opposites – are inseparable and arise together from the same source. I also rejoice in seeing that absolute truth manifests on earth in so many glittering facets, so many different jewels in Indra's Net. Welwood is a brilliant jewel.

~ 1379 ~

Many years ago I visited a beach that had very big waves. The beach was in a sheltered bay, and beyond the waves crashing on the shore, the water was reasonably calm. I successfully managed to swim out beyond the shore break by using the undertow to carry me through the incoming wave before it crested. I went out about fifty yards behind the waves and paddled around for a while. Then I looked back toward shore, and my heart jumped. Looking down from the top of the wave to the beach below was like looking down from the top of a three-story building.

How am I going to get back to shore without getting pounded into the sand and breaking my neck? After my initial panic, I thought the problem through. I realized that if I stayed just behind the crest of the wave, I could be propelled forward by the force of the wave and it would deliver me onto the shore unscathed.

That's exactly what happened. I rode the top of the wave to the shore after the wave crashed in front of me; I simply glided onto the beach and walked up to dry land, as smooth and easy as stepping off an escalator. It was as if God held me in his hand and gently lowered me down to earth.

This is what spiritual surrender is like. I could not control the processes of nature and make the waves stop, but I could return safely to shore if I followed the wave's rhythm, surrendering to its power and using its energy to propel me. By allowing my will to find synchrony with the wave's (God's) irresistible will, I could ride the wave safely, even though just a small difference in my position, being slightly out of sync with the wave, could have resulted in serious injury. The force of my own will is no match for the force of nature, but if I trust in the wisdom of the wave, we can work together.

It's a kind of aikido, reading the signs and signals, not resisting obstacles but deftly dodging them, harmonizing with their power and turning them to your service. As evil can be harmonized with good.

~ 1380 ~

When we mix together all the colors of paint on an artist's palette, the result is a black blob. But when all the separate colors of the visible light spectrum are brought together, the opposite happens; we call the resultant wave "white light." But white light is not really white – it is *invisible*.

The pictorial representation of yin/yang is an interlocking pattern of black and white elements. If we were to attempt to blend these elements together in the material world, they would produce a shade of gray, much as white cream in black coffee makes a light brown mixture. But if we blend the opposite extremes of yin/yang together in the spiritual realm, in the eternal singularity without form or substance, we get a result like invisible white light. The image disappears altogether. This is the Great Void, the emptiness, the sum total, the zero-sum balance, of all that is.

PART 58
Circling the Globe
January 2019 – May 2019

~ 1381 ~

A while ago I wrote that the process of life and the process of death are the same process. (~1209~) I have devised a pictorial way to demonstrate this:

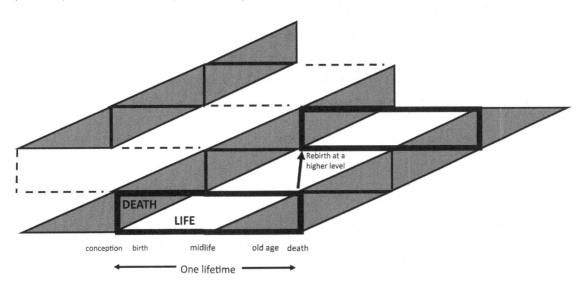

At conception you are more dead than alive, in the darkness and stillness of the womb, more in touch with the spirit realm than the earthly one. At birth you open your eyes, feel your mother's touch, drink her milk, and begin to perceive the many splendored sights, sounds, textures, and flavors of duality. You are now alive, but until your consciousness arises, memories form, and your ego takes over, you are still in touch with God and the spirit realm where you were before you were born, innocent and free from sin.

In midlife you are at your physical and mental peak. Your senses are at their sharpest; your physical strength and stamina are at their height; you have completed your education and are intellectually powerful; you are socialized and have learned how to handle your emotions and function in community with others. You are fully alive in the body and in the world.

As you age, you notice your senses fading, your strength and health declining, and your thoughts turning away from the world and toward the spirit. Your body and mind increasingly walk both the path of life and the parallel path of death.

This pattern has no timeframe. One complete lifetime could take a week for an insect, or hundreds of years for a tree. The process is endless and inexorable. Early death, whether by abortion, disease, or accident, does not end the process. We just push the reset button and start again. It is also conceivable that even a very short human life could be a complete one, having processed through all the stages and accomplished its life purpose in record time.

Imagine this pattern in multi-dimensions, spiraling endlessly around the surface of a globe in an innumerable series of births and deaths, until eventually reincarnation ends, karma ends, and a buddha is thrown off the wheel of samsara, off the globe, into the Void.

With this final awakening at the end of the last incarnation, the pendulum flies off its hinges, the taut rubber band snaps, the moth flies into the flame, the iceberg melts into the ocean, and the soul melds into the spirit. And then, from inside the globe, another soul emerges to jump on the merry-go-round and begin the cycle.

~ 1382 ~

I have begun my journey to a workshop with Caroline Myss. My angels are with me, says *Angel Numbers 101*.[34]

I checked into my hotel room at my first stop – building 4, 4th floor, room 441.

> **Angel Number 4** – The angels are with you. They send you the number 4 to reassure you that they've heard your prayers and are helping you.

> **Angel Number 44** – The angels are giving you extra comfort, love, and support right now. Ask them for help with everything, and listen to their guidance through your intuition.

> **Angel Number 441** – The angels and archangels say that your thoughts are manifesting rapidly into material form, so be sure to only think about your desires. Ask the angels for help in staying positive.

Next hotel room, at the workshop – room 336.

> **Angel Number 3** – The ascended masters are helping you – usually this means an ascended master you feel close to – for example, Jesus, Quan Yin, a saint, or some other spiritual/ religious figure.

Angel Number 33 – You have a strong and clear connection with one or more ascended masters, who have answered your call and your prayers. Keep talking to them, as they're helping you with your present situation.

Angel Number 36 – The ascended masters ask you to keep your thoughts focused on spirit, and release any material worries to them.

Angel Number 336 – Your prayers for help with material needs have been heard and answered by the ascended masters.

Next hotel room, on my way home – same hotel as the first, same building, same floor, room 442.

Angel Number 442 – The angels and archangels are urging you to stay positive, as your optimism supports them in answering your prayers.

First airport gate F4.

Next airport gate D41 and seat 14D

(I don't know the meaning of the retrograde order, but there must be one.)

Angel Number 1 – Stay positive. Everything you're thinking about right now is coming true, so be sure that you're only thinking about what you desire. Give any fears to God and the angels.

Angel Number 14 – Lean upon the angels to help you maintain a positive outlook. This will keep your own demeanor optimistic and bright.

Angel Number 41 – The angels ask you to keep very positive thoughts, as everything you say and think is manifesting into form rapidly.

Next hotel room – 4th floor, room 463. (The airline put me up when my last flight was delayed.)

Angel Number 463 – You've attracted major help with your prayers! You have ascended masters, guardian angels, and the archangels working on answering your prayers.

The Number 3 adds the ascended masters to my Number 4 angels; the Number 1 adds a sense of urgency; the Number 6 tells me to let go of worldly worries. Sounds right.

~ 1383 ~

Dream: *I am in a beautiful ornate room, cathedral-like, made of dark wood. There are two large heavy doors that I prop open. There is another set of outer doors, and when both sets of doors are open, you can see into the room. Inside the room, many people are helping me with a project involving large smooth stones, like river rocks. Then I am outside digging, and under a thin layer of asphalt I find the stones.*

Then I am up in the air, piloting an airplane, having a great time and enjoying the view. My plane suddenly goes into a vertical dive. I look for the fuel gauge wondering if I am out of fuel, but couldn't find it. I look for a flat area on the ground, hoping to land safely. I get the plane leveled off, flying just above the ground. I was about to scrape the treetops when I woke up.

From dreammoods.com:

Room – To dream that you are in a room represents a particular aspect of yourself or a specific relationship. Dreams about various rooms often relate to hidden areas of the conscious mind and different aspects of your personality. If the room is welcoming or comfortable, then it signifies opulence and satisfaction in life. To dream that you find or discover a new room suggests that you are developing new strengths and taking on new roles.

Door – To see an opened door in your dream symbolizes your receptiveness and willingness to accept new ideas/concepts.

Stones – To see a stone in your dream symbolizes strength, unity, and unyielding beliefs. Look at the shape, texture and color of the stone for additional significance. Some stones also carry sacred and magical meanings.

Digging – To dream that you are digging indicates that you are working hard to uncover the truth in a problem that is haunting you. You are preoccupied with trying to find out something about yourself, your reputation, or your self-identity.

Airplane – To see or dream that you are in an airplane indicates that you will overcome your obstacles and rise to a new level of prominence and status. You may experience a higher consciousness, newfound freedom and greater awareness. To dream that you are flying an airplane suggests that you are in complete control of your destination in life. You are confident and self-assured in your decisions and accomplishments. To dream that a plane crashes suggests that you have set overly high and unrealistic goals for yourself. To see an airplane landing in your dream signifies completion of a journey or some task.

My room having doors which I purposely keep open suggests that I am letting knowledge in and out, allowing outsiders access to the room. This seems to be in accord with my new mentoring mission. I dig for truth and find the sacred stones.

I am indeed in control as I fly the plane of my life. My plane loses altitude but does not crash. It also does not land, so I guess my journey is not unrealistic but is not yet completed.

~ 1384 ~

My brother walks like an old man. His joints are failing – neck, hips, knees, ankles. He has had three surgeries in the last four years to fix various parts, and is awaiting two more. He is younger than me, but he is falling apart while I stay pretty much together. He says the reason is that he has eaten too much junk food all his life. While I don't discredit the effect of diet, I see the problem from a different angle.

He has spent the last forty years in a dysfunctional marriage, trying to appease a wife whose negativity, petulance, and woundology have kept him in a near-constant state of hypervigilance, always on guard to prevent or mitigate the tirades that inevitably plague his household. (I credit Emily's behavioral disorder for helping me understand and forgive my sister-in-law's similar but milder condition.) Adding to this emotional disease is his vulnerability to pseudo-religious influences that have taught him not to love, but to hate and fear. The atmosphere in his house is one of unremitting tension, judgment, criticism, and acculturated despair.

As I watch so many people pass through my life, I witness their poignant struggles with pleasure and pain, good and evil, life and death. I see them flailing away, not knowing where to turn. It is so hard for them to let down their guard and open to the love of God, being afraid to see the illusion of life, to let go in unsupported thought, to surrender to God – even when prayers to God are constantly on their lips.

Compassion is "suffering with," knowing feelings of frustration and angst but also knowing the divine love that is the way out of suffering and seeking to light that path of liberation. This is the bodhisattva call.

~ 1385 ~

Marriage has nothing to do with love. It is about lust, about providing a protective family to care for the children who inevitably come when young people act out their urges. This is why Jesus said that people are not married in heaven; divine love has no use for marriage and its baggage of worldly concerns.

With this realization I have come to another interpretation of this Bible passage: "Have you not read that he who made them from the beginning made them male and female, and said, 'For this reason a man shall leave his father and mother and be joined to his wife, and the two shall become one flesh'?" (Matthew 19:4-5 RSV) In what way do a man and woman combine to become literally *one* flesh – together in one body? When they make a baby. A person is in fact half his mother and half his father – his parents become, literally, "one flesh."

~ 1386 ~

The mind lets go of everything that's fabricated and caused, that arises and passes away. That's how it gains release. The *Brahmanimantanika Sutta* describes this state of release as "consciousness without surface," a consciousness that, unlike ordinary consciousness, is not experienced through the six senses. In other words, it's not engaged in any world, in any sense of the term. The *Kevatta Sutta* adds that this consciousness is free from name and form, which means that—unlike, say, the infinitude of consciousness experienced in formless state of concentration—it's not involved in any sort of fabrication. In both of these discourses, this consciousness is presented as something that even the devas in the highest heavenly worlds don't know. After all, they're still in their worlds, whereas this consciousness is where no world finds a footing. It's the world's cessation.

In the *Atthi Raga Sutta*, the image used to illustrate this consciousness is of a light beam that doesn't land on any object. Though bright in and of itself, it doesn't participate in the world in any way, and so can't be detected as existing, not existing, both, or neither. Its release is that total. – Thanissaro Bhikkhu, "Going Beyond Mind's Fabrications," *Bodhidharma*, Winter 2018

This image of a light beam that doesn't land on anything sounds like a spaceman's perception of light from outer space. Our spaceman can see the sun and the illumination of the earth when the sun's light lands on it; that is, when sunlight enters the world of name and form. But he cannot see anything illuminated in the empty space between the sun and the earth. In outer space where there is no atmosphere, no particles in air to reflect light, the light of the sun does not land on anything. This is eternity – the Great Void, emptiness – from which duality comes and in which it operates. That the same beam of sunlight can be undetectable in space but detectible on earth elegantly shows how the invisible God is made visible in the world, and how consciousness of name and form gains release.

"… this consciousness is presented as something that even the devas in the highest heavenly worlds don't know. After all, they're still in their worlds, whereas this consciousness is where no world finds a footing." Jesus knew this consciousness: "The foxes have holes, and the birds of the air have nests; but the Son of man hath not where to lay his head." (Matthew 8:20 RSV)

~ 1387 ~

CULTURAL AND SPIRITUAL RELIGION

Everybody has a cultural religion – the religion, or lack of one, that we grew up with. As adults, we practice the prayers, rituals, and doctrines that are the sociocultural overlays of our childhood religion, but the simplistic images of gods, heaven, life, and death that we learned as children rarely take us to the place where the great spiritual lessons lie.

Few people dig deep into spirituality. That's because spiritual religion hurts. The path to the narrow gate, to the hole in the log in the ocean, goes through rivers of fire. Trials and temptations must be overcome. Everything must be given up. When a crisis hits and the simple religion of our childhood fails to rescue us, faith can be lost and our cultural religion abandoned. Serious spiritual seekers often take a different path than the one their cultural religion provided because its superficial rules and dogmas corrupt or obscure the deep spiritual message of that religion. They seek a cleaner lens, and sometimes find the same universal truth, arrive at the same Source, along a different path. (e.g., Ravi Zacharias [~1259~])

~ 1388 ~

Rita no longer says she loves me. I tell her that I love her, but there is no echo coming back. She "loved" me when I was loaning her money, but when I refused to loan her even more money last year, distance came between us. Even though my refusal to loan her money, my refusing to enable her continuing financial dependency, catalyzed events that have brought her into financial health, our closeness cooled.

When she asked me for a new loan to replace her old broken-down car, she had a crazed look about her, like a drug addict desperate for a fix and willing to do anything to get it. It was that desperation, not the loan request itself, that caused me to deny her the loan. Since no loan was forthcoming, she was forced to find a healthier solution – selling some inherited possessions that she didn't need but had been holding for purely sentimental reasons. Yet today, when she repaid her previous loans in full, thanks to the more secure financial condition I had led her to, she denied having been in financial crisis, still blind to the fact that her financial house of cards was on the verge of tumbling down. She claimed only that she had been concerned about having a vehicle to get to work.

Like Emily, although to a much milder degree, Rita used me and then threw away the pretense of love when it was no longer useful. Rita is much closer than Emily to overcoming the causative trauma of childhood abuse, but she is still wrapped in her wounds and the deep fear they engender. I saw through her wounds, brought the light of love to bear on them, and like Emily, she recoiled from my light. Her life is healthier now, thanks to the wheels that my loan refusal set in motion, but she is still groping in the darkness.

But then, as one light dims another one brightens. The Unnamed One invited me to dinner while he is in town next month. Perhaps he is awakening ever so slowly to the true nature of my love and wants it near him again. The living die, and the dead are raised. Lives and loves come in and go out of my life in a kaleidoscope of patterns and colors.

UPDATE: A little while after I wrote the above entry, Rita called. She said, "Did I ever thank you for not giving me the loan I wanted? I'll say it now – thank you. I realize you did me a big favor." And then she added, "I love you."

~ 1389 ~

EMPTINESS

I once described the difference between scripture and revelation in terms of limits, like the difference between an infinitely sided polygon and a circle. (~150~) This also describes the jump of consciousness from duality to eternity.

The infinitely sided polygon contains an infinite number of angles, but when we take the quantum leap to a circle, all angles disappear. There are no angles at all, yet every angle is contained therein. Infinite fullness becomes emptiness. In the same sense, eternity is not just the sum total of all things – the entire contents of duality – but the explosion and implosion of everything out of and into nothing.

Heaven and nirvana are not the same as eternity. They are the conscious awareness of eternity in duality. A knowing that has nothing to do with knowledge.

From the *Heart Sutra*: "Here, Sariputra, form is emptiness and the very emptiness is form; emptiness does not differ from form, form does not differ from emptiness; whatever is form, that is emptiness, whatever is emptiness, that is form, the same is true of feelings, perceptions, impulses and consciousness ..."

~ 1390 ~

In his discussion with Nicodemus, Jesus said, "Truly, truly, I say to you, unless one is born of water and the Spirit, he cannot enter the kingdom of God." I have expounded at length about what Jesus meant by "Spirit" in this context, but what did he mean by "water"? Later in his gospel, John explains:

> Now when the Lord knew that the Pharisees had heard that Jesus was making and baptizing more disciples than John (although Jesus himself did not baptize, but only his disciples), he left Judea and departed again to Galilee. He had to pass through Samar'ia. So he came to a city of Samar'ia, called Sy'char, near the field that Jacob gave to his son Joseph. Jacob's well was there, and so Jesus, wearied as he was with his journey, sat down beside the well. It was about the sixth hour.

> There came a woman of Samar'ia to draw water. Jesus said to her, "Give me a drink." For his disciples had gone away into the city to buy food. The Samaritan woman said to him, "How is it that you, a Jew, ask a drink of me, a woman of Samar'ia?" For Jews have no dealings with Samaritans. Jesus answered her, "If you knew the gift of God, and who it is that is saying to you, 'Give me a drink,' you would have asked him, and he would have given you living water." The woman said to him, "Sir, you have nothing to draw with, and the well is deep; where do you get that living water? Are you greater than our father Jacob, who gave us the well, and drank from it himself, and his sons, and his cattle?" Jesus said to her, "Every one who drinks of this water will thirst again, but whoever drinks of the water that I shall give him will never thirst; the water that I shall give him will become in him a spring of water welling up to eternal life." (John 4:1-26 RSV)

I find the reference to the well of Jacob and Joseph meaningful. The life of Joseph, who was thrown into a well by his brothers, presaged the life of Christ, who was also thrown into the abyss by his brethren and, like Joseph, arose from the well of hell to reign in heaven.

~ 1391 ~

Dream last night: *My right eye was stuck closed and I was having trouble getting it open. I was commiserating with a friend who was having the same problem. She indicated that she had heard of a solution to the problem. We were both trying to get our eyes open, with limited success.*

From dreammoods.com:

> **Eyes** – To see your own eyes in your dream represents enlightenment, knowledge, comprehension, understanding, and intellectual awareness. Subconscious thoughts may be

coming to the surface. The left eye is symbolic of the moon, while the right eye represents the sun. To dream that your eyes are injured or closed suggests your refusal to see the truth about something. You may be expressing feelings of hurt, pain or sympathy. To dream about someone else's eyes indicates an emotional or intimate connection with that person. It also signifies a mutual understanding.

My left eye is open, seeing God with form as reflected in the moon, but God without form, the direct light of the sun, is still elusive. Is Martha my female friend in the dream? Or Josie? Or Cecilia? There are very few women I know with whom I might have an intimate connection or mutual understanding at a high spiritual level. That I saw my closed eye and also my friend's suggests that we are at similar stages of enlightenment, knowledge, awareness. We both want to get our right eyes open, but something holds us back.

~ 1392 ~

If you asked twenty good men today what they thought the highest of the virtues, nineteen of them would reply, Unselfishness. But if you had asked almost any of the great Christians of old, he would have replied, Love. You see what has happened? A negative term has been substituted for a positive, and this is of more than philological importance. The negative idea of Unselfishness carries with it the suggestion not primarily of securing good things for others, but of going without them ourselves, as if our abstinence and not their happiness was the important point. I do not think this is the Christian virtue of Love. The New Testament has lots to say about self-denial, but not about self-denial as an end in itself. We are told to deny ourselves and to take up our crosses in order that we may follow Christ; and nearly every description of what we shall ultimately find if we do so contains an appeal to desire. If there lurks in most modern minds the notion that to desire our own good and earnestly to hope for the enjoyment of it is a bad thing, I submit that this notion has crept in from Kant and the Stoics and is no part of the Christian faith. Indeed, if we consider the unblushing promises of reward and the staggering nature of the rewards promised in the Gospels, it would seem that Our Lord finds our desires not too strong, but too weak. – C.S. Lewis, *The Weight of Glory* [86]

It is important to differentiate positive "desire" in Lewis' Christian context from negative "desire" in the Buddhist sense of the first poison. The Buddha discovered, as Lewis implies, that neither the Selfishness of hedonism nor the Unselfishness of asceticism is an end in itself. The meaning of "desire" as Lewis meant it – the desire for the rewards in heaven that Christ promised – is the same urge that caused the Buddha to give up both hedonism and asceticism and sit under the bodhi tree. The Buddha took up the cross of Christ with all its pleasure and pain, surrendered his attachment to and avoidance of all earthly things, and reaped the reward of awakening promised in the Gospels.

"To desire our own good and earnestly to hope for the enjoyment of it," as Lewis described it, is not to desire our own pleasure or happiness in the worldly sense, but rather to desire the eternal Joy, Compassion, Loving-kindness, and Equanimity that transcend simple earthly pleasure, good, and enjoyment. The highest and best good we could possibly desire for ourselves is reunion, reconnection, with the unity that is God. This is the reward promised in the Gospels.

~ 1393 ~

We must simply accept it that we are spirits, free and rational beings, at present inhabiting an irrational universe, and must draw the conclusion that we are *not derived from it*. We are strangers here. We come from somewhere else. Nature is not the only thing that exists. There is 'another world', and that is where we come from. And that explains why we do not feel at home here. A fish feels at home in the water. If we 'belonged here' we should feel at home here. All that we say about 'Nature red in tooth and claw', about death and time and mutability, all our half-amused, half-bashful attitude to our own bodies, is quite inexplicable on the theory that we are simply natural creatures. If this world is the only world, how did we come to find its laws either so dreadful or so comic? If there is no straight line elsewhere, how did we discover that Nature's line is crooked? C.S. Lewis, *Present Concerns* [79]

We, as physical beings, *are* derived from the universe. There is no denying that human anatomy and physiology correlate with that of our mammalian relatives. Genesis says that Adam came from the dust of the earth, as the Buddhists say we came from the earth as an apple comes from an apple tree – not created out of nothing, but raised out of all that came before.

But if we consider that Lewis is not talking about our physical selves, but our God-selves, there is new meaning. In that sense, we did indeed come from somewhere else, from the nothingness that is the Godhead.

A fish feels at home in the water. We humans, as physical forms, feel at home in the air. But neither the fish nor the man is merely a physical form. Each is imbued with the same Spirit from which each came and to which each will return. When the physical form awakens to its spiritual nature, one and inseparable, the body will feel at home wherever it is, knowing that it belongs anywhere and everywhere.

Lewis can be reconciled by knowing that both the spirit self and the physical self are true. The line that God drew from eternity through Nature is both straight and crooked.

~ 1394 ~

Many times I have asked why so many troubled people come into my life and are drawn into my love. I am seeing more clearly now that karma would have it no other way.

> My life fell apart, and Rimpoche held me close as I cried on his chest like a little child sobbing in her mother's arms. As I gathered myself together, he said matter-of-factly, "You know, this is just samsara. You can't take it personally." – Cyndi Lee, "Taking Refuge," lionsroar.com 2/15/19

Caroline Myss puts the same idea in terms of archetypal patterns:

> You have to understand, and here's what's so healing, there was nothing personal about this relationship; if you understand the archetype in that person, you have to understand that, while you feel very personal about it, you can't take it personally because he would have done this to anyone, and he's going to go on to do it again and again and again. You have to understand, it wasn't personal. – Caroline Myss, Hay House World Psychic Summit 2017 [130]

My prime archetype is the bodhisattva/empath/wake-up-fairy/healer/teacher. Sociopathic archetypes and other such troubled souls gravitate toward me, and I toward them, as the karma directs. I surrender to God, the karma, and know that good and evil are not personal.

Caroline says that awakening is "the impersonal experience of your own life." It is the egoless experience of divine wisdom arising within you. It's not personal.

~ 1395 ~

> This instruction on prajnaparamita is a teaching on fearlessness. To the extent that we stop struggling against uncertainty and ambiguity, to that extent we dissolve our fear. The synonym for total fearlessness is full enlightenment—wholehearted, open-minded interaction with our world. By learning to relax with groundlessness, we gradually connect with the mind that knows no fear. – Pema Chödrön, "Bodhichitta: The Excellence of Awakened Heart"[180]

The feeling of groundlessness that I felt at the beginning of this journal, the sense of being untethered, lost in space, abandoned by God – the feeling of intensely horrific fear that set me on my spiritual journey – I can now experience as its polar opposite, as the eternal groundlessness of peaceful emptiness, of oneness with God – of no fear. The cursed helplessness of abandonment morphs into the blessed helplessness of surrender.

Nothing changes with enlightenment. Our spiritual journey arrives at the same place it started. What seemed to be hell was all along and at the same time, heaven.

~ 1396 ~

Another dream: *I was wandering around a big old house gathering up piles of trash. I had huge collections of it. Trash cans were everywhere, some full, some empty. I began searching the piles, trying to remember where I put something. I came upon a big mailbox inside the house, so full I could barely open it, but it was neatly labeled with typewritten notes listing its contents.*

From dreammoods.com:

House – To see a house in your dream represents your own soul and self. To see an abandoned house in your dream implies that you have left behind your past. You are ready to move forward toward the future. To dream that you are cleaning your house signifies your need to clear out your thoughts and get rid of old ways.

Garbage – To dream that you are throwing away garbage suggests that you are kicking your old negative habits and throwing away your bad characteristics and unwanted traits. To see piles of garbage in your dream represent rejected or unwanted aspects of yourself.

Garbage Can – To see a garbage can in your dream symbolizes unwanted ideas, thoughts or memories. It is time to rid yourself of the baggage.

Search – To dream that you are searching for something signifies the need to find something that is missing or needed in your life. The dream may be analogous to your search for love, spiritual enlightenment, peace, or a solution to a problem.

Mailbox – To see a mailbox in your dream represents important information that you are about to receive. If the mailbox is full, then it indicates that you have not digested or accepted these messages.

Label – To see or read labels in your dream indicate that you have unknowingly exposed certain private matters, due to your carelessness and neglect.

This dream took place in the dark, so I know it has to do with the subconscious. I am indeed throwing away lots of stuff, old habits, past baggage. Maybe the searching had to do with something I threw away before I meant to.

The mailbox I saw was the big public kind that you put outgoing mail into, not the small home mailbox that the postman delivers to. Perhaps the stuffed mailbox represents lots of backed-up information I have yet to deliver (this unpublished book?), mentoring yet to be done.

The labels on the mailbox are curious. If the mailbox messages are outgoing, perhaps the labels (the table of contents of this book?) mean that I am exposing private matters, but not unknowingly due to carelessness, rather, as in this book, quite intentionally.

~ 1397 ~

This sin has been described by Saint Augustine as the result of Pride ... From the moment a creature becomes aware of God as God and of itself as self, the terrible alternative of choosing God or self for the centre is opened to it. This sin is committed daily by young children and ignorant peasants as well as by sophisticated persons, by solitaries no less than by those who live in society: it is the Fall in every individual life, and in each day of each individual life, the basic sin behind all particular sins: at this very moment you and I are either committing it, or about to commit it, or repenting it. – C.S. Lewis, *The Problem of Pain* [56]

Being born into duality is eating of the Forbidden Tree, becoming "aware of God as God and of itself as self." Lewis' choosing God, not self, for the center is the same as the Islamic surrender to God, the Zen idea of no-self, and Jung's annihilation of the ego. They may use different words and images to describe their understanding, but all mystics come from and go to the same place.

~ 1398 ~

My astrological reading: *"You are romantic, peace-loving, compassionate, and considerate, and you live to love! Your life path mission is to achieve balance between giving and receiving. Sympathetic and caring, you are a born counselor, and your life path number symbolizes the principles of nurturing and harmony. You are the teacher, the trainer, and the parent. You will love any job where you can make life more comfortable, easy, and luxurious for others."*

My Buddhist message: *An image of flowers is seen ... you look at a vase of flowers from the front ... the flowers look fresh and vibrant ... but looking from another angle, you see wilted flowers ... people recognize you as one who sees the buddha-nature and also the suffering ... as one who can listen completely, with compassion ... the Buddha is helping you, always with you.*

I am bombarded from all sides with messages that confirm my calling as a servant, teacher, healer, and compassionate counselor.

The Buddhist service today was about merit transfer, which sends love and healing to all in one's sphere, making no distinction between friend and foe. The compassion and loving-kindness of the Buddha is for everyone. Jesus agreed:

> You have heard that it was said, "You shall love your neighbor and hate your enemy." But I
> say to you, love your enemies and pray for those who persecute you, so that you may be sons of
> your Father who is in heaven; for he makes his sun rise on the evil and on the good, and sends
> rain on the just and on the unjust. (Matthew 5:43-45 RSV)

~ 1399 ~

In the September 8, 1997 issue of *The New Yorker*, a story appeared about a Wall Street investor's battle with terminal cancer.[xvi] Before the cancer, Kirk, the investor, had been a shrewd, aggressive player of the stock market, buying and selling quickly, making short-term deals that netted short-term profits. Long-term concerns – like death – were far from his normal routine.

His efforts to fight his disease were equally aggressive. He arrived in Dr. Jerry Groopman's office after everyone else had given him just weeks to live. But his will to live was strong, and he was determined to try every experimental treatment available.

As he embarked on his new extreme treatment regimen, however, he began to know fear – fear of oblivion, of loss of self:

> "I didn't expect to be so afraid, Jerry." He paused. "I'm not sure why. I rarely feel afraid.
> Maybe it's because I know that this is my last chance and I'll probably die, and after death …
> It's just nothingness."
>
> Now I thought I understood why he had insisted on treatment. "So then it would be the same
> as before we were born," I said. "Is that terrifying, to be unborn? That's what my father used
> to say to comfort me as a child when I asked him about death."
>
> Kirk said, "See if you still find that enough comfort when you're the one in this bed. Nothingness,
> No time. No place. No form. I don't ask for Heaven. I'll take Hell. Just to be."

The treatments worked. Kirk's cancer went into remission and virtually disappeared. It was hailed as a miracle by the hospital staff and the medical community.

[xvi] Jerome Groopman, "The Last Deal," *The New Yorker*, September 8, 1997

But Kirk's attitude had changed. His previously assertive and aggressive tone gave way to a more bland and resigned one. The doctor ruled out depression, exhaustion, and other to-be-expected emotional disturbances as possible reasons.

Before the cancer, Kirk had been a rabid reader of newspapers and investment magazines, looking for potentially profitable deals, but after the remission he lost interest in the news:

> Newspapers used to be a gold mine for me. They're filled with disconnected bits of information – a blizzard in the Midwest, the immigration debate in California, the problems of West Germany absorbing East Germany. For you, Jerry, those articles might be about the lives or fortunes of individuals and nations. For me, they mean nothing beyond information for deals and commodity trading. I never really cared about the world's events or its people. Not deep down inside.

> When I went into remission I couldn't read the papers because my deals and trades seemed pointless, because I was a short-term investor. I had no patience for the long-term. I had no interest in creating something – not a product in business or a partnership with a person. And now I have no equity. No dividends coming in. Nothing to show in my portfolio.

> How do you like my great epiphany? No voice of God or holy star but a newspaper left unread in its wrapper.

> The remission meant nothing, because it was too late to relive my life. I once asked for Hell. Maybe God made this miracle to have me know what it will feel like.

Dr. Groopman encouraged Kirk to share his thoughts about his wasted life with his family:

> Kirk, you can't relive your life. There is no time. But your wife and children can learn from you. And when you're gone the memory of your words may help guide them.

Is any life really wasted? Even a "self-absorbed, uncaring shit," as Kirk described himself, can be a guide, during life and afterward. As Emily, in all her narcissism and deep psychic pain, was a guide for me.

The cancer returned, and Kirk died after a four-month remission. The doctor's final note:

> I composed in my mind a eulogy – addressed, as eulogies are, to the living. The words I chose were not from a holy text but from Kierkegaard: "It is perfectly true, as philosophers say, that life must be understood backward. But they forget the other proposition, that it must be lived forward."

Live life forward in duality; understand life backward in eternity.

~ 1400 ~

CBS News: "Scientists unveil first image of black hole in all its dark glory:"

> The accepted reality of black holes is relatively new, but the concept is not. John Mitchell, an English country parson and accomplished scientist, first suggested the possibility of "dark stars" in 1783. Einstein's relativity equations predicted the inevitable existence of black holes in 1915, although the famous physicist initially did not believe such objects could be real. But in 1916, German astronomer Karl Schwarzschild calculated an exact solution to Einstein's equations that showed how black holes could form.
>
> The image captured by the Event Horizon Telescope shows a black central core—the event horizon—surrounded by a lopsided ring of light emitted by particles racing around the black hole at nearly the speed of light. It closely resembles what astronomers expected based on simulations running the equations of Einstein's general theory of relativity.
>
> For truly massive stars, enough gravity is available to overcome all known nuclear forces, and core collapse proceeds to the point where it vanishes from the visible universe, leaving behind nothing but an enormously concentrated "gravity well" of deeply distorted space.
>
> The black hole's mass defines the size of its event horizon, the zone from which nothing, not even light, can escape. If a photon, dust particle—or a spaceship—crosses the event horizon, it is forever lost to the universe. Nothing can escape the gravitational clutches of a black hole.
>
> By definition, black holes are invisible. But they can be detected by the radiation streaming away into space from gas and dust particles being sucked in. As such material approaches the event horizon, it is accelerated to enormous velocities and as the particles jostle together, heat—and high-energy radiation—is generated.[181]

My suspicions seem to be confirmed – a black hole is a portal connecting duality and eternity – a stunning physical explanation and actualization of the mystical metaphors and visions of invisible emptiness, timelessness, awakening, and God.

A black hole is the narrow gate, the hole in the log in the ocean, that few will find. When you cross the black hole's event horizon, you are involuntarily sucked in, pulled like a spaceship locked in a tractor beam; there's no going back. This is where the irreversible eighth bhūmi bodhisattva is, in total surrender, unsupported thought, letting go of everything in this world, giving everything back to the otherworldly Source. "If a photon, dust particle—or a spaceship—crosses the event horizon, it is forever lost to the universe." The iceberg melts in the warm ocean; the moth flies into the flame; the buddha attains *anuttara samyak sambodhi*.

The high-energy radiation generated at a black hole is the invisible light of God's love, the Holy Spirit, the cherubim's fiery sword guarding the Tree of Eternal Life, or a bodhisattva returning to the illusion of the universe to bring it back to the reality of the Void, to be recreated and sucked back again into the black hole of eternity.

Quantum mechanics (mathematics of the very small) and gravity (mathematics of the very large) meet in a black hole. Looking out from inside a black hole, you would see a distorted universe, in both time and space. Time would play out unbelievably fast in front of your eyes. Gravitational forces stretch space and everything in it; everything stretches into a long string one atom thick, and then the very atoms themselves are pulled apart. The heart of the black hole, the infinitesimal singularity, is where this journey terminates. Everything is compressed until it is nothing, yet still exists. This is eternity, the Godhead, the mysterious Source.

Creation (duality) has a beginning (the Big Bang) and an end (a black hole). Creation rises and falls, emerges and is destroyed, endlessly. But the Godhead/Source is without beginning or end; it is the emptiness from which came the Big Bang and the infinitesimal singularity at the far extreme of a black hole.

The not-religious-but-nevertheless-spiritual Einstein has again been proven to have made the jump to light speed – unintentionally and effortlessly leaping from science to religion and to the mystical place where they meet. Interesting that the first suggestion of black holes came from a "country parson." The journey of artists, scientists, philosophers, and parsons is one and the same journey.

~ 1401 ~

I had another strange trilogy of dreams last night: *The first and most involved one was on an airplane. This was an unusual plane, however; there were no separate seats or seat belts, no overhead compartments or narrow aisles. The cabin of the plane was like a lounge with couches and carpets, and the restroom was like a luxurious public restroom in a fancy hotel. I barely noticed that I was flying.*

In the second dream I was inspecting the overworked fingers of my massage therapist, saying, "Take care of your hands."

The third dream found me on stage looking for my seat in the band just before a show. The stage setup was not what I was expecting. I kept trying to assemble my instrument but putting the pieces together the wrong way.

From dreammoods.com:

> **Lounge** – To dream that you are in a lounge suggests that you need to stop and take a break from some problem or issue in your waking life.
>
> **Bathroom** – A bathroom relates to your instinctual urges. Alternatively, a bathroom symbolizes purification and self-renewal. You need to cleanse yourself, both emotionally and psychologically.
>
> **Hand** – To dream of your hands represents your relationships with those around you and how you connect with the world. Hands serve as a form of communication and can represent authority, hate, protection, justice, etc., depending on the gesture. Perhaps you need to lend a helping hand to someone.

All the dreams took place in darkness, signifying the subconscious. To be in an airplane is to overcome obstacles and rise to higher consciousness. Do the more comfortable surroundings mean that I am feeling greater ease and comfort up in the spiritual heights, finding purification and self-renewal?

I wonder if the massager's hands are Martha's. I have been concerned for her lately, sensing that she is under stress from massaging other people's problems and needs support in handling her own.

Am I returning to my old job – my old life – but not finding things as I remembered them, not remembering how the pieces fit together? I no longer fit in. I have moved on.

~ 1402 ~

A few days ago I saw a film documentary, *Free Solo*, about Alex Honnold, a master rock climber who climbed El Capitan without ropes or safety gear of any kind. One small slip and he would be dead. But he didn't slip and he didn't die. He got to the top unscathed, his incredible ascent recorded in great detail by a very nervous film crew.

The film was a study of the psychology of facing danger. How can someone even think about doing such a dangerous thing without being overcome with fear? There had to be something in this man's brain that allowed him to take overwhelming danger in stride. He submitted to an MRI scan of his brain while being shown images of dangerous situations to see what was happening in his head. Sure enough, the MRI showed a lack of activity in his amygdala, the part of the brain that controls emotion. (~1225~) This abnormal brain condition put him in the perfect mental state to take huge risks involving potentially terrible consequences without fear. Indeed, he was not afraid to fall to his death, commenting that if he died, it would be all right.

The world would go on. His wife would be sad, but she would go on. (Love, like fear, was also muted in his underactive amygdala.)

I couldn't help but think about Emily's overactive amygdala, the extreme opposite of Alex's condition, where emotions rage out of control. Emily takes risks impulsively, thoughtlessly, driven and enslaved by hot emotions run amok. Alex takes carefully calculated risks, not being subject to the mindless cacophony that hot emotions produce. Because of his high level of skill and preparedness, he considered the risk of his free climb to be relatively low, even though the consequences of a mistake would be very high. He was able to succeed because he was able to live totally in the moment, never losing focus, never losing mental or physical control, confident in his ability and powers of concentration.

Those of us who live between these emotional extremes are considered normal, knowing both fear and love at manageable levels. But we miss out on achievements that can only be accomplished at the extremes – Honnold's fabulous climb at one extreme, Mahler's bipolar-inspired symphonies at the other. The sacrifice of the people at the extremes is that they cannot know the healthy expression of worldly love and fear; both extremes suffer distortions of these feelings, underwhelming and passionless at one end, overwhelming and uncontrollably passionate at the other. Both extremes are distanced from the full spectrum of life and love, for opposite reasons.

> Why else were individuals created, but that God, loving all infinitely, should love each differently? And this difference, so far from impairing, floods with meaning the love of all blessed creatures for one another, the communion of the saints. If all experienced God in the same way and returned Him an identical worship, the song of the Church triumphant would have no symphony, it would be like an orchestra in which all the instruments played the same note. – C.S. Lewis, *The Problem of Pain* [56]

Divine love finds us all perfected in eternity, beyond the amygdala.

~ 1403 ~

APOLOGY AND FORGIVENESS, Part 10

> I find that when I think I am asking God to forgive me I am often in reality (unless I watch myself very carefully) asking Him to do something quite different. I am asking Him not to forgive me but to excuse me. But there is all the difference in the world between forgiving and excusing. Forgiveness says, "Yes, you have done this thing, but I accept your apology, I will never hold it against you and everything between us two will be exactly as it was before." But

excusing says, "I see that you couldn't help it or didn't mean it, you weren't really to blame." –
C.S. Lewis, *The Weight of Glory* [86]

Lewis makes a good point about the difference between forgiving and excusing, but he neglects to compare these acts with another important one: forgetting. God does not just forgive sin, he forgets sin: "I will forgive their iniquity, and I will remember their sin no more." (Jeremiah 31:34) This passage implies two levels of salvation: Forgiving iniquity, which is a quality of duality, and forgetting, which in this context is a quality of eternity.

Lewis described excusing in the worldly context of our egoistic desire to disavow sin. There is another way to view excusing that reflects an enlightened understanding of the compulsive-impulsive behaviors of fear, anger, or ignorance: not blaming or judging these acts to be sins. This is excusing in the context of sinless eternity, where the law and sin, right and wrong, are gone, thus making forgiveness unnecessary. (see the story of spilled milk: ~1305~)

God in his eternal oneness can easily forgive and forget, but forgetting can be difficult and dangerous for people living in the world. An abused child can forgive and even excuse, but forgetting can lead to repression and deeper darkness. Such victims, for the sake of their own survival, dare not forget and go back to a relationship "exactly as it was before." This is akin to my forgiving and excusing – but not forgetting – Emily's destructive behavior. In this world, that is. In eternity everything is forgiven, forgotten, and ultimately excused in the divine wisdom. All is exactly as it was before, as it is supposed to be, as it eternally is.

~ 1404 ~

My angel card draw (same card came up twice): *"Victory!" – Archangel Sandalphon: "Your prayers have been heard and answered. Have faith."*

This is the first (and second) time the "Victory!" card has appeared.

~ 1405 ~

The pastor told me that something I wrote inspired his sermon today. It had to do with God's love and Christ's redemption being not just general, but personal – meant for everyone, but also specifically for *you*. A broad invitation to grace, and also an intimately personal one.

Talk about mentoring! I am becoming a teacher of teachers. I wonder about the reduced frequency of spirit messages coming my way lately. Am I losing touch with my guardian angels? Caroline Myss said that sometimes silence is an answer to prayer; you already know all you need to know. I am sensing that now I am becoming less a receiver of spiritual messages than a sender of them. Has the ninth bhūmi arrived? The tenth? The back of my 5th chakra is tingling.

This morning I had an unexpectedly deep conversation with a member of the Sunday school group who, based on my previous encounters, I had thought was not receptive to my heretical ideas. But maybe he was, after all.

~ 1406 ~

Cecilia is again lamenting the hate and violence in the world, wondering what we can do to counter it.

Dear Cecilia,

I am horrified that Buddhists kill Muslims in Myanmar, Muslims kill Christians in Sri Lanka, Christians kill Muslims in the Middle East, Jews kill Muslims in Palestine, Hindus and Muslims kill each other in India and Pakistan, Christians kill other Christians in Ireland and all over the place – all in the name of their respective gods.

The thing that gets me past the horror and despair of these killings is knowing that both my Christian congregation and my Buddhist sangha embrace the multiplicity of cultures that surround them, welcoming the different and unknown, not fearing them. I feel just as at home with the Muslims, Daoists, Jews, Shamanists, Hindus, Eckankarians, and all other people who honor universal spiritual truths. These people, not the terrorists, represent most of the earth's population. Sadly, there are many other people whose religious train got derailed and fell off the track of truth.

Fear, not religion, is the root of violence. Love is the antidote to fear. Killing abates only when love, which belongs to all religions but is the special province of none, liberates the fearful from their fear. We are on the right track when we seek to remove the fearmongers from public office, but much more needs to be done. We must remove fear from the hearts of those who put the fearmongers in office in the first place. Rather than ask them, "Why did you vote for so-and-so?" let's ask, "What frightens you?" And then look for ways to address their fear. A tough ask, I know, but until we plumb the depths of this fear, more tyrants will arise.

Yours in Christ, in Gassho, Namaste,

Betty

Dear Betty,

Thanks for this thoughtful (as always) comment. After all the readings on Good Friday about God being on our side, and unless you worship like me I'll tear you limb from limb … and that's after seeing the light, Nebuchadnezzar! I'm trying to keep my own fear of these wingnuts in check, but I admit it's not easy.

Cecilia

"Unless you worship like me I'll tear you limb from limb" pretty well describes all theocracies, including Christian, Islamic, and Buddhist ones, sad to say. The interpretation of scripture is in the eyes and ears of the beholder.

Sadly true. In the reports on Sri Lanka, militant Buddhists are prominently mentioned. Now we have the wealthy lost Muslim young men. How does wealth or lack of it factor into being radicalized?

Going on the assumption that your question is not just rhetorical – I don't think wealth or lack of it need have any causative behavioral effect. Yes, a lot of impoverished people become embittered and hateful, but how do you explain the many who come from the same background and go the other way? And of course, how do you explain many of our current leaders who come from privilege, with no hardship to blame for their bad behavior? Both Jesus and the Buddha made the point that access to heaven/nirvana is not related to earthly wealth or status. Both rich people and poor people must come to that realization, from opposite directions, if they are to find peace.

Preacher Betty the Heretic

Dear Preacher,

I was actually wondering if wealth encouraged this kind of extremism, more than poverty. But of course, both conditions harm the soul (for different reasons), and that's the causative factor.

You're my kind of heretic!!

Cecilia

Does a monk's vow of poverty harm his soul? Does my having more money than I need harm my soul? (I give most of my excess away, to be sure my soul stays pure!) Wealth plays to a person's greed; poverty plays to his fear. (Greed, fear, and ignorance – the Three Poisons.) When a person is able to rise above greed and fear, the presence or absence of wealth has no soul effect. This is the Buddhist concept of "unsupported thought" and Jesus' remark that it is easier for a camel to go through the eye of a needle than for a rich man (i.e., a greedy man who covets his wealth) to enter the kingdom of God.

You are as good a sparring partner as Ignacio was! You sharpen the edge on my mighty swift sword. Thank you.

~ 1407 ~

LIBERATION THEOLOGY AND THE PROSPERITY GOSPEL

The above conversation caused me to think about the divergence and convergence of liberation theology and the prosperity gospel. Liberation theology is guided by scripture that says the faithful should minister to the poor and liberate them from the bondage of poverty. The prosperity gospel is guided by scripture that says the faithful will be rewarded. Both doctrines have been perverted for opposite political purposes, but both are true, although not necessarily in the ways they are usually interpreted.

The true liberation of liberation theology is not liberation from poverty, but from the fear of hardship that poverty brings. The true reward promised in the prosperity gospel is not material wealth, but release from the bondage of greed that prevents their return to oneness with God. When the poor surrender their fear of poverty, they open the way for God to lift them up; God will clothe them as he clothes the lilies of the field. When the rich surrender their attachment to wealth, they understand that the money and possessions that come to them are not theirs; they belong to God and are placed in their care to do God's will. Those who have wealth are reservoirs, holding tanks for God's wealth, to be meted out as God directs. God deposits wealth with us as we deposit money in a bank.

As for the rich in this world, charge them not to be haughty, nor to set their hopes on uncertain riches but on God who richly furnishes us with everything to enjoy. They are to do good, to be rich in good deeds, liberal and generous, thus laying up for themselves a good foundation for the future, so that they may take hold of the life which is life indeed. (1 Timothy 6:17-19 RSV)

The result of liberation theology and the prosperity gospel in tandem is a society in which everyone has enough to comfortably subsist and maybe a little bit more. Everyone is liberated, and everyone prospers. No crushing poverty, no opulent wealth. It is the discovery of heavenly blessings through liberation from both greed and fear.

~ 1408 ~

And what of an end of consciousness? Some Buddhist scholars of the past maintained that upon attaining the state of nirvana the continuum of one's mental and physical existence would cease. However, an absurd consequence of this view is that there would be no one to experience the state of nirvana. The individual instances of consciousness that we experience throughout life—perceptions of all we see and feel as well as thought processes we've engaged in—will cease when our physical being expires at death. However, our fundamental quality of clarity and knowing—the essential nature of consciousness—does not end at death; its continuum is unceasing.

There also exists a very subtle physical body, referred to in Buddha's Vajrayana or tantric teachings, that acts as the basis for our most subtle consciousness. Just as the continuum of our subtle consciousness has no beginning or end, so the continuum of this most subtle physical aspect of self is also beginningless and endless. – The Dalai Lama, "Seeing Ourselves Clearly"[182]

I am awestruck by the Dalai Lama's description of the "very subtle physical body," different from the body of existential thoughts and perceptions, acting as "the basis for our most subtle consciousness." This so beautifully explains the mystery of what I have experienced in tantric love, a "most subtle physical aspect of self," a state in which my body is not my own, but is inhabited by a beginningless and endless consciousness of love. Most subtle indeed, and clearly different from the worldly sensations that cease when our physical being expires at death. Here is the source of healing and miracles, like the hormonal changes that occurred in my physical body in response to the consciousness that does not end. Could this be what the early Christians meant by the resurrection of the "body"?

~ 1409 ~

I am beginning to see yet another layer of the education that Emily gave me – learning to accept things I do not and can never understand. As hard as I try, I cannot get inside the mind of someone with severe mental illness, someone for whom abhorrent behavior is normal and natural; someone who knows there is a difference between right and wrong, but for whom the line of demarcation between them is invisible.

Emily is not a bad person; she means no harm, wants to be "good" or at least perceived to be so, but cannot control the biological and psychological forces that drive her in the opposite direction. My deeply empathic heart feels her pain, and I can have compassion for her and forgive her abuses – even thank her for them and the lessons they teach – but my mind can never really grasp what it is to process thoughts as she does.

A new book has crossed my path, *Women Who Love Psychopaths*, that is helping me crawl inside the sick mind. The authors explain that psychopaths and sociopaths discover as children that they do not have the same emotions or moral conscience as other people. They are punished when they behave outside acceptable norms and quickly learn that they must somehow appear "normal."

> [Mimicking and parroting] This adaptive skill set of The Dark Triad [psychopaths, sociopaths, and narcissists], which is developed early in life and honed to perfection in adulthood, is predicated on the need to "hide in public." There is an ocean of difference between "awareness" and "insight." The brains of people with personality disorders have been impaired in the areas of empathy and insight. An awareness of their problems can seem to come with all the bells and whistles of insight when it really isn't insight at all.
>
> Let me tell you a story, relayed to me by a psychopathic client:
>
> *Pete the Pathological had an older sibling, Nick the Normal, who was not laden with the problems of no empathy, lack of insight, or a limited range of emotional experiences. One day the boys came home from school. Their mom was sitting on the couch crying, with a black eye, saying that their father had beaten her, packed his things, and left. Nick the Normal went to his mother and hugged her. He got ice for her eye, and then he sat down with her to help problem-solve the situation. Pete the Pathological stood off to the side just watching in an uncaring and bored way, while thinking to himself, "Good! I always hated that bastard. Glad he's gone." He offered no emotion or solutions, proceeded to pick lint off his pants and thought about whether this opportunity would give him time to slip away to play baseball.*
>
> *The mother instructed the boys to go outside so she could pull herself together. As soon as they were outside, Nick lit into Pete. "What's wrong with you? She was bruised and*

bleeding and you just stood there like a stump." And POW, Nick the Normal punched Pete the Pathological right in the face.

Pete told me in therapy that it was at that moment he recognized he didn't feel what he should feel, like others did. He learned a powerful lesson with that punch—that if you don't act like others, there are consequences. Pete the Pathological said he practiced certain phrases, inflecting different tonality in his voice to match Nick's. He even stood in the mirror to imitate the emotions that *should* appear on his face *as if* he were experiencing that emotion.[183]

I can imagine Emily practicing this same way to become the consummate actress that I witnessed as her public persona. This kind of mimicry is also a tool in cognitive behavioral therapy – behave as if you actually feel the emotion you want to feel.

I watched Emily trying to use this technique, going through her repertoire of staged acceptable behaviors with me during one of her narcissistic rages. But because she was already out of control, her attempt to playact at normalcy failed. In this failed attempt I saw that she is not a bad person; she knew she was being abusive and wanted to stop. But as hard as she tried, she couldn't. This is the other side of the coin of understanding: It is just as hard for her to put herself into a healthy state of mind as it is for me to put myself into a sick one.

~ 1410 ~

LOVE, Part 15

> Even while we kill and punish we must try to feel about the enemy as we feel about ourselves—to wish that he were not bad, to hope that he may, in this world or another, be cured: in fact, to wish his good. That is what is meant in the Bible by loving him: wishing his good, not feeling fond of him nor saying he is nice when he is not. – C.S. Lewis, *Mere Christianity* [76]

Lewis is right about love being more than fondness or niceness. But he fails to take the next step toward true divine love. It is not enough to just wish your enemy's good; you must stop seeing him as evil. Letting go of anger and vengeance is a good first step, but judgment must also be let go. We must stop seeing the enemy as "bad" and hoping that he may be cured. Nothing is good or bad, and nothing needs to be cured. Divine love makes no judgments. All is a reflection of God, and all is well.

I see this progression along the path to divine love:

Acceptance – realizing that there is no end to evil, and we must accept its presence in our lives.

Forgiveness – realizing that those who do evil are not always in control of their behavior, and it's not personal; it's archetypal. We forgive them because they know not what they do.

No judgment – realizing that the line between good and evil is not as clear as we thought it was, that one person's vice is another's virtue, and that all things come from God. We refrain from judging the behavior or character of another.

No separation – realizing that everything is a mix of good and evil, light and dark, vice and virtue. We are not separate from the matter, energy, and forces around us. Karma – you reap what you sow – means that we participate directly or indirectly in creating the conditions that affect us. The worshipper is not separate from the worshipped. The abused is not separate from the abuser.

~ 1411 ~

TO MRS. JOHNSON, 2 March 1955: As MacDonald says, 'the time for saying comes seldom, the time for being is always there.' What we practice, not (save at rare intervals) what we preach, is usually our great contribution to the conversion of others. – C.S. Lewis, *The Collected Letters of C.S. Lewis, Volume III* [87]

As the Hindus say, "Those who speak do not know, those who know do not speak." So, when do wise and knowing people speak? They all do, from Lao-tzu to Lewis, sometimes reluctantly, but even those who caution us about speaking, are speaking. The wise and knowing speak when their disciples ask them to, like the Buddha, or when God tells them to, like Jeremiah. They speak not to convert anyone to anything, because universal truth belongs to all, but simply to convey or relay helpful information. The listener may do whatever he wishes with the information received.

> "We are told," said Camilla, "to pray to his image, and then he himself will come from behind us and lay his hundred hands upon our heads and breathe into us the greater life so that we shall live no longer with our own life but with his. No one has ever dreamed it was the Unicornman. We were told you bore stings not for us but for our enemies."
>
> "But do those who have been through it never tell?"
>
> "How could they tell?"
>
> "Why not?"
>
> "But they don't speak."
>
> "You mean they are dumb?" said Scudamour.

"They are – I don't know how it is with them, "said the girl. "They go about their business needing no words because they live with a single life higher than their own. They are above speech." – C.S. Lewis, *The Dark Tower* [135]

Jesus said that a tree is known by its fruit. Actions speak louder than words.

~ 1412 ~

When they had finished breakfast, Jesus said to Simon Peter, "Simon, son of John, do you love me more than these?" He said to him, "Yes, Lord; you know that I love you." He said to him, "Feed my lambs." A second time he said to him, "Simon, son of John, do you love me?" He said to him, "Yes, Lord; you know that I love you." He said to him, "Tend my sheep." He said to him the third time, "Simon, son of John, do you love me?" Peter was grieved because he said to him the third time, "Do you love me?" And he said to him, "Lord, you know everything; you know that I love you." Jesus said to him, "Feed my sheep." (John 21:15-17 RSV)

When Jesus used the word "love" the first two times, in the original Greek translation the word for "love" is *agape* (ἀγάπη, ἀγαπᾷς divine love). When Peter said, "love," the Greek word is *phileo* (φιλῶ, brotherly love) all three times. Jesus asked Peter the question the second time, again saying *agape*, hoping that Peter would awaken to the difference between *agape* and *phileo*. But Jesus was getting nowhere and finally relented, used the word *phileo* the third time, and accepted that Peter's awakening would not happen in that conversation. Jesus knew, however, that Peter would awaken to the difference after Peter's conditional filial love allowed him to deny Jesus three times, and after that, when divine love lifted him to unconditional surrender and his own cross of sacrifice.

Jesus spoke in terms of eternity, but his disciples could not understand: "The kingdom of the father is spread upon the earth and men do not see it." Jesus often relented and spoke in terms that people who are stuck in duality can understand. This is how he presented the Sermon on the Mount and the Lord's Prayer, in metaphorical terminology that recognized the limitations and dangers of language.

In researching the Greek words for love, I came upon this alternate interpretation of the John 21 passage:

One of the most common conversations around the uses of the word "love" comes from John 21:15-17. Jesus asks Peter if he loves Him three separate times. The first two times, the Bible uses the *'agape'* form of love, which is understood to be a general meaning of the word. This love is not based on merit of the person loved, but rather unconditional and based on them as an image bearer of Christ. This love is kind and generous. It continues to give even when the other is unkind, unresponsive and unworthy. It only desires good things for the other and is compassionate.

But the third time that Jesus asks Peter if he loves Him, He uses '*phileo*,' which speaks of affection, fondness and liking the other. This love is companionable and relational. It's brotherly and friendship love.

While *agape* is a more universally understood meaning of love that is shown to a person from no doing of their own, I'm intrigued that Jesus chose to use '*phileo*' as a way to force Peter to think deeper. He wanted to know if Peter loved Him not just because of who He was in God, but rather that they had built a deep and intimate friendship. He wanted to know that Peter cared about Him as a person and a brother. He wanted Peter to know what true reconciliation looked like and it required both kinds of love. – Gary Edmonds, "Agape and Phileo Love: We Need Both"[184]

In my interpretation, Jesus does not force Peter to think deeper; it worked the other way around: *Jesus the Christ* came up from the depths (or down from heaven) to meet Peter where he was at the superficial level of duality. But I can also see this other interpretation as equally valid: Jesus realized that he couldn't lift Peter to eternity, so *Jesus the Man* met Peter on the earthly plane, shifting his description of love from eternal to worldly perspective, validating Peter's worldly understanding of love and accepting that God's will could be done ("Feed my sheep") from that worldly place, even without conscious awareness of eternity.

Yes, true reconciliation requires both kinds of love, *agape* in heaven and *phileo* on earth. The paradox is that once you know *agape*, *phileo* is subsumed in it. You can live in heaven and on earth, in eternity and duality, at the same time.

I realize now that my relationships with The Unnamed One and Emily were like this relationship of Jesus and Peter. I loved them in *agape*, but the only love they could return was *phileo*. Martha called me a wake-up fairy; I could wake up my loves to the existence of *agape*, but not bring them to the actual experience of it. They were not ready to say "yes" to the angel in the spaceship. In this life I must be satisfied with *phileo*.

Or – maybe Jesus didn't say *phileo* the third time. Maybe the Greek author/translator just made a mistake.

> Words are but symbols for the relations of things to one another and to us; nowhere do they touch upon absolute truth. Through words and concepts we shall never reach beyond the wall of relations to some sort of fabulous primal ground of things. – Friedrich Nietzsche, *Philosophy in the Tragic Age of the Greeks*

~ 1413 ~

I reached for a file folder on my desk and accidentally knocked my box of angel cards onto the floor. They fell into two separate piles, with these two cards exposed, facing up:

"Teaching and Learning" – Archangel Zadkiel: "Keep an open mind, and learn new ideas. Then, teach these ideas to others."

"Life Review" – Archangel Jeremiel: "Take inventory of your life, and resolve to change or heal anything that is unbalanced."

My Buddhist message today: *Whether you know it or not, you have taken a positive step forward … closer to the buddha realm … your heart tells you to leave the place of comfort to bring comfort to others … someone is waiting for you … your smile … give a cool drink when it is hot, a hot drink when it is cold.*

~ 1414 ~

I think all Christians would agree with me if I said that though Christianity seems at first to be all about morality, all about duties and rules and guilt and virtue, yet it leads you on, out of all that, into something beyond. One has a glimpse of a country where they do not talk of those things, except perhaps as a joke. Everyone there is filled full with what we should call goodness as a mirror is filled with light. But they do not call it goodness. They do not call it anything. They are not thinking of it. They are too busy looking at the source from which it comes. But this is near the stage where the road passes over the rim of our world. No one's eyes can see very far beyond that: lots of people's eyes can see further than mine. – C.S. Lewis, *Mere Christianity* [76]

Lewis may not have known he was doing it, but in the above statement he validated Jesus' gospel – the good news that in "something beyond," the law and sin – "duties and rules and guilt and virtue" – are dead. The love of God, the light of God that fills the mirror, is not called anything, not even goodness. (The Dao that can be named is not the Dao.) The "rim of our world," where you can see the place beyond, is the edge where I sit, where duality and eternity meet. Lewis sits there, too, and very few eyes can see further than his.

~ 1415 ~

Dreamtime: *I am with a group walking down the street looking for a restaurant. We go into a restaurant and sit down. The place is almost empty. Our group engages in lively conversation and doesn't notice that no one has come to take our food orders. I go to the kitchen to inquire. Only the dishwasher is there. I say, "We would like to get some dinner!" She nods in agreement, but no cook seems to be around. In the meantime, the restaurant has filled up with many people, all eating their dinners.*

From dreammoods.com:

> **Restaurant** – To dream that you are in a restaurant suggests that you are feeling overwhelmed by decisions and choices that you need to make in your life. Alternatively, it indicates that you are seeking emotional nourishment outside of your social support system.

> **Eating** – To dream that you are eating with others signifies harmony, intimacy, merriness, prosperous undertakings, personal gain, and/or joyous spirits. Food can represent love, friendship, ambition, sex, or pleasure in your life.

Dreammoods isn't much help in this case, since the difficulty with decisions and choices at a restaurant usually comes with the menu, which we never got in my dream. Perhaps I was seeking emotional nourishment outside my social support system, and the others in my group, possibly representing my social support system, were seeking nourishment with me. Why were other diners being fed, but for me and my group there was no cook in the kitchen? Was I looking for nourishment that no restaurant could provide? Or was the kitchen empty because I have already received all the nourishment I need?

Perhaps I can interpret this one on my own: This dream reflects my impatience waiting for new spiritual signs; my friends and I are hungry for more. Others are being fed, but we continue to wait. *Anutpattica dharma shanti.* Patience.

PART 59
Everything Hurts
May 2019 …

~ 1416 ~

We are happy—if not happiest—when we are living in harmony with our inner nature. We feel honest and clear. … You are confident about being loved and loving—not in return, just loving because of the quality of person you are. At the core of this life philosophy is a deep understanding that you are a part of Nature and you reside within the cycles and laws of Nature. – Caroline Myss, https://www.myss.com/happiness-as-a-force-of-nature/

Indeed, all my spiritual awakenings over the last thirty years, like the Buddha touching the earth, have been for the purpose of bringing me into harmony with Nature and my inner nature, my buddha-nature. When I faced my anxiety at the farm a couple years ago, I said to myself, "I can breathe and nothing hurts." I was happy. That's all I need.

The real test will be when I can't breathe and everything hurts. Will I still be happy? The silver lining to that dark cloud is that when I really can't breathe, whatever hurts won't hurt for very long. I'll be dead.

~ 1417 ~

Metta, or loving-kindness, is essentially about protection—protecting oneself and each other from inner and outer harm. I was actually surprised to discover that the Buddha said clearly that while it's best to balance caring for self and others, if that's not possible, protecting oneself comes before protecting others! – Trudy Goodman, "Time to Say Goodbye," *Lion's Roar*, March 2019

I am heartened to know that the Buddha agrees with the Christians who say I should protect myself from abuse to protect God's investment in me. (~1213~/~1328~)

This commentary on the *I Ching* says much the same thing in practical Confucian-like terms, justifying the position of self-preservation I had to assume with both Emily and The Unnamed One:

遯 *Hexagram 33: Retreat* – Do not see retreat as surrendering the battle to the enemy. It is a good strategy to allow the multitude of negative forces that have been stirred to finally die down again. It is wise to retreat simply and without compulsive apology. You have no reason to feel guilty for retreating. It is not your responsibility to stay. Although with this strategy you may forfeit some things, to engage would be far worse.

There are times when retreat is the only course of action. That time is now. You cannot fix it. You cannot advance it. You cannot even understand it. Consider the eternal virtues of heaven, its everlastingness, its solitude and fortitude, and consider the eternal virtues that are yours alone. Slip into the eternal principles of heaven, and away from the daily flux. – "Mini Ching," *Harper's Magazine,* July 2013, from "How to Be Good When You're Lost," by Sheila Heti

And yet, the vulnerability of divine love never ends. There are lots of martyrs who liquidated God's investment when they were called to a sacrificial level of service. I will keep protecting God's investment for now, but a bodhisattva gives up self for a life of service, and God's investment in me will need to move from a savings account to a checking account eventually.

~ 1418 ~

Imagine yourself as a living house. God comes in to rebuild that house. You thought you were going to be made into a decent little cottage, but He is building a palace. He intends to come and live in it Himself.

The command 'Be ye perfect' is not idealistic gas. Nor is it a command to do the impossible. He is going to make us into creatures that can obey that command. He said (in the Bible) that we were 'gods' and He is going to make good His words. If we let Him—for we can prevent Him, if we choose—He will make the feeblest and filthiest of us into a god or goddess, a dazzling, radiant, immortal creature, pulsating all through with such energy and joy and wisdom and love as we cannot now imagine, a bright stainless mirror which reflects back to God perfectly (though, of course, on a smaller scale) His own boundless power and delight and goodness. The process will be long and in parts very painful, but that is what we are in for. Nothing less. He meant what He said. – C.S. Lewis, *Mere Christianity* [76]

Yes, of course, Lewis is right – as far as he goes. When he takes the next step – the quantum leap to eternity – he will know that we are already gods – we *are* God – the palace is already and always built, and God is already and always in it. To be made "perfect" is to be the finished palace, to awaken to this eternal truth and live every moment in its light.

The stainless mirror metaphor that Lewis uses to describe our awakened state is the same as that used by the Buddhists. And his recognition of the painful part of the process is the

Buddhist First Noble Truth. As I come to know more about Lewis the Mystic, I see that his spiritual journey and mine (and everyone's) come from and go to the same place. The journey, in three stages:

1. Unconscious, asleep, no-self.

2. Semi-conscious, seeing the ego-self in the mirror, the mind creating time, space, memory, and thought.

3. Fully conscious, awake; seeing the God-self in the mirror, all dust removed; liberated from time, space, memory, and thought; once again no-self.

~ 1419 ~

HEALTH, Part 19

My heart arrhythmia is still with me. I first noticed the main symptom, irregular heartbeats, shortly after Lou died. One of the causes is stress, which clearly applies in my case. The condition gradually abated as I recovered from Lou's death, but reappeared to varying degrees with new stresses, especially with Emily's abusive rages.

The doctor says it is nothing to worry about, but recently my symptoms have become more severe, and chronic. I have been having more and more trouble with any kind of physical activity. The least bit of exertion makes my chest and legs ache, and I am quickly winded. I am otherwise healthy, and although my life is increasingly sedentary, I don't think I am that badly out of shape.

A while ago I described my bout of "broken heart" syndrome when Emily raged at me the last time. My heart has been battling stress-induced adrenalin rushes for decades now, when Lou died and with each bout of divine love thereafter. My vocation as a performer has kept a background of regularly recurring stress going for more than fifty years. Knowing the deep spiritual meaning of all these stressors helps to mitigate them, but still, my body is weary of the endless struggle. My heart remains broken.

~ 1420 ~

ON DEATH

> Basically, the four noble truths come down to the fact that we and everything else will die, and we suffer because we don't want to accept that. We could go so far as to say that samsara is nothing but the denial of death, and enlightenment is accepting it. ... An old Zen admonishment goes, "Don't put a head on top of your head," meaning don't put a false self on top of your true self. And don't put a false reality on top of true reality. Because in a terrible irony, denying death deadens life. – Melvin McLeod, "This World of Dew," *Lion's Roar*, November 2021

> In a thousand ways, most of them not entirely conscious, we hold on to the hope that something of this self, somehow, will remain, and we hold on to that even as everything we touch slides away like sand in running water. ... Slay the demons of hope and fear, my teacher told me. That meant accepting my anxiety, my fear. It meant coming to see that hope and fear are one thing: fantasies of the unborn future. Hope pulls and fear pushes and together they keep us stuck in what has not happened, living a half-life of imaginary events. – Sallie Jiko Tisdale, "Everything Dies," *Lion's Roar*, September 2021

> Eternity is in everything. We're stuck with it. It's even in dying, which can be unpredictably full of intimacy, beauty, comedy, pain, boredom, awe—all in all, truly something not to be missed. ... Well, what are we then? A piece of the vastness. And each piece of the vastness is all of the vastness. – John Tarrant, "Where, Oh Where Will I Go?" *Lion's Roar*, September 2021

> At the moment of your death, you will not see yourself as letting go of life, but simply enjoying it at a higher level. – *Conversations with God* [23]

At the beginning of this journal, I was terrorized by the idea of oblivion, the idea that nothing whatever continues after death. I now understand that fear of death is really fear of oblivion, the eternal loss of any semblance of self as we know ourselves on earth. But with awakening, we know that 1) the self is only an illusion, a phantom that is better done without; 2) the spirit – the "vastness" – is eternal, with us now and in the hereafter, complete in its entirety, without diminution; and 3) life and death are the same continuous process, each progressive stage to be enjoyed at higher and higher levels.

Hope and fear are the first and second poisons of the unborn future. I will not allow them to deaden my life here and now.

~ 1421 ~

When I started reading *One Hundred Years of Solitude* [185] by Gabriel Garcia Marquez, I thought it was boring. Inane stories about alchemy, discovering ice, and various people sleeping with various other people. I thought, I'll keep reading for a while and see if it picks up a bit. It didn't. I put the book away for a few days. But then I started wondering what happened to the guy strapped to a tree because he was crazy. I continued reading. Then I was hooked.

The book is like a dreamy soap opera. The characters are woven through a series of events that could only happen in a dream – tying a guy to a tree for so long that when you untie him he doesn't want to leave the tree, a girl eating dirt, a man who is killed but keeps turning up, an insomnia plague, invisible doctors, a massacre that allegedly never happened – yet the author weaves enough plausibility into the story that you are constantly on the edge between waking and dreaming. This is literary art, the same kind of phantasmagorical art I try to create in my music, making the listener wonder if the sounds come from this realm or some other.

Marquez covers the gamut of human existence in this book, including war, politics, sex, wives, concubines, religion, violence, illness, death, food, and the full range of human emotion. The pendulum swings wildly from one extreme to the other – wealth/poverty, war/peace, truth/lies, destruction/construction, flexibility/rigidity, separation/reconciliation, joy/sorrow. An undercurrent of exposed hypocrisy runs through the book in the juxtaposition of religious ceremonies and symbols – weddings, funerals, masses, Ash Wednesday ashes – with rampant killing, adultery, lying, and all manner of sin. The word "solitude" creeps into the text often enough to remind us that in all the myriad human interactions depicted in the book, real or fanciful, everyone comes from and goes to a place of solitude.

Eventually we readers get over the discomfort of being on the cusp between dreaming and waking, on the edge of insanity, and just accept where we are. By the end of the book the weirdly impossible becomes the expected and commonplace, and we learn to live calmly in Marquez' improbable Alice-in-Wonderland world. I wonder how many readers know that this state of existence is not found only in literary fantasy. It is the very illusion we live every day in our allegedly real lives.

~ 1422 ~

MARA and MAYA

Māra comes from the Sanskrit form of the verbal root *mṛ. Māra* is a verbal noun from the causative root and means "causing death" or "killing." *Māra* is the demon who tempted Prince Siddhartha (Gautama Buddha) by trying to seduce him with the vision of beautiful women who, in various legends, are often said to be Mara's daughters. In Buddhist cosmology, Mara is associated with death, rebirth and desire. Nyanaponika Thera has described Mara as "the personification of the forces antagonistic to enlightenment."

Māyā, literally "illusion" or "magic," has multiple meanings in Indian philosophies depending on the context. In ancient Vedic literature, *Māyā* literally implies extraordinary power and wisdom. In later Vedic texts and modern literature dedicated to Indian traditions, *Māyā* connotes a magic show, an illusion where things appear to be present but are not what they seem. *Māyā* is also a spiritual concept connoting that which exists, but is constantly changing and thus is spiritually unreal, and the power or the principle that conceals the true character of spiritual reality. – *Wikipedia*

Jennie Lee, in *Breathing Love*,[186] gives a practical description of Maya:

When our souls come into bodily form, the one energy or consciousness that comprises the universe has the experience of being separate and unique. The force that creates this experience is called *maya* in Sanskrit, and is described as a veil of illusion that makes us believe we are different and incomplete, therefore needy of the love of others to make us whole. Maya is the dividing force of creation in opposition to love, the unifying force.

I have used the word "Mara" in this journal to describe my adversary in my spiritual battle, the tempter of both the Buddha and the Christ, the antagonist to enlightenment. Mara is not so far from Maya, the dividing force of creation, antagonistic to the unifying force of love. Both Mara and Maya urge us to keep up the illusion of duality, to fall into patterns of greed and fear that reinforce the divisions. Thus, Mara is the personification of the principle of Maya.

Jennie goes on to describe what happens when Mara is vanquished:

All experience of separation ends when our only desire is simply to *be* the love that we already are. Both in relationships and in meditation, this is the natural movement of the heart toward Source. As soon as we surrender the personal "I," love appears as our very own divine Self. It fills us and sustains us and enables us to walk through life with a consciously loving and ever open heart, elevating us to a state of joy unparalleled by material acquisitions, accomplishments, or relationships. Everything in the material world changes and passes away, so it cannot be the final truth. That which is *eternal* is, and love is eternal. Therefore love is the ultimate reality, the most *real* experience we share as human beings.

~ 1423 ~

As I walked up to the door of the post office, I looked down and saw a white feather wafting across the sidewalk in front of me. I saw many other bird feathers nearby, so I gave it only a passing thought.

But then, upon returning to my car, I was startled to see a small white feather in an unlikely place – nestled next to my car door window just above the door handle. It was as if the spirits said, "Sending one feather across her path was too subtle. She didn't pay attention. Let's put one right in front of her where she can't miss it."

Now I'm paying attention.

~ 1424 ~

HEALTH, Part 20

It seems that my heart arrhythmia has gone away. For the last week my heartbeat has been strong and regular. I am no longer fatigued by normal bodily locomotion, and my muscle aches and pains that I thought were inevitable effects of aging are much reduced. I have also lost my excess appetite. I eat mostly from habit rather than hunger. What changed?

Perhaps I have finally healed from my three years of torture with Emily. It only took two and a half years.

~ 1425 ~

Today the Bible study group tackled the book of Judges, learning about the judges, prophets, warriors, and rulers – people like Othniel, Ehud, Shamgar, Deborah, Barak, and Jael – who populated the promised land of the Israelites after Moses freed them from slavery in Egypt.

There emerged in this history a recurring pattern: God would set down rules; the Israelites would break them; God would be upset and stir up the Canaanites to make war with the Israelites; then God would raise up a savior to defeat the enemy and bring peace to the land.

And then the Israelites would mess up again, and there would be another war and another great leader to vanquish the enemy, followed by another forty-year generation of peace.

This ever-repeating historical cycle brought home to me why Jesus was necessary. It was as if God had said:

> *This crime and punishment thing isn't working. I give them laws and the people break them. I set the Canaanites on them to make war but they don't learn anything from it; I just have to send in a strongman to end the war. They stay peaceful for a while, but then after a generation or two they go back to sinning again.*

> *I have to break this cycle. It seems that people who are not yet awakened to heavenly realms cannot bear the burden of the law; they are caught up in greed and fear and are unable to turn away from temptations of the flesh. Salvation by works is too hard for them. I will show them the Way to salvation by faith. I will make a new covenant with the people; those who choose to walk the Way will be freed from the law and sin. I will not judge them; I will not remember their sins; they will make war no more.*

> *I will incarnate myself and walk the earth with them, proclaiming this gospel. I will show the people by example how to live a sinless life, how to surrender their greed and fear to the power of divine love. The Way will not be easy. There will be ridicule and rejection, pain and sacrifice. But in this journey there awaits perfected eternal life, once again oneness with me in the Garden of Eden.*

Of course, this story is ridiculous. God – the Godhead, that is – never says anything.

~ 1426 ~

Interdependent co-arising can happen simultaneously and also sequentially. Life in space and time is a state of constant change, an inexorable cycle of rising and falling from one side of duality to the other. The Book of Judges in the Bible chronicles recurring sequences of good and evil leapfrogging over each other from one generation to the next in ancient Palestine. A look at modern history shows that after the pestilence of the Spanish flu and World War I came the prosperity of the Roaring Twenties, followed by a horrible era of economic collapse and an even more devastating World War II, followed by another period of relative calm and prosperity while the foundation for the next disastrous era was being laid.

It seems that each cycle of recurring tension goes to even greater extremes than the previous one, leading to massive societal collapse every few thousand years. History records the fall of the Roman Empire and the resulting Dark Ages as such a collapse. Current news reports are filled with stories about climate change, political corruption, socio-economic oppression, and environmental destruction on a global scale. Perhaps we are near the next great cataclysm.

The same cycle plays out in microcosm in each individual life. Each life cycle goes through periods of strife and hardship followed by relative comfort and peace, then returning to strife, and then again to peace. However, given the infinite layers of existence always in play, in both the microcosm and macrocosm, nothing is pure light or pure dark. As each large cycle plays out, there are glimmers of light in times of darkness and dark shadows in times of light.

~ 1427 ~

My friend Josie, whom I have been supporting financially from time to time, has suddenly become a loquacious e-correspondent. Her chronic illness is acting up and her spirit has begun to gravitate toward me. In her recent correspondence she wrote: "I have a ways to heal, yet have a wonderful healing team, amongst which is you; if you do not mind, I include you. *Just turning my attention toward you helps.*" I am wondering if the feather on my car might have been a harbinger of this new surge from Josie.

I am humbled that this lady, a highly elevated spirit herself, could be helped by just turning her attention toward me. She says, "I have been spending time in mental companionship with you." Others have told me that my spiritual power is magnetic, even though I feel wholly inadequate. I seem to scare the people I thought I was supposed to help. I will go slow with Josie and try not to scare her.

~ 1428 ~

The good is uncreated; it never could have been otherwise; it has no shadow of contingency; it lies, as Plato said, on the other side of existence. It is the *Gita* of the Hindus by which the gods themselves are divine, the *Dao* of the Chinese from which all realities proceed. But we, favoured beyond the wisest pagans, know what lies beyond existence, what admits no contingency, what lends divinity to all else, what is the ground of all existence, is not simply a law but also a begetting love, a love begotten, and the love which, being between these two, is also imminent in all those who are caught up to share the unity of their self-cause life. God is not merely good, but goodness; goodness is not merely divine, but God. – C.S. Lewis, *Christian Reflections* [39]

Lewis starts this passage in perfect accord with the unified thought of the sages of all ages and places. Then he careens off the path into an attitude of Christian superiority that distances him from the wisdom he is trying to impart. (John Wesley, alas, did the same thing.) But then, at the end, he returns to the essential truth: "God is not merely good, but goodness; goodness is not merely divine, but God." God is love – not merely loving, but love itself.

~ 1429 ~

Can I find a way to be grateful for pain, fear, and evil? It is relatively easy to forgive when bad things happen by accident and nobody gets hurt, like spilled milk. We understand how these events have a necessary place in the cosmos. But what about heinous acts that cause grievous harm, or the intractable pain of severe illness, or paralyzing fear such as gripped me after Lou died? Forgiveness and acceptance of such things is much harder. Gratitude for such suffering is hardly the first reaction that comes to mind, if it comes at all.

I know how to be grateful for the psychological torture that Emily and The Unnamed One inflicted on me, even though their unskilled behavior was often intentional and knowingly hurtful. I have learned their lessons and am grateful for them. Perhaps the same kind of gratitude can also apply to even more severe manifestations of darkness.

This is the highest gratitude, gratitude for the whole of life. But it is not me, the human being, who is grateful. It is my God-self thanking me, the human being, for my existence. Through me, through my consciousness, the invisible God gets to experience all the colors of the rainbow, to have a channel through which divine love can flow, and also to witness how everything fits together in eternity. This deep gratitude, known as appreciative Joy in Buddhism, describes the condition of Adam and Eve before the Fall, when they were separate from, yet one with, God.

I am God – coming apart, coming together, like an accordion, making music by coming apart and coming together.

~ 1430 ~

The Dalai Lama, in his new book, *Following in the Buddha's Footsteps*, has brought me renewed peace with my experience of tantric love:

> Tantric texts discuss certain behaviors that reflect a person's having overcome polarities and preconceptions regarding such things as cleanliness or beauty. The conduct of very advanced tantric practitioners may reflect this. It is often said that their behavior cannot be spoken of

in terms of precepts because their level of spiritual realization is beyond the preconceptions of inherent good and evil. We must properly understand what this means. Such people are no longer under the influence of ignorance and other afflictions; it is in that sense that they are beyond good and evil. It does not mean that they may transgress precepts at will, with no harmful results. Rather, because they have profound wisdom of ultimate reality, their minds are so thoroughly disciplined that the very purpose of precepts—to tame the unruly mind—has already been fulfilled. Having understood emptiness and dependent arising, they have great respect for ethical conduct. Although such practitioners may act unconventionally on occasion and outwardly appear to be acting contrary to precepts, no mental defilement is involved, and their actions do not harm others.[190]

This is exactly the state of being born again of the spirit that Jesus introduced to the Jews, and the state of sinlessness that Paul described in Romans, being no longer under the law (which, like the precepts, was intended to tame the unruly mind). When Jesus and his disciples healed and harvested on the sabbath, apparently "acting contrary to precepts" (Jewish law), they were not acting in defiance of the law, but from a place above the law, of "profound wisdom of ultimate reality:" "The sabbath was made for man, not man for the sabbath." (Mark 2:27 RSV)

I had always intuitively known that my experience with tantric love – spiritual love, divinely ordained, rule-breaking, erotic, oblivious to precepts, beyond good and evil, beyond the law and sin – was righteous. But my conditioning from earlier in life left me with a small lingering doubt, wondering if I could in fact be such a "very advanced tantric practitioner." The Dalai Lama has so precisely described my tantric experience that I no longer have any doubts. This realization is not prideful; it is incredibly humbling.

~ 1431 ~

Emily has been silent for over two months. She did not respond to my last two emails. Then today in the mail there was a package from her, a birthday gift, with a note:

Happy Birthday. Enjoy this little gift. Light and Joy.

Why? Is she trying to be caring and considerate, or feeling some kind of obligation? Or is she keeping me on the string in case she might again want something from me? I am grateful for her reappearance, but also distrustful. Joy in reawakened love, sorrow in renewed despair.

~ 1432 ~

In reading and re-reading the beginning of this journal, words I wrote thirty years ago, I am struck by how much I intuitively knew even then, before the concepts of duality and eternity had fully entered my consciousness. I often think that I am haplessly wandering through life, still mostly unconscious. The Buddha said to think of him as one who is awake. I think of myself as one who is still asleep but can hear the faint sound of an alarm clock going off!

Last week I strained my back and was almost immobile for about four days. That cleared up just in time for my right knee to go out. I am again slightly crippled, but I'll take knee pain over back pain any day. As these body parts break down, I just wait and let them have their way with me. They seem to clear up on their own – so far. I always remind myself, however, that my pains and ailments could return as quickly and suddenly as they left; everything neat turns messy and everything messy turns neat, and my body is not the real me.

~ 1433 ~

THE SUTRA OF THE GIRL MARVELOUS WISDOM

In the 6th century *Sutra of the Girl Marvelous Wisdom*, an eight-year-old girl's buddhahood is challenged in the belief that only males can become buddhas:

> Marvelous Wisdom does not believe her female body is a problem [to achieving Buddhahood] because her buddha-land will be one in which there is nothing called "woman." It is not, then, that her buddha-land does not have women, rather, her buddha-land does not have gender.
>
> And yet, despite making such an impassioned declaration regarding the genderlessness of her own forthcoming buddha-land, Marvelous Wisdom does indeed transform her female form and take on a male body. Why does she do it? The answer to this problem lies not in her body but in her audience.
>
> She changes her sex, then, not as a condition of her impending Buddhahood but as a means of teaching those in the assembly about the ultimately empty nature of physical forms. She changes her sex because, as a highly attained being, she can, but also because the act stands as a proof of the veracity of her claim to Buddhahood to an assembly that cannot escape their own limited perception, which sees a female body as lesser than a male one. – Stephanie Balkwill, "Becoming a Buddha: Lessons from Little Girls," *Buddhadharma*, Fall 2019

This Buddhist misogyny parallels so well the Christian scriptures of Peter and Paul concerning the subservience of wives to their husbands, reflecting the low status of women in the culture of their time and place. Yet, as in Buddhist history, there are many female Christian "buddhas" – Teresa of Avila, Hildegard of Bingen, Marguerite Porete, Hadewijch, Catherine of Siena, and of course, Mary Magdalen and Mary the mother of Jesus.

In the story of Mary and Martha (~1375~), Jesus defended Mary's desire to hear his teaching, saying, "Mary has chosen the good portion, which shall not be taken away from her." Jesus understood the spiritual equality of women and their rightful place in heaven just as the true mystics of all cultures do. It was necessary for Jesus to be born a male for the same reason that Marvelous Wisdom changed her female body to male, because in the misogynist society of 1st century Palestine, a savior in female form would have been disbelieved and dismissed just as the female form of Marvelous Wisdom was.

> Shimon Kefa said to them,
> Miryam should leave us.
> Females are not worthy of life.
> Yeshua said,
> Look, I shall guide her to make her male,
> so she too may become a living spirit resembling you males.
> For every female who makes herself male
> will enter the kingdom of heaven.
> (Gospel of Thomas 114)

Just as the Girl Marvelous Wisdom changed her anatomy to gain credibility in her androcentric society, so Jesus enabled women in his society to do so.

We traditionally depict Jesus in a male body, but outside of the worldly cultural context, gender is meaningless. Jesus was both masculine and feminine, and neither, genderless, like Marvelous Wisdom in her genderless buddha-land.

Carl Jung describes the ever-present feminine inside the male body:

> In Eastern symbolism the square—signifying the earth in China, the *padma* or lotus in India—has the character of the *yoni*: femininity. A man's unconscious is likewise feminine and is personified by the anima. The idea of the anima as I define it is by no means a novelty but an archetype which we meet in the most diverse places. It was also known in alchemy, as the following scholium proves: "As the shadow continually follows the body of one who walks in the sun, so our hermaphroditic Adam, though he appears in the form of a male, nevertheless always carries about with him Eve, or his wife, hidden in his body."[77]

All human fetuses start out as female. The genes that trigger the transformation of genitalia from female to male kick in around the seventh week of gestation.[xvii] Indeed, every man was once a woman, and she still lives hidden inside. Sometimes she comes out of hiding, in metaphor, as Eve emerged from Adam's rib, and Radha came out of Krishna.

Marcus J. Borg writes in *Meeting Jesus Again for the First Time*:

> In Jewish wisdom literature, wisdom is often personified in female form as "the Wisdom Woman." Consistent with this personification, wisdom is a feminine noun in both Hebrew (*hokmah*) and Greek (*sophia*). The use of Sophia language to speak about Jesus goes back to the earliest layers of the developing tradition. It is also, as we have seen, widespread across the tradition. According to the synoptics, Paul, and John, that which was present in Jesus was the Sophia of God. The multiplicity of images for speaking of Jesus' relationship to God (as *logos*, *Sophia*, Son—to name but a few) should make it clear that none of this is to be taken literally. They are metaphorical. This is important to understand in a tradition whose Christological and devotional language has been dominated by patriarchal imagery. It is useful to realize that the dominance of father/son imagery reflects the fact that Trinitarian thinking took shape in a patriarchal and androcentric culture.[68]

All of this demonstrates the ubiquitous power of the feminine, even in the androcentric cultures of both East and West. As the Jews, Greeks, and Christians used female imagery to depict Wisdom, in the trinity of Buddhism, the Buddha is flanked by Wisdom (Prajnaparamita) and Compassion (Avalokiteshvara), both of whom are often given female form.

> Be it woman, or be it man for whom
> Such chariot doth wait, by that same car
> Into nirvana's presence shall they come.
> – *Samyutta Nikaya Sutra*

~ 1434 ~

I attended a luncheon today honoring a friend's long life of service. A lady sitting at my table leaned over and said, "You look like a nun. You have the aura." I was startled, but pleased that my buddha-nature is visible to others.

Last month I attended a business workshop at a Catholic university. During a break a man came over to me and asked if I was a member of a religious order. What could I say? No ... but in a much deeper sense ... yes.

[xvii] https://www.ncbi.nlm.nih.gov/books/NBK222286/

I enlisted four of my trusted spiritual advisors to help me edit this book. None of them have responded in any significant way to my drafts, neither positively nor negatively. Their silence has led me to think that my mystical life story – my hero's journey, as Joseph Campbell calls it – is not meant to be edited. The complete and unabridged account of my journey stands as is, without critique or comment. So here it is – the life of Christ, the Word of God – exactly as I am called to transcribe it.

~ 1436 ~

THE BLIND LEADING THE BLIND

> "Let them [the Pharisees] alone; they are blind guides. And if a blind man leads a blind man, both will fall into a pit." (Matthew 15:14 RSV)

The Pharisees condemned Jesus because he challenged their literal interpretation of scripture under the Mosaic purity system of their 1st century culture,[68] which had caused them to think in worldly, not Godly, terms. Many modern Christian fundamentalists with their blinding literal interpretations have led their flocks into the same demonic pit.

Scripture is a chicken and egg thing. You can find God there, but you have to already know God to recognize him. A preacher/teacher cannot lead his flock to heaven if he is blind to it. The Buddha explained:

> They ask, "All these many brahmins preach different paths leading to union with Brahma. Do all these paths lead to the same place?"
>
> The Buddha responds with a question of his own: "Have any of these teachers seen Brahma face to face?"
>
> "No, they haven't," admits Vasettha.
>
> "Has their teacher or their teacher's teacher seen Brahma face to face?"
>
> Vasettha says no.
>
> "Well then," answers the Buddha, "all these brahmins are teaching a path they do not know or see. It is as if three blind men are leading one another."[188]

The Pharisees denounced Jesus for bringing sight to a blind man on the sabbath, questioning whether such healing could be from God. Some of the Pharisees said, "This man is not from God, for he does not keep the sabbath." (John 9:16 RSV) The man healed of his blindness said:

> "Never since the world began has it been heard that any one opened the eyes of a man born blind. If this man were not from God, he could do nothing." They answered him, "You were born in utter sin, and would you teach us?" And they cast him out. (John 9:32-34 RSV)

Jesus rebuked the Pharisees, pointing out that their narrow interpretation of scriptural law and their delusional claim of spiritual authority gave them a false sense of sight:

> Jesus said, "For judgment I came into this world, that those who do not see may see, and that those who see may become blind."

> Some of the Pharisees near him heard this, and they said to him, "Are we also blind?" Jesus said to them, "If you were blind, you would have no guilt; but now that you say, 'We see,' your guilt remains." (John 9:39-41 RSV)

To say that you see the light of God but speak and act contrary to that light is to remain guilty. The Roman soldiers who killed Jesus were guiltless because in their blindness they did not know what they were doing: "Father, forgive them, for they know not what they do." The Pharisees, on the other hand, were guilty because they knew what they were doing.

Misinterpretations of scripture or not interpreting at all, taking the words literally, can only lead to more profound ignorance. Such misreadings do not bring people closer to God; they create an even greater distance from him. They do not polish the mirror; they put more dust on it, adding limits and barriers to transcendence. The devil quotes scripture with the best of them, and as John Wesley said, is "convinced that every title of Holy Scripture is true." These sincere but blind and misguided preachers are devils in angels' clothing.

> The most important thing I say to people who come to my classes is: please don't attach to my words, to my thoughts. There are two kinds of thief. There's the mind thief and there's the object thief. Please watch out for the mind thief – spiritual leaders, teachers, and all that. Don't be scared by the material thieves, they only take material things. But the mind thieves, they can steal the whole of your life. People tell me that I am a Buddhist leader but I tell them, don't be attached to this idea, don't even trust my words. Just practice and then you'll see what I'm talking about. – Danette Choi [195]

Danette Choi's view is like that of Krishnamurti, who dissolved his Order of the Star in 1929 and said, "I do not want followers, and I mean this. The moment you follow someone, you cease to follow Truth. I am not concerned whether you pay attention to what I say or not."

I fear that most preachers and religious teachers are mind thieves.

~ 1437 ~

Yesterday I met with a group that practices mindfulness meditation. I got into a conversation with a psychologist who disputed my claim that mindfulness, while useful in most cases, doesn't work in states of acute panic when the brain fills with white noise and nothing can penetrate the pain. I soon realized that we were talking apples and oranges; the psychologist didn't understand how the kind of panic I was talking about differed from the kind he was used to seeing in his clinical practice, such as agoraphobic panic attacks.

While agoraphobia is more serious than the usual background stress that most people have, it still falls into a category that I call chronic anxiety – an ongoing fear that sometimes erupts into an acute phase that is the overt panic attack. This kind of panic is a response to sensory stimuli and can be reversed by removing the stimuli; e.g., by the agoraphobic going home, or the claustrophobic moving to an open space. And indeed, as the psychologist suggested, mindfulness can be helpful in reducing the level of panic while in the panic-inducing environment.

The kind of panic that is resistant to mindfulness is deeper, more spiritual, and extrasensory; a kind of existential anguish that is truly hell. It resists every effort of the mind to control it. It is akin to the feeling that C.S. Lewis described as "a sudden jab of red-hot memory" that makes all commonsense vanish "like an ant in the mouth of a furnace."

I associate this kind of anxiety most often with the experience of death. People like C.S. Lewis (and me) discover it when a deep spiritual love is lost. Others when they themselves are facing critical illness or death. When this anxiety is repressed, it can manifest as other forms of panic (e.g., claustrophobia) or mental disorder (e.g., depression). But the unique etiology of these manifestations must be recognized if a real cure is to be found – a cure that lies along a different path than the therapeutic or pharmacological route that is usually taken.

The last day of the life of Christ is a perfect depiction of both kinds of panic. When Jesus prayed his prayer of primal fear in Gethsemane, asking God to spare him the suffering he knew was coming, he experienced the normal human anxiety that comes with foreboding, a kind of anxiety that most people experience in the course of life. This kind of anxiety responds to mindfulness, as it did for Jesus when he finally said, "Thy will be done," and it carried him through the trials and tribulations up to his crucifixion.

But then, hanging on the cross, a different kind of panic arose – literally all hell broke loose. He said, "My God, my God, why hast thou forsaken me?" He experienced true hell – defined as separation from God – the ultimate negative polarity of dualism where the tether to anything at all seems to be broken. Nobody was better at mindfulness than Jesus, but it was no help to him at that moment. Mindfulness cannot succeed in this situation – must not succeed – if surrender, annihilation of the ego, and awakening are to happen. Jesus, and all of us, must descend to hell (separation from God) before we can ascend to heaven (oneness with God). This is not unlike the Buddha needing to experience both extremes of hedonism and asceticism before his awakening could happen.

This doesn't mean that mindfulness can't return, as it did for Jesus when he said, "It is finished." I'm just saying that we shouldn't try to short-circuit the journey to hell and back. Let the panic rage. It must be felt, acknowledged, responded to, and learned from before we let it go. Otherwise we are repressing or denying it, taking the third poison, using mindfulness to divert us from the pain rather than to find peace within it.

Anthony de Mello said that people go to the doctor for relief, not a cure. Most people try mindfulness meditation in search of relief from their pain – physical, emotional, or psychic. Mindfulness can work for this purpose, just as hypnosis, valium, heroin, psychic readings, acupuncture, prayer, and other kinds of meditation can. Mindfulness used for relief, like some religious practices, provides a distraction from that which bothers us, but this is only allopathic medicine, treating the symptoms, providing relief but not a cure.

The hellish pain that I have described cannot be relieved. There is no relief in hell, but there can be liberation – a cure. If mindfulness meditation is used to facilitate awakening, to disarm the ego and surrender absolutely everything, including life itself, to God, it can be a tool to get out of hell once the value of the hellish experience has been received. Mindfulness used in this way is a form of true religion – "re-ligare," to link back – enabling consciousness of eternal unity while still in the world of duality. But this return to mindfulness can and should only happen after the initial experience of hell is allowed to come and go without relief. Otherwise, the effect is only delusion, not awakening.

> Our sadness, our loneliness, our fear, and our anxiety are not mistakes. They are not obstacles to our path. They are the path. The freedom we long for is not found in the eradication of these but rather in the information they carry. – Jody Hojin Kimmel, "Feeling Our Way to Awakening," *Buddhadharma* Winter 2020

~ 1438 ~

Render therefore to Caesar the things that are Caesar's, and to God the things that are God's.
(Mark 12:17, Matthew 22:21, Luke 20:25 RSV)

The conversation that elicited this comment by Jesus was about paying taxes, symbolized by a coin with Caesar's image on it. This verse is often used to validate the separation of church and state. We are created in the image of God; we have God's image stamped on us, not Caesar's. Worldly governments are of no concern to the eternal God.

However, Gandhi said, "Those who say spirituality has nothing to do with politics do not know what spirituality really means." This is also true. Politics and spirituality intersect in duality as a quest for social justice. Most of those who practice civil disobedience, many of whom are religious leaders, many of whom are martyred for the cause, are called to do so as bodhisattvas, reflecting and expressing their highest buddha-natures/God-selves.

But we must remember that good and evil, justice and injustice, must coexist in duality. C.S. Lewis gives us a pragmatic explanation of how things can go wrong at the political-spiritual nexus:

> Theocracy is the worst of all governments. If we must have a tyrant, a robber baron is far better than an inquisitor. The baron's cruelty may sometimes sleep, his cupidity at some point be sated; and since he dimly knows he is doing wrong, he may possibly repent. But the inquisitor who mistakes his own cruelty and lust of power and fear for the voice of Heaven will torment us infinitely because he torments us with the approval of his own conscience, and his better impulses appear to him as temptations. And since Theocracy is the worst, the nearer any government approaches to Theocracy the worse it will be. – C.S. Lewis, *On Stories* [13]

Esther Hicks/Abraham says that all politics is outside the vortex. To find God we must be in the vortex. Render to Caesar what is Caesar's from our position in duality, then find the vortex where we can give our eternal God-selves to God.

~ 1439 ~

HOW ARE SPIRITUAL MESSAGES TRANSMITTED?

DOCTRINAL – *in the mind*: studying sutras, scripture, and commentaries, often in a seminary, monastery, or under a master teacher/guru. This is usually the first and sometimes the only way that people come to know God and the cosmic mystery. Sometimes insight can come through such study, especially in metaphorical messages like poetry and parables.

Because messaging via intellectual channels depends on words and thoughts, it is vulnerable to misinterpretation and misunderstanding — ever-present dangers when verbal language is involved. Because authors and translators necessarily must intercede between the message and its recipient, doctrinal transmission is at best indirect and imprecise.

EXPERIENTIAL – *in the body*: physical space-time events that are natural phenomena, perceived by the senses, operating within the laws of nature, for example:

Rain, rainbows, wind, earthquakes, eruptions

Animal and human messengers (birds, turtles, gurus, shamans)

Symbolic objects, sounds, and images (a song, picture, feather, stone, number, amulet, rune)

A book falling open to a particular page

Hearing your name or "your song" while walking through the mall

Sitting next to an unexpectedly significant person on a bus or airplane

These kinds of phenomena derive their meaning from synchronicity — the appearance of a powerful prophetic or symbolic object or event at the exact moment you need it. In this way, seemingly ordinary objects and events become miracles. Nothing is an accident or coincidence; timing is everything. C.S. Lewis describes this phenomenon:

> *TO VERA GEBBERT, 23 March 1953*: Now as to your other story, about Isaiah 66? It doesn't really matter whether the Bible was open at that page through a miracle or through some (unobserved) natural cause. We think it matters because we tend to call the second alternative 'chance.' But when you come to think of it, there can be no such thing as chance from God's point of view. Since He is omniscient His acts have no consequences which He has not foreseen and taken into account and intended. Suppose it was the draught from the window that blew your Bible open at Isaiah 66. Well, that current of air was linked up with the whole history of weather from the beginning of the world and you may be quite sure that the result it had for you at that moment (like all its other results) was intended and allowed for in the act of creation. 'Not one sparrow,' you know the rest (Matthew 10:29). So of course the message was addressed to you. To suggest that your eye fell on it without this intention, is to suggest that you could take Him by surprise. Fiddle-de-dee! This is not Predestination: your will is perfectly free: but all physical events are adapted to fit in as God sees best with the free actions He knows we are going to do. – C.S. Lewis, from *The Collected Letters of C.S. Lewis, Volume III* [87]

The plaque on my wall that says, "Faith is not belief without proof, but trust without reservations" came to me out of the blue, serendipitously appearing in an unsolicited mail order catalog. I had never gotten such a catalog before, and despite my purchase of the plaque, no more such catalogs ever came after that.

SPIRITUAL – *in the soul*: metaphysical, supernatural phenomena, operating beyond the laws of nature.

Epiphanies, visions, voices, and trances are examples of supernatural messaging. Because these experiences are beyond nature, there is no way to adequately describe them using language or other space-time modes of communication. They cannot be explained by the natural laws of biology, chemistry, or physics. They tend to be personal and private, not witnessed simultaneously by others as natural phenomena often are.

Such spiritual communication enters into and emanates from us through trans-dimensional portals like the chakras:

1st chakra – instinct, pre-consciousness: This is the pure innocence of the natural world, still one with God in the Garden of Eden, sinless, acting in accord with innate nature.

2nd chakra – head knowledge: mental, messaging via the mind, such as artistic (Bach) or scientific (Einstein) imagination and creativity.

3rd chakra – gut knowledge: clairsentience, intuition.[xviii]

4th chakra – heart knowledge: where divine love arises.

5th chakra – aural and tactile: clairaudience, hearing voices, incoming messages at the back of the 5th chakra, outgoing through the front, from the mouth (speaking in tongues).

6th chakra – visual: the third eye, clairvoyance, visions (Bernadette of Lourdes).

7th chakra – epic and lucid dreams, trances, epiphanies (Teresa of Avila).

Joseph Campbell described how lower and higher chakras – sensory and extrasensory perception, respectively – reinforce each other and work together. (~643~) When the 4th chakra of divine love opens, the energy of the 1st chakra rises to the 7th, the 2nd to the 6th, and the 3rd to the 5th. The sinless innocence of the 1st chakra in duality becomes the sinless innocence of unity with God in eternity. The creativity of the 2nd chakra becomes infused with divine imagination

---

[xviii] The masculine is linear and rational, the feminine global and intuitive. Intuition is the essence, the fruit of dharma itself, which nourishes and liberates through quantum shifts of intuitive insight. This is why the *Heart Sutra*, the supreme text of direct, intuitive awakening, points beneath cognition, beyond both attainment and knowledge. This is not the knowing of the clinical observer, where all is "out there." Instead, it is this immediacy of direct experience that inducts us into the greater mystery, where all phenomena are miraculous appearance. – Thanissara, "Reclaiming the Sacred Feminine," *Buddhadharma*, Fall 2019

and inspiration. The power of the 3rd chakra becomes the omnipotence of surrender to truth. What starts as mundane worldly work becomes God's work. Physical life awakens to eternal life.

~ 1440 ~

Rosanne Cash: Where's the line between self-love and self-indulgence?

Sharon Salzberg: At one point, this fabulous writer, Susan Griffin, said something to me that was really amazing: "You have to stop thinking of yourself as the person writing this book and think of yourself as the first person who gets to read it." – "Loving Your Inner Critic," *Lion's Roar*, September 2019

This so captures the essence of my experience with this book – reading it, not writing it. Many times I have found comfort reading the words I wrote decades earlier, marveling at the wisdom that came not from me, but through me, before I had any idea I was writing a book. This God-given wisdom precludes any self-indulgence and at the same time promotes self-love – love of the indwelling God-self, the true author of this book.

~ 1441 ~

In the film *Jesus Christ Superstar*, a scene depicts Jesus being swarmed by throngs of lepers reaching out to him and begging for help:

CROWD
See my eyes, I can hardly see.
See me stand, I can hardly walk.
I believe you can make me whole.
See my tongue, I can hardly talk.

See my skin, I'm a mass of blood.
See my legs, I can hardly stand.
I believe you can make me well.
See my purse, I'm a poor, poor man.

Will you touch, will you mend me Christ?
Won't you touch, will you heal me Christ?
Will you kiss, you can cure me Christ?
Won't you kiss, won't you pay me Christ?

JESUS
There's too many of you … Don't push me.
There's too little of me … Don't crowd me.
LEAVE ME ALONE!

Sometimes I feel like that, overwhelmed by the enormity of pain, struggle, and sorrow around me. I am a bodhisattva hearing the world's cries, wanting to help, but knowing that in the big picture I am helpless. Evil cannot be ended in this world, only dodged, circumvented, or finessed somehow. All I can do is slice the world's pain into small manageable pieces, stay in the moment, and stand by for instructions.

> When I consider how my light is spent,
>   Ere half my days, in this dark world and wide,
>   And that one Talent which is death to hide
>   Lodged with me useless, though my Soul more bent
> To serve therewith my Maker, and present
>   My true account, lest he returning chide;
>   "Doth God exact day-labour, light denied?"
>   I fondly ask. But patience, to prevent
> That murmur, soon replies, "God doth not need
>   Either man's work or his own gifts; who best
>   Bear his mild yoke, they serve him best. His state
> Is Kingly. Thousands at his bidding speed
>   And post o'er Land and Ocean without rest:
>   They also serve who only stand and wait."
>   – John Milton, "Sonnet 19"

~ 1442 ~

APOLOGY AND FORGIVENESS, Part 11

The topic for the theology discussion group today was sin, evil, and forgiveness. I couldn't help but bring up my understanding of Romans 7:7-8, that when we rise above the law, there is no sin and thus nothing to forgive. These dear friends, sincere seekers of truth and wisdom, could not grasp this idea. I wonder how I can engage these people in such discussion without causing more confusion than I dispel.

In contemplating how I might reach these good people, I am beginning to see the process that leads to understanding the eternal sinless condition. I see four stages, which roughly correspond to the different kinds of forgiveness in the Jewish tradition (~1244~):

1. In the beginning, we respond reflexively to sin and evil with anger and a desire for revenge, retaliation, punishment – an eye for an eye. There is no recognition of a relationship between the perpetrator and the victim, no basis from which forgiveness might arise. This is a lower chakra response arising from the second poison of fear.

2. At some point, we learn socially acceptable behavior and stop acting out our anger. We no longer inflict physical or emotional violence on those who hurt us, but underneath we are still seething, harboring resentment and frustration. We neither forgive nor forget. But in holding back our blind rage, we move from a crude desire for retaliation to a more nuanced desire for justice. This is somewhat like *mechilah* in the Jewish tradition.

3. When the 4th chakra opens, we see that sin and evil are more complicated than we thought. We recognize the pain sinners feel that leads to their sinful behavior (sometimes our own sinful behavior). We gain sympathy, even empathy. We learn to love our neighbors as ourselves. We learn to forgive. Like the Jewish *selichah*.

4. When we awaken the higher spiritual chakras, we see our own participation in the causation of hurtful or sinful acts around us. We see how dark clouds can have silver linings. We see that all things come from God and are eternally right: "In everything God works for good." (Romans 8:28 RSV) The past is forgotten: "I will remember their sins and their misdeeds no more." (Jeremiah 31:34, Hebrews 10:18 RSV) Divine love washes over all good and evil, all vice and virtue, and all are cleansed. No use crying over spilled milk. No forgiveness necessary. Like *kapparah*.

~ 1443 ~

I have given up on the Buddha. That is to say, I have given up on the Enlightened One, the Blessed One, the omniscient Lord of people and gods who works miracles, knows unknowable things, and continues to exert his power from beyond. When I ask Buddhists to explain why I should accept their revered sage as a modern-day life-adviser, I am typically offered only articles of faith (claims to be believed in or rejected) and rarely good (that is, examinable and testable) reasons.

But along the way, something unexpected happened. I met one of the world's most gifted teachers. He is Gautama, the human figure behind the fanciful facade of the Buddha. Like the Stoics, Epicureans, and Platonists in ancient Greece and Rome, Gautama instructed in the manner of a philosopher, a lover of wisdom. He taught and modeled a viable way to human flourishing, and did so rooted firmly in everyday life. – Glenn Wallis, "Gautama vs. the Buddha"[189]

I like the way the author dismisses the exalted, sacred image of the Buddha and prefers to learn from everyday man Gautama. I think Christians could learn from this. It is the human Jesus – not the worshipped, exalted, divine Christ – who teaches, wanders the byways of Palestine, and shows us the Way to salvation by dying on the cross. Like Gautama, the human Jesus is the real teacher. Not Christ the Divine, the omniscient Lord and Master, but Jesus the man, rooted firmly in everyday life. Jesus is not to be worshipped; he is to be followed.

~ 1444 ~

PASTOR: *Every week when I preach, I grieve more about what I DON'T say than what I DO say.*

BETTY: Why don't you just say it? Let it out and you won't grieve anymore. Just tell the truth as it is revealed to you. There is a price to be paid for truth-telling, to be sure, but it is the price of God's grace, well worth paying. Jump in the heretic pool with me – the water's fine!

I worry more about how my words might drown out the greater truth already on the lips of those who are listening.

It is quite the opposite – your words inspire the greater truth to come forth in the hearts and to the lips of the congregation, as they have many times for me. All who hold pieces of the truth – you, me, Caroline Myss, C.S. Lewis, and many of the folks around us every day – are sacred messengers of the God who puts words in our mouths as he did in Jeremiah's. The truth – greater or lesser – cannot be drowned out.

I fret about the inadequacy of words to communicate the vastness of love, and am learning to let go of the anxious suspicion that I might be full of shit.

You may be full of shit – but it's Holy Shit!! Seriously … wisdom is in your words. After all, God put the words in your mouth, right? Words are indeed inadequate, but they are all we have (along with hugs). Don't worry, I'll tell you when shit happens (but it won't).

I can only hope the Holy Spirit will help. What I DO know is the words I express with certainty today will need to be rounded up and herded over a cliff someday because God will reveal something new, something deeper, something brighter than I could know today.

The something new, deeper, and brighter is always *additive* to the wisdom and truth we already know. Nothing need be thrown over a cliff. With new insight we just understand more clearly the truth we have always known and, even if haltingly, expressed. This is the huge lesson I am learning by writing a book encompassing so many years of spiritual seeking. When I go back and read things I wrote decades ago, I am stunned by how much truth I intuitively knew before the deep meaning of it had entered my consciousness – before I knew I knew what I knew.

Perhaps this is why so many pastors end up in therapy.

Pastors, psychologists, social workers, and anyone who feels responsible for the bodies, minds, and souls of other people. I have had my own bouts of self-doubt and fear that my spiritual authority is as potentially harmful as it is helpful. In session with my intuitive friend Martha, this exchange took place:

> *"More and more, people will look to you for guidance and advice," she said. "Someday you will hear that someone's life was forever changed by something you said."*
>
> *"But this is frightening," I replied, "What if I say the wrong thing and ruin someone's life?"*
>
> *"Not possible," she replied. "If you feel compelled to say something, that means it is coming from God, the Source, and needs to be said, even if it is something the other person doesn't want to hear."*

Perhaps the main reason that pastors end up in therapy is the cognitive dissonance they feel when the words they speak, in keeping with the liturgy of the Church, conflict with what they really believe, often in light of new understandings and even divine revelation. They discover a clear distinction between the teachings of Jesus and the teachings of the Church. The way out of therapy is to let go of the dogmas and doctrines of the Church and simply speak the truth as it is revealed. Of course, doing so may invoke the wrath of the Church, as Jesus, Marguerite Porete, Anthony de Mello, Joseph Campbell, and many other ancient and modern mystics found out. But hey, that's pretty good company to keep!

Many years ago, I saw a film on TV about a priest who lost his faith. He couldn't pray the Lord's Prayer because the words stuck in his throat. He was in deep despair and searched for a way back to God. At the end of film, he tried to say the prayer again, but he still choked on the words. I, too, choke on the Lord's Prayer, not because I have lost my faith, but because I have found it – trusting in a God above the one addressed in the Prayer.

~ 1445 ~

This was my response to the Lord's Prayer in church this morning:

Our father who art in heaven
And everywhere

Hallowed be thy name.
A rose by any other name would smell as sweet.

Thy kingdom come
Already here

Thy will be done
Doing it

On earth as it is in heaven.
Same place.

Give us this day our daily bread
Got it, thanks

And forgive us our sins
Nothing to forgive

As we forgive those who sin against us.
Nothing to forgive.

Lead us not into temptation
Too late (been there, done that)

But deliver us from evil.
Delivered.

The words and images of the Lord's Prayer come from a cultural perspective rooted in dualism. The need for this worldly approach is the same as in this Buddhist view of building merit:

In some Buddhist teachings it's said that you should accumulate merit so you'll have a better rebirth. Isn't that rather selfish? Yes it is, and that's okay. You could say that in Buddhism the definition of skillful means is "whatever works." In other words, the teachings have to meet people where they are. For example, someone who isn't ready for the truth of emptiness is taught that karma is real, even though ultimately, it's not. The same is true for our motivations. If people live morally and with loving-kindness in hopes of a better rebirth, that can only benefit themselves and others, no matter what happens after they die. Later they may develop a more selfless or sophisticated motivation, but that's what works for them now. – "Beginner's Mind," *Lion's Roar*, January 2020

I hear the Lord's Prayer from the cusp of duality/eternity, understanding that most people are not there yet. Jesus had to use concepts and language understandable to people who are at the beginning of their spiritual journey, still firmly planted in duality. Jesus, like the prophets before and after him, had to do "whatever works."

~ 1446 ~

GRACE THROUGH FAITH, OR WORKS? OR BOTH?

Faith alone:

> We ourselves, who are Jews by birth and not Gentile sinners, yet who know that a man is not justified [reckoned righteous] by works of the law but through faith in Jesus Christ, even we have believed in Christ Jesus, in order to be justified by faith in Christ, and not by works of the law, because by works of the law shall no one be justified. For I through the law died to the law, that I might live to God. I have been crucified with Christ; it is no longer I who live, but Christ who lives in me; and the life I now live in the flesh I live by faith in the Son of God, who loved me and gave himself for me. I do not nullify the grace of God; for if justification [righteousness] were through the law, then Christ died to no purpose. (Galatians 2:15-21 RSV)

Faith with works:

> But someone will say, "You have faith and I have works." Show me your faith apart from your works, and I by my works will show you my faith. You believe that God is one; you do well. Even the demons believe—and shudder. Do you want to be shown, you shallow man, that faith apart from works is barren? Was not Abraham our father justified by works, when he offered his son Isaac upon the altar? You see that faith was active along with his works, and faith was completed by works, and the scripture was fulfilled which says, "Abraham believed God, and it was reckoned to him as righteousness;" and he was called the friend of God. You see that a man is justified by works and not by faith alone. For as the body apart from the spirit is dead, so faith apart from works is dead. (James 2:18-26 RSV)

Paul and James are talking about two different kinds of works. There is a crucial difference between works under the law (ego-driven, to build merit, intended to *cause* grace/enlightenment)

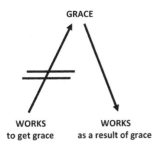

GRACE

WORKS
to get grace

WORKS
as a result of grace

and works above the law (God-driven, to serve others, the *effect* of grace/enlightenment).

Works as described by Paul in Galatians are prescribed by the law and are motivated by a desire for God's grace. Works as described by James are acts of selfless service and sacrifice, done without pride or ego, as prescribed by God, not to build merit or get salvation. These works are evidence of true faith, arising spontaneously and unconsciously motivated by "Christ who lives in me." Only cheap grace and false faith come without works.

This is not to denigrate works under the law; they have an essential place in the journey toward grace and enlightenment. As I quoted earlier from Buddhist teaching, "If people live morally and with loving-kindness in hopes of a better rebirth, that can only benefit themselves and others, no matter what happens after they die. Later they may develop a more selfless or sophisticated motivation, but that's what works for them now." Thus, there is no harm in intentional good works for altruistic, albeit selfish, purposes. But they won't get you through the narrow gate.

Works under the law, in and of themselves, cannot bring grace, but like study and contemplation, they can put one into a state of alignment with and receptivity to spirit that paves the way to grace. When the gift of grace is bestowed on the faithful servant, a more selfless or sophisticated motivation arises and transforms good works into God's works.

Steps Along the Way from Good Works to God's Works

On the temporal plane:

1. *Recognition of duality*

   Awareness of karma
   "Whatever a man sows, that he will also reap." (Galatians 6:7)

2. *Attempts to get on the good side of duality*

   Building merit
   Works under the law (to gain favor with God, as in Galatians 2:15-21)

On the eternal plane:

3. *Recognition of the equality of opposites and the impossibility of eliminating evil*

   Walking the Middle Way

Loving your enemies, turning the other cheek
Works above the law (in selfless service, as in James 2:18-26)

4. *Awakening to the Godhead where opposites disappear*

No karma, no building merit: "Bodhisattvas do not accumulate merit."
All works arise spontaneously; none are judged as good or evil: no try, no law, no sin

Shinran, the founder of Shin "Pure Land" Buddhism, said that lack of faith, lack of reliance on Other-Power (the Godhead), drives us to keep striving, to persist in trying to make ourselves worthy through discipline and good works. This desperate effort just digs us deeper into our spiritual predicament since it is rooted in ego-clinging. This describes works under the law as in Galatians 2:15-21.

But both Shinran and Dogen, founder of the Soto Zen school, were convinced that enlightenment is already and always achieved, and thus spiritual practice, prayer, and good works are an upwelling within oneself of Other-Power. These practices do not lead toward awakening but express it; they are not to earn our liberation but to enact it. This describes good works as a result of grace, as in James 2:18-26.

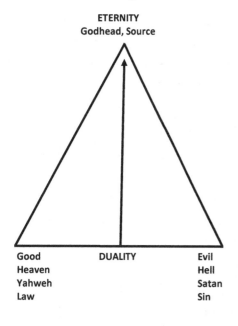

This triangle shows that being on the "good" side of duality gets you no closer to eternity than being on the "evil" side. Some might say that the triangle should be adjusted to raise the good side closer to eternity. But no; both good and evil are contained in duality and must co-arise equally. The path to eternity – the Middle Way between the pairs of opposites – is revealed when, through the power of divine love, we realize that good and evil, rising and falling together, are both manifestations of God and must be accepted as such. As one moves toward eternity along the Middle Way, the distance between the extremes of duality is shortened; both good and evil are reduced in amplitude until they finally disappear in the eternal singularity.

At this point it is possible to fully understand and spontaneously follow Jesus' instructions: "But I say to you, do not resist one who is evil. But if any one strikes you on the right cheek, turn to him the other also." (Matthew 5:39 RSV); and "You have heard that it was said, 'You shall love your neighbor and hate your enemy.' But I say to you, love your enemies and pray for those who persecute you, so that you may be sons of your Father who is in heaven; for he makes his sun rise on the evil and on the good, and sends rain on the just and on the unjust." (Matthew 5:43-45 RSV)

I do not seek out opportunities to do God's work; they come to me. My life of service as a truth-teller is again coming to the fore. There are interpersonal challenges throughout my sphere, people struggling with poverty, illness, self-doubt, anger, all kinds of frustration, and they are taking it out on each other (and sometimes me). My truth is stirring up dust in some quarters and settling it down in others. I am alternately a rabblerouser and peacemaker, depending on the situation. I do it all with love, knowing that often it will be necessary for me to turn the other cheek.

Esther Hicks/Abraham's definition of "service" is "the influence of Source resonating with you. Stay in resonance with who you really are." Shakespeare said, "To thine own self be true." Just by being who I am, resonant with Source, not by doing anything in particular, I am living a life of service. Lao-tzu said, "The Dao, by doing nothing, leaves nothing undone." John Milton said, "They also serve who only stand and wait." Anthony de Mello said, "My business is to do my thing, to dance my dance. If you profit from it, fine; if you don't, too bad!"

One of the new musicians in my group took me to lunch yesterday, wanting to pick my brain, learn about the group's history and get direction for the future. "I wanted to talk with you," she said, "because you just have an aura about you." When I get mired in day-to-day worldly concerns, observations like hers remind me that my life is not of this world.

~ 1447 ~

HEALTH, Part 21

My heart arrhythmia is back with a vengeance. My pulse is very slow and refuses to speed up in response to exercise. Now just the mild exertion of walking the aisles at the grocery store is too much. Walking up one flight of stairs makes me stop to catch my breath. No pain, just weakness and exhaustion. I also have a new ache in my hip and another one in my neck. The upside of all this is that I hardly notice my sore knee anymore.

I am an empath. I take on the suffering of others. Whose heartache am I feeling now? Or is it my own, the first harbinger of blessed death? Now that this book is almost done, perhaps my march to the scaffold has begun. That's okay with me.

As Jesus was hanging on the cross, a priest mocked him, saying, "He saved others, he cannot save himself." (Mark 15:31 RSV) C.S. Lewis said, "Others can do for us what we cannot do for ourselves, and one can paddle every canoe except one's own." Jesus could have saved himself (in the worldly sense) if his ego had been in charge. He could have avoided his fate had he not spoken truth to power, not challenged the Pharisees, and not accepted the sacred duty to which he was called. But in so loving his life, he would have lost it (in the eternal sense): "For whoever would save his life will lose it; and whoever loses his life for my sake and the gospel's will save it." (Mark 8:35 RSV) Jesus surrendered his ego to God, his body to the Romans, lost his life, and saved it.

I can save others, but I cannot save myself. My life and health are in God's hands. I am a bodhisattva taking upon myself the pain of others, as God commands. I treat my body respectfully as the temple of my soul, but I know that there is no treatment for any of my ailments, no diet or exercise or lifestyle that will make any difference in my health. I hesitate to seek treatment for my heart condition because maybe God wants me to slow down and is limiting my heart function to be sure I do. When God wants me to speed up again, my heart will jump back into action. I surrendered control of my body and soul to God, and I will be either healed or killed as God commands.

The heart – the heart chakra – is the entry and exit point of divine love in the physical body. It is the seat of the God-self, the buddha-nature, the place from which the Buddha touches the earth. When I no longer have need or use for my body, my heart will just stop and I will be absorbed back into the earth. To borrow a metaphor from C.S. Lewis, the weary river of my life will have made its way safely to sea.

UPDATE, a month later: For no apparent reason, my arrhythmia is much improved. Not gone, but I am again energetic and fully functional. I guess God is not quite done with me and is holding me in a little backwater on my weary river's journey to the sea.

~ 1448 ~

Have this mind among yourselves, which is yours in Christ Jesus, who, though he was in the form of God, did not count equality with God a thing to be grasped, but emptied himself, taking the form of a servant, being born in the likeness of men. And being found in human form he humbled himself and became obedient unto death, even death on a cross. (Philippians 2:5-8 RSV)

In a YouTube video[xix] with Esther Hicks/Abraham, she said, "I'm so free, I can choose bondage."

[xix] https://www.youtube.com/watch?v=XOLaiBwve68&feature=youtu.be

This really hit home for me. I remembered a line from one of the Jesus movies, when Jesus goes to visit John the Baptist in Herod's prison: "I go to free him *in his cell*." Even in bondage, the awakened soul remains free.

All my friends wanted me to get away from Emily, not understanding why I stuck with her for so long, tolerating her abuse. Most people thought my love was just the typical lovesick clinging that is the opposite of freedom. But no – I freely chose bondage with her, not in dependency, but in service, staying in the fire with her – and in the vortex – for our mutual spiritual benefit. Only when the flames got so hot that my love could no longer reach her and my own body was being consumed did I pull away.

A few days ago, Emily sent me an email out of the blue (not just the usual response to mine, sent out of polite reciprocal obligation) asking if I was okay and wanting to know if I needed anything. A slender thread still connects us.

~ 1449 ~

A dream last night:

Scene 1 – An old man with a white beard is telling me strange things. He has some metal objects, like embossing stamps or branding irons, with odd symbolic patterns. He says, "I will not hurt you," but I am suspicious, a little fearful, and move away from him.

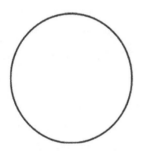 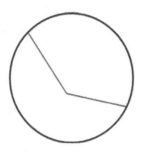 

Scene 2 – The man is asleep. I quietly move toward him, pick up one of the metal objects, and run away.

Scene 3 – I am in an auditorium with a big crowd of people. Suddenly the old man appears on the stage carrying the three metal objects and three pieces of paper. He sends one of the papers to me and says in a kind, gentle voice, "This one's for you." The paper has the image of the empty circle embossed on it, with an image of the man's face in the corner. He sent the other papers to others in the auditorium. I woke up as he was telling us what the symbols mean.

From dreammoods.com:

Man – To see an old man in your dream represents wisdom or forgiveness. The old man may be an archetypal figure who is offering guidance or insight.

Auditorium – To dream that you are in an auditorium indicates that there is something that you need to learn from others. Pay attention to those around you.

Circle – To see a circle in your dream symbolizes perfection, completeness, immortality and/or wholeness. To see circles within circles in your dream indicate that you are well protected or that you are being overly guarded. You may need to let down your defenses.

A circle is the Buddhist calligraphic symbol for enlightenment. Zero, a closed circle without beginning or end, is the number for God. My esoteric message at the Buddhist temple today was *"… continue the teaching."* My dream reminds me that I need to learn from the old man and carry forth his wisdom. The scene in the auditorium was my mystical graduation ceremony.

~ 1450 ~

HEALTH, Part 22

DROWNING

I went snorkeling in the ocean, as I had done so many times before. I puttered around the reef for a while, then started back to shore. I took off my mask and prepared to walk up onto the beach.

The next thing I knew, I was lying face down in the water, breathing water. I dragged myself up to the shore, gasped for air, and called for help. The last thing I remember is two lifeguards pulling me up the beach, urging me to continue coughing up the water in my lungs.

TO THE EDGE AND BACK AGAIN

Then my consciousness moved to a higher plane. From a distance I saw an ambulance, lights flashing, next to the lifeguard station, but I have no memory of being inside the ambulance. Then I saw two of my friends talking to someone in a hospital bed. I was looking down from above, objectively observing the scene but not in it.

Then in a sudden psychic shift, in a split second, as if waking from a dream, I entered the scene and realized that I was the person they were talking to … the person in the bed is ME!!! The transition from one perspective to the other was quick, instantaneous, like changing channels on the TV. The dispassionate detachment that characterized my visions of the ambulance and the conversational scene in the hospital morphed into a horribly passionate reality.

Neale Donald Walsch wrote in *Conversations with God*, "At the moment of your death, you will not see yourself as letting go of life, but simply enjoying it at a higher level." My soul left my body for the time between the beach and my revival in the hospital, while fate (From All Thoughts Everywhere) determined whether I should continue enjoying life at a higher level or go back to the world. Dozens of people played a role in my drama, onstage and backstage, determining my fate as I jumped from one realm to another on the razor's edge.

My friends later told me that the question had been put to me whether I wanted to continue life-saving treatment or pull the plug. I chose life. At that point my soul, my consciousness, returned to my body. My mission on earth was not yet complete. A bodhisattva must always return.

THE ULTIMATE EMPATH

I have often wondered about my generally excellent health, wondering if it is possible for me to understand the physical suffering of others without having experienced the same level of suffering myself. Many years ago I wrote, "As I watched the cross of Christ being carried through the sanctuary, I wondered if my paralyzing terror after losing Lou and my existential anguish after finding you will not be enough suffering in this life to satisfy God's demands. I sensed that my bodhisattva duty, like Christ's, may require of me a final crushing sacrifice." (~279~)

Was this it? The tube in my throat made it impossible for me to speak or make any sound at all. My hands and feet were strapped down so I couldn't move. I was helpless, immobile, and I couldn't do anything about it, not even cry out. Once my initial panic began to subside, I knew that I had no choice but to surrender to the forces around me and find peace in the midst of the storm. This wasn't exactly crucifixion, but it served the same spiritual purpose.

MEDICINE

So often I have resisted what I call "medical interference" (~1165~), wanting my life to ebb and flow as nature, not medical science, directs. I tend to ignore small symptoms of disease, and I ignored the progressively more serious symptoms of my heart arrhythmia, expecting that my heart would just stop when the time was right. (~1105~/~1419~/~1447~)

But the time wasn't quite right. The fact that I fainted in the water right in front of the lifeguard station and regained consciousness just in time to crawl out of the water on my own were signs that I was supposed to be rescued, not to die. The time was right for my education in physical suffering, but not yet for death. Sometimes "medical interference" is meant to be. This isn't the first time that God had to smack me upside the head to get my attention, but it was certainly the most dramatic.

One might think, in view of this experience, that I would now be more concerned about my health and want more ongoing medical attention. But no. Nothing has changed. I still have no fear of death — in fact, I welcome it as much as ever. I still trust my body to be in control of itself and know how and when to shut down. The spirits will tell me when it is time to die, as they told me that this was not the time, and I will not resist. My life has been full of synchronicities directed by spiritual forces, and the end of my life will be no different.

LESSONS

Ever since the long-lingering respiratory ailment I suffered after Lou's death, I have dreaded anything that makes breathing difficult. Thus, my greatest bodily fear has been drowning. Yet, when I regained consciousness in the water, feeling water going in and out of my lungs, it felt almost good. Not unpleasant at all. Because I was unconscious when I started breathing water, there was no panic, no choking reflex, nothing in my body or mind to resist the flow of water instead of air into my lungs. My mind let go, my bronchi relaxed and surrendered control. In yet another miraculous serendipity, I became one with the water. I no longer fear drowning.

The Six Dharmas of Naropa, from Vajrayana (Tantric) Buddhism, describe practices meant to awaken a most subtle consciousness (see the Dalai Lama's description: ~1408~) that remains unchanging in our ever-changing world, through all states of mind, from waking to dreaming, sleeping, and dying. During my ordeal, especially in my out-of-body experience, I felt my most subtle consciousness moving through all four states, in and out of the bardo.

I trust the karma. Nothing is an accident, and everything in the end is right. Life is an illusion and dissolves into the dust from which it came. In this world everything changes, and nothing can be grasped. We all participate in some way in causing everything that happens to us, and there is always a lesson to be learned. Patience, acceptance, tolerance, forgiveness, surrender. Whatever happens, all is well.

On my first morning home from the hospital, I was awakened by the sound of a dove cooing outside my window, as if to welcome me back to life in the world. During my hospital stay I heard no birds, saw no trees, felt no warmth of the sun. I now see more clearly the illusion of life in space and time, but also the preciousness of every moment, not knowing which moment will be my last.

The steadfast care I received during this ordeal, from friends and complete strangers, revealed the depth of love that flows among us. All the people in my sphere are treasures. Not because of what they do for me, but because of the essence of who they are, each one a unique aspect of God. Divine love connects us all.

UPDATE: I now have a pacemaker that regulates my heart's electrical system and should prevent future fainting and dizzy spells. I am fully recovered. But I am not the same person who entered the water that fateful day. I am the ghost of Betty, her avatar. I am living on borrowed time, and the Door of Death is now open wide for me.

FURTHER UPDATE: Four months after this incident, I visited my Buddhist spirit guide, wanting to know more about the meaning of my near-death experience. He said that gratitude was indicated – for my rescue and for lessons learned – and that an ancestor was involved, a female. The day of the accident was my mother's 100th birthday. My mother died of heart disease; perhaps we celebrated her centennial by making sure my heart condition was taken care of. Thanks, Mom.

~ 1451 ~

Jesus said, "You always have the poor with you." We can try to end poverty, but we will fail. It is the same with curing disease or ending warfare. We may succeed occasionally, for a little while, but in the end, death is inevitable. Resistance is futile. (see "Lazy Self-Defense:" ~995~) We may relieve a little suffering in one place, but it rises up again somewhere else.

Rather than fight against evil, Jesus said, "Resist not evil." Turn the other cheek. Find peace in bondage, even choose it, and willingly serve from that place of darkness. Jesus taught us how to do it.

Lao-tzu said, "Because the sage always confronts difficulties, he never experiences them." Don't swim against the current or try to change it. Just go with it, knowing that everything is as it is meant to be. Confront your fear, face it, and it goes away. The movie *Jesus Christ Superstar* expressed this so succinctly: "To conquer death, you only have to die." That's why I no longer fear drowning.

~ 1452 ~

THINKING AND THE MIND, Part 10

> Once we've transcended the delusion of existence, the next step on the Madhyamaka path is to return to the middle. In fact, Madhyamaka means "Middle Way." From the perspective of the Madhyamaka, both existence and nonexistence are extreme positions; the absolute truth is beyond any extreme, beyond any view of existence or nonexistence. While the absolute truth refutes existence, it also goes beyond nothingness, beyond nonexistence. At this stage, we experience the absolute truth, free from concepts of existence or nonexistence. There is nothing to hold on to, not even a real or correct view.
>
> The Prasangika school asserts the inseparability of the two truths and cautions against drawing too sharp a distinction between them. They are of one nature right from the beginning. When you see relative truth, its nature is absolute truth. Nothing separates the two. We can't find any instance of relative truth, no matter how solid and real it seems, that exists separate from or outside of the absolute truth. To the extent that we see a form, hear a sound, or experience a thought as being vividly clear and real, to that same degree we can also experience them as empty. – Dzogchen Ponlop Rinpoche, "Through the Lens of Madhyamaka"[191]

This is wonderful stuff, but contemplating ideas like this makes my brain hurt. It is like the hurt that comes from sensory overstimulation or overexertion. The mind, like the body, sometimes needs to sit down and take a load off. There is a place where I understand, where I "know," but that's not the place where my brain is.

There are still thoughts that keep coming up and turning my brain to mush: Why is there anything at all? What is behind and beyond nothingness? Who made God? What is the substrate upon which eternity rests?

> Attention, in the Buddha's vocabulary, is a matter of what questions you focus on trying to answer. Inappropriate attention focuses on questions like, "Is the world eternal? Is it not? Who am I? Do I exist? Do I not?" These questions trap you in what the Buddha calls a "thicket of views." To insist on answering them is like being shot with an arrow and refusing to get it removed until you've found out who shot it and how it was made. You'd die. – Thanissaro Bhikkhu, "Things You Need for Your Journey"[192]

My mind is trapped in a thicket of views. The mountains are, after all, only mountains, and the waters, only waters.

~ 1453 ~

Meanwhile, where is God? This is one of the most disquieting symptoms. When you are happy, so happy that you have no sense of needing Him, so happy that you are tempted to feel His claims upon you as an interruption, if you remember yourself and turn to Him with gratitude and praise, you will be—or so it feels—welcomed with open arms. But go to Him when your need is desperate, when all other help is vain, and what do you find? A door slammed in your face, and a sound of bolting and double bolting on the inside. After that, silence. You may as well turn away. The longer you wait, the more emphatic the silence will become. There are no lights in the windows. It might be an empty house. Was it ever inhabited? It seemed so once. And that seeming was as strong as this. What can this mean? Why is He so present a commander in our time of prosperity and so very absent a help in time of trouble?

I tried to put some of these thoughts to C. this afternoon. He reminded me that the same thing seems to have happened to Christ: 'Why hast thou forsaken me?' I know. Does that make it easier to understand?

Not that I am (I think) in much danger of ceasing to believe in God. The real danger is of coming to believe such dreadful things about Him. The conclusion I dread is not 'So there's no God after all,' but 'So this is what God's really like. Deceive yourself no longer.' – C.S. Lewis, *A Grief Observed* [3]

My sense of abandonment by God is the heart of this journal. Lewis felt abandoned when Joy died, as I did when Lou died, as Jesus did when he was dying. But the effect of abandonment is not learning dreadful things about God, although both dreadful and wonderful things are indeed aspects of God's worldly manifestation. We must know abandonment in the darkness of hell before we can know oneness with God in the light of heaven.

Release from our separation anxiety comes when we realize that there is no separate God outside ourselves to either support us or abandon us. This is an illusion of time, space, thought, and emotion. In both good times and bad, our view of God is what the reactionary response of our body-mind shows us. God is always with us, inside us. There is no bolted door, no empty house, except for the Great Void, the Emptiness in which we and God are always found.

~ 1454 ~

That time of year thou mayst in me behold,
When yellow leaves, or none, or few, do hang
Upon those boughs which shake against the cold,
Bare ruined choirs, where late the sweet birds sang;
In me thou seest the twilight of such day

As after sunset fadeth in the west,
Which by and by black night doth take away,
Death's second self that seals up all in rest;
In me thou seest the glowing of such fire
That on the ashes of his youth doth lie,
As the deathbed whereon it must expire,
Consum'd with that which it was nourish'd by;
This thou perceiv'st, which makes thy love more strong,
To love that well, which thou must leave ere long.
  – William Shakespeare, "Sonnet 73"

I have often said it is my curse, that I love too well. Shakespeare explains in this sonnet what I mean by that. Love and loss – knowing that everything one loves must be lost – "makes thy love more strong." What I have learned in the years since Lou and all my other loves is that the strongest love, divine love, is never really lost. The yellow leaves, the setting sun, the ashes of youth, and the expiring fire will all rise again in the fullness of time, their spirits continuing uninterrupted in the endless eternal continuum.

In the realm of divine love, I have discovered that I have not loved too well, but rather, I have loved just right, completely, in eternal perfection. Divine love is both a curse and a blessing, and neither. It is God, the Dao, the Emptiness, the Source, the Force. It is all there is.

Epilogue

Death is not extinguishing the light, but putting out
the lamp because the dawn has come.

– Rabindranath Tagore

By the time you read this, I will probably be dead. Did I win the final battle with Mara? Did I reach *anuttara samyak sambodhi*? Did I make it through the narrow gate? Does it matter? Regardless, somehow I had to finish this book, leaving the final questions unanswered.

But yet, all questions are already answered in the place where there are no questions and no need for answers. Knowing that past is present is future, I can rest assured that the dawn has come.

Afterword

Don't be dismayed at good-byes.
A farewell is necessary before you can meet again.
And meeting again, after moments or lifetimes,
is certain for those who are friends.

Richard Bach writes in *Illusions* [47] that we are all illusions. Only love is real.

There is no end to this book.
It, too, is an illusion
to be continued and continued and continued
in the timeless eternity
that is the reality of divine love.

Gentle reader, we are friends, and will meet again.

The End

(as we think of endings in this world)

First in the Series:

Volume One
The First Awakenings

Volume Two
Soul of Darkness

Volume Three
Love Is God Is Love

Volume Four
The Mystic Milieu

Next in the Series:

Cast of Characters

Each of the five volumes of *Love and Loss* can stand alone, but for those who read later volumes without having read the earlier volumes, it may be helpful to know the roles played by the recurring characters introduced early on:

Lou – my husband and first karmic love

The Unnamed One – my second karmic love

Emily – my third karmic love

Jean & Joan – the twins who reawakened my ability to love

Archie – a brief but meaningful love object

James – my rude office colleague who taught me to see through bad behavior

Ignacio & Cecilia – my Christian angels

Kathy – my niece who hears me in her dreams but is afraid to listen

John – Lou's favorite brother

Elaine – John's wife and my Buddhist angel

Natalie – John's and Elaine's daughter

Joe – a business associate and my atheist angel

June & Marilyn – a lovely gay couple who understood my pain

Vincent, Arthur, & Danny – Emily's on-again, off-again lovers

Martha & Rita – my intuitive angels

Hugh & Josie – my shamanic angels

Patrick – my best friend in the band

Acknowledgments

One of the great virtues I have discovered in my life's journey is gratitude. I am grateful for all the joy and all the sorrow, and especially for all those who helped me learn and grow through the joys and sorrows. There are so many over the decades who gave me encouragement, comfort, understanding, and support, whose tender care kept me from falling off a cliff of despair. Some of these people go back thousands of years, others are alive and with me now. I cannot thank my contemporaries by name or the anonymity of this book would be destroyed. But you know who you are! Thank you all so much. A few of these angels are characters in the book; you do not know their true names, but you know their true souls.

Of course, at the top of the gratitude list are the heroes of this book, my karmic loves, to whom I literally owe my life in the spirit. Fanning out from them, I also thank their families, ancestors, and descendants to and from whom our eternal love will always flow. Speaking of ancestors and descendants, I humbly thank my parents, who raised me well, kept every door of opportunity open, and prepared my heart and mind to welcome the wisdom of every place and every age. And I thank my siblings and their children, who had the temerity to challenge my beliefs and make me think about the difference between what is true and what I *think* is true, testing the mettle of my ideas in the fire of their skepticism.

This story includes many different religious and philosophical perspectives. I pay homage to the many branches of the Judeo-Christian tradition, as well as the Eastern traditions of Buddhism, Hinduism, and Daoism; the Greco-Roman gods and goddesses; several ancient indigenous religions; and various world philosophies with little or no religious basis. My spiritual growth would not have been possible without major input from luminaries in all the arts and sciences. I am therefore especially indebted to the writers of the Bible, the Hindu, Daoist, and Buddhist scriptures, and the work of, among many others: William Shakespeare, Albert Einstein, Dave Brubeck, Pang-yun, John Wesley, Deepak Chopra, Joseph Campbell, John Milton, Jacobo Timerman, Felix Mendelssohn, Robert Olson, Martin Luther King, Jr., Carol Burnett (and her fabulous comedic cast), Kahlil Gibran, Anthony de Mello, Plato, Henrietta Lacks, St. Francis of Assisi, Sandi Patti, Martin Heidegger, Dietrich Bonhoeffer, Marianne Williamson, T. S. Eliot, Lao-tzu, David Oistrakh, C. S. Lewis, Socrates, Wayne Dyer, Thomas Hardy, the Dalai Lama, Jorge Luis Borges, Brené Brown, Vince Gill, Carl Jung, St. Augustine, Thich Nhat Hanh, Alan Watts, J. S. Bach, Doreen Virtue, Alexander Pope … and on and on and on … and the myriad artists, scientists, authors, philosophers, and other great souls of every age who influenced them.

I must give a special nod to the filmmakers. Like most people of my generation, I came of age watching movies, and I marched faithfully in step with my contemporaries as the movies moved from theaters to television to videocassette to DVD to the Internet. A great film is a work of art, like great literature, stage plays, and opera, with which they often share common themes and subject matter. I owe the screenwriters, actors, directors, producers, designers, cinematographers, composers, musicians, and all the creative people who make movies a debt of gratitude for putting deep spiritual messages into sounds and pictures – dramas, musicals, and documentaries – that can reach into the hearts of the masses. I will name the movies that I can remember contributing to my spiritual growth, but I know there are many more that escape my recollection: *Song of Bernadette, Star Wars (all episodes), It's A Wonderful Life, Gandhi, Guess Who's Coming To Dinner, Flight, The Buddha, Sophie's Choice, The Last Samurai, Mary and Tim, Einstein's Universe, The Heart Is A Lonely Hunter, Judgment At Nuremberg, Avatar, Romeo and Juliet, West Side Story (R&J modernized and musicalized), Invasion of the Body Snatchers, Julia, The Shawshank Redemption, Titanic, WarGames, Inherit The Wind,* and the Jesus flicks: *Greatest Story Ever Told, Jesus of Nazareth, Jesus Christ Superstar, King of Kings, Ben-Hur.*

Everyone who has passed through my life, in person or through writings, art, music, or historic legacy, has added a piece to my spiritual puzzle. Some pieces are larger than others, but each piece is essential to completing the puzzle. The final piece I must add myself.

Virtually all of my thoughts and opinions in this book were developed with inspiration from the great work of others, as reflected in the references below. I do not claim to be a Bible scholar, Zen master, psychologist, or an expert in history, literature, art, science, or humanities. I am a layperson relating what inspiring works of art, science, religion and philosophy say to me, amplified by my own experience and revelation. No religious or scholarly authority has formally endorsed my interpretations. However, like the infinitely connected jewels in Indra's Net, all ideas are connected to all others. I claim no originality in any of the thoughts herein; as Goethe said, "Everything has been thought of before; the task is to think of it again."

As is the case with most diaries, in this journal I am talking to myself. In that private environment of my own heart and mind, there were no holds barred, no subjects off limits, no level of intimacy too deep. Under normal circumstances the deeply personal thoughts, feelings, ideas, analyses, and speculations herein would only be shared with the most intimate confidants, if at all. I am sharing this journal now because the miraculously abnormal circumstances of my life demand it. So my final acknowledgment goes to the Source, however you know it, and to you, the readers of this book, who have all become my most intimate confidants and who are yourselves miraculous manifestations of the Source.

A Word About Sex

I thought long and hard about how much sexually explicit material to include in this book. I knew I had to include some; the evolution of my sexuality, as concerns the crossing from spirit to flesh and back again, is central to my story. In such stories, the sexual questions are the ones usually left unanswered, in deference to modesty, privacy, and propriety, yet are the ones on everyone's mind:

What is the role of sex in divine love? When does "having sex" become "making love"? How does a widow for whom joy in sex has ended find satisfaction with a man whom she has never even seen naked? And with a woman thousands of miles away? How does the eternal creative union of Shiva and Shakti play out in real life – and in real-life body chemistry? How do the urges of the body, the thoughts of the mind, and the wisdom of the spirit each play a role in the act of sex, and in the larger sense, of creation? What is tantric love? How does love in the spirit feel in the body?

I knew I had to answer these questions, so I left most of the sexy stuff in, taking a chance that more readers would be grateful and enlightened than offended or titillated.

A Word About Money

The proceeds I receive from the sale of this book after the cost of its production will be donated to nonprofit organizations doing work that is consonant with my spiritual direction. I offer my personal life experiences seeking to enrich the lives of others, not to enrich my own. I have enough money.

Betty Hibod
2020

References & Citations

1. Paulo Coelho, *Manuscript Found in Accra*, trans. Margaret Jull Costa. (Vintage Books/Random House, New York 2013).

2. Joseph Campbell, *Transformations of Myth Through Time*. (Harper & Row, New York 1990).

3. C.S. Lewis, *A Grief Observed*. © 1961 by C.S. Lewis Pte. Ltd. (Bantam/Seabury Press, New York 1963).

4. St. Augustine, *Confessions*, trans. R.S. Pine-Coffin. (Penguin Books, Harmondsworth, England 1961).

5. Jacobo Timerman, *Prisoner without a Name, Cell without a Number*, trans. Toby Talbot. (University of Wisconsin Press, Madison 1930).

6. Joseph Campbell, *The Power of Myth*, transcript of the PBS documentary hosted by Bill Moyers. (Apostrophe S Productions, Inc., New York 1988). Used by permission.

7. Alan Watts, *The Way Of Zen*. Excerpt(s) from WAY OF ZEN by Alan Watts, copyright © 1957 by Penguin Random House LLC, copyright renewed 1985 by Mary Jane Watts. Used by permission of Pantheon Books, an imprint of the Knopf Doubleday Publishing Group, a division of Penguin Random House LLC. All rights reserved.

8. *www.dreammoods.com*. © 2000-2014 Dream Moods, Inc. All rights reserved.

9. Robert Olson, *An Introduction To Existentialism*. (Dover Publications, Inc., New York 1962).

10. Kahlil Gibran, *The Prophet*. (Alfred A Knopf, New York 1923).

11. *wikipedia.com*. Descriptions of the ten bhūmi used in this book are from the Avatamsaka Sutra, as illuminated in commentaries at wikipedia.org: http://en.wikipedia.org/wiki/Ten_bhūmis.

12. Abhaya, http://www.freebuddhistaudio.com/search.php?q=kshanti&r=10&o=ya&b=p&l= en&at= audio&lang=en.

13. C.S. Lewis, *On Stories: And Other Essays on Literature*. © 1982, 1966 by C.S. Lewis Pte. Ltd. All rights reserved.

14. Anita Moorjani, *Dying To Be Me.* (Hay House, Carlsbad CA 2012).

15. C.S. Lewis, *God in the Dock.* © 1970 by C.S. Lewis Pte. Ltd. All rights reserved.

16. Paraphrased from *Traveling the Path of Compassion: A Commentary on the Thirty-Seven Practices of a Bodhisattva* by His Holiness the Seventeenth Karmapa (KTD 2009), translated by Ringu Tulku Rinpoche and Michele Martin. (*from the January 2010 issue of Shambhala Sun*).

17. The Enneagram Institute, www.enneagraminstitute.com. Copyright 2014, The Enneagram Institute. All Rights Reserved. Used with permission.

18. Martin Heidegger, *An Introduction to Metaphysics*, trans. Ralph Manheim. (Yale University Press, New Haven 1959).

19. Cyndi Dale, *The Complete Book of Chakra Healing.* (Llewellyn Publications, Woodbury MN 1996, 2009).

20. Rebecca Skloot, *The Immortal Life of Henrietta Lacks.* (Crown Books 2010).

21. Hsuan Hua, *The Chan Handbook.* (http://psychology.wikia.com/wiki/Dhy%C4%81na_in_Buddhism)

22. http://www.africa.upenn.edu/Articles_Gen/Letter_Birmingham.html.

23. Neale Donald Walsch, *The Complete Conversations with God.* (Putnam/Penguin Group, New York 2005).

24. Viktor Frankl, *Man's Search for Meaning*, Part One, "Experiences in a Concentration Camp." (Pocket Books, pp. 56–57. via *Wikipedia*).

25. Thich Nhat Hanh, *The Thich Nhat Hanh Collection* ("Peace Is Every Step," "Teachings On Love," "The Stone Boy" and other stories), trans. Mobi Warren and Annabel Laity. (One Spirit, New York 2004).

26. Deepak Chopra, *How To Know God.* (Harmony Books/Random House, New York 2000).

27. C.S. Lewis, *Miracles: A Preliminary Study.* © 1947, 1960, 1996 by C.S. Lewis Pte. Ltd. All rights reserved.

28. Joseph Campbell, *The Inner Reaches of Outer Space.* (Novato, CA; New World Library 2002, pp. 39, 41, 43, 86-87, 92, 93-94, 101-102, 103). Quotations from *The Inner Reaches of Outer Space* by Joseph Campbell, copyright © 2002; reprinted by permission of Joseph Campbell Foundation (www.jcf.org).

29. Abbot George Burke, *Dharma for Awakening* (http://www.ocoy.org/dharma-for-christians). Used by permission.

30. https://en.wikipedia.org/wiki/Jiddu_Krishnamurti.

31. Marianne Williamson, *Enchanted Love*. (Touchstone/Simon & Schuster, New York 1999).

32. Tim Flannery, "Only Human: The Evolution of a flawed species." (*Harper's Magazine*, December 2014).

33. Thich Nhat Hanh, *Living Buddha, Living Christ*. (Riverhead Books, New York 1995).

34. Doreen Virtue, *Angel Numbers 101*. (Hay House, Carlsbad CA 2008).

35. Doreen Virtue, "Hermetic Philosophy and the Seven Hermetic Principles." (https://www.youtube.com/watch?v=8t3AkVvFuqk); and *The Kybalion*. (The Yogi Publication Society, Chicago 1912, 1940).

36. Chögyam Trungpa, *Transcending Madness*. (Shambhala Publications, Boston 1992).

37. Marsha Linehan, http://www.nytimes.com/2011/06/23/health/23lives.html?sq=linehan&st= cse& scp=1&pagewanted=all.

38. Cognitive Behavior Therapy: http://psychology.about.com/od/psychotherapy/a/cbt.htm.

39. C.S. Lewis, *Christian Reflections*. © 1967, 1980 by C.S. Lewis Pte. Ltd. All rights reserved.

40. Joseph Campbell, *A Hero's Journey: Joseph Campbell on His Life and Work*. (New World Library, Novato CA 1990, pp. 101, 107-108). Quotation from *The Hero's Journey* by Joseph Campbell, © 2003, reprinted by permission of the Joseph Campbell Foundation (www.jcf.org).

41. Marianne Williamson, https://www.youtube.com/watch?v=4-ZLkxlV1O8.

42. Thich Nhat Hanh, *Going Home: Jesus And Buddha As Brothers*. (Riverhead Books, New York 1999).

43. https://en.wikipedia.org/wiki/Tantra; and http://www.scribd.com/doc/166511911/The-Songs-of-Radha-from-the-Gita-Govinda-erotic-poetry#scribd.

44. Anthony de Mello, *Awareness*. (Center for Spiritual Exchange, New York 1990).

45. https://myfattyjourney.wordpress.com/2010/08/18/paulo-coelho/.

46. Paulo Coelho, *The Alchemist,* trans. Alan R. Clarke. (HarperCollins, New York 1993).

47. Richard Bach, *Illusions: The Adventures of a Reluctant Messiah.* (Dell/Random House, Inc., New York 1977).

48. Julien Green, *God's Fool: The Life and Times of Francis of Assisi,* trans. Peter Heinegg. (HarperCollins, New York 1985).

49. Shari Y. Manning PhD, *Loving Someone with Borderline Personality Disorder.* (The Guilford Press, New York 2011).

50. Doreen Virtue, from the Angel Intuitive Workshop, September 26-28, 2014.

51. Dietrich Bonhoeffer, *The Cost of Discipleship,* p. 84, 86 (1949), trans. Barbara Green and Reihhard Krauss. (2001).

52. https://en.wikipedia.org/wiki/Metatron.

53. Dietrich Bonhoeffer, *Letters & Papers From Prison.* (Touchstone/Simon & Schuster, New York [1953, 1967, 1971] 1997).

54. F.C. Happold, *Mysticism.* (Penguin Books, Harmondsworth, England 1963, 1970).

55. Marianne Williamson, "Reparations for Slavery: The Role of Repentance in Politics," an address at Harvard Divinity School, February 19, 2019.

56. C.S. Lewis, *The Problem of Pain.* © 1940, 1996 by C.S. Lewis Pte. Ltd. All rights reserved.

57. Dr. Henry Cloud and Dr. John Townsend, *Beyond Boundaries.* © 2014 Zondervan; all rights reserved. via Bible Gateway, https://www.biblegateway.com.

58. Anthony de Mello, "A Rediscovery of Life." (https://www.youtube.com/watch?v=8b8TLQh4Q84, https://vimeo.com/9718009).

59. Miguel Serrano, *C.G. Jung & Hermann Hesse: A Record of Two Friendships,* trans. Frank MacShane. (Shocken Books, New York 1966).

60. David Ray Griffin, ed., *Deep Religious Pluralism.* (Westminster John Knox Press, Louisville, KY 2005).

61. Joseph Campbell, *Thou Art That.* (New World Library, Novato CA 2001, pg. 13, 29-30, 82, 99) © Joseph Campbell Foundation (jcf.org) 2001. Used with permission.

62. John Wesley Sermons, "On Divine Providence." (http://www.umcmission.org/Find-Resources/John-Wesley-Sermons/Sermon-67-On-Divine-Providence#sthash.xGIJNxd5.dpuf). "On Faith." (http://www.umcmission.org/Find-Resources/John-Wesley-Sermons/Sermon-106-On-Faith#sthash.ffTUN2RE.dpuf).

63. A. H. Maslow, "A Theory of Human Motivation." (1943) Originally Published in *Psychological Review*, 50, 370-396 (http://psychclassics.yorku.ca/Maslow/motivation.htm).

64. McLeod, S. A. (2014) "Maslow's Hierarchy of Needs." (www.simplypsychology.org/maslow.html).

65. http://hinduism.about.com/od/scripturesepics/a/lovelgends_4.htm.

66. http://mohitinhere.blogspot.com/2005/08/mysterious-radha-and-her-last-meeting.html.

67. Madhuri Guin, http://www.dollsofindia.com/library/radhakrishna/.

68. Marcus J. Borg, *Meeting Jesus Again for the First Time.* (HarperOne/HarperCollins, New York 1995).

69. Anthony de Mello, https://www.goodreads.com/author/quotes/54195.Anthony_de_Mello

70. Anthony de Mello, http://lazarus.trinityjanesville.org/demello.htm.

71. Anthony de Mello, http://www.demellospirituality.com/the-way-to-love-excerpts/.

72. Congregation for the Doctrine of the Faith, Joseph Card. Ratzinger, Prefect, "Notification Concerning the Writings of Fr. Anthony de Mello, SJ." (http://www.ewtn.com/library/CURIA/CDFDEMEL.HTM).

73. Diane K. Osbon, *A Joseph Campbell Companion.* (HarperCollins, New York 1991). *Reflections on the Art of Living, A Joseph Campbell Companion.* © Joseph Campbell Foundation (jcf.org) 1991. Used with permission.

74. John B. Cobb, Jr., "Whitehead and Mind-brain Relations: How Psychology and Physiology are Connected." (http://www.jesusjazzbuddhism.org/whitehead-and-mind-brain-relations.html).

75. Jay McDaniel, "A Process Appreciation of Islam: Interpreting Some Key Ideas in the Islamic

Tradition in a Process-Relational Way with help from Yusuf Islam." (http://www.jesusjazzbuddhism. org/beautiful-islam.html).

76. C.S. Lewis, *Mere Christianity.* © 1942,1943, 1944, 1952, 1980 by C.S. Lewis Pte. Ltd. All rights reserved.

77. C. G. Jung, *Dreams*, trans. R. F. C. Hull. (Princeton University Press, Princeton NJ 1974).

78. Tenzin Gyatso, His Holiness the XIV Dalai Lama, *Commentary on the Thirty Seven Practices of a Bodhisattva*, trans. Acharya Nyima Tsering. (Library of Tibetan Works and Archives, Dharamsala 1995).

79. C.S. Lewis, *Present Concerns: Journalistic Essays.* © 1986 by C.S. Lewis Pte. Ltd. All rights reserved.

80. Dr. Wayne W. Dyer, *Change Your Thoughts - Change Your Life.* (Hay House, Inc., P.O. Box 5100, Carlsbad, CA, 92018, 800-654-5126, www.DrWayneDyer.com).

81. *Shambhala Sun*, v. 24, n.3, January 2016. (Lion's Roar Foundation, 1790 30th St, Suite 280, Boulder CO 80301). All Rights Reserved.

82. Mahasi Sayadaw, "The Promise of Nibbana." http://www.lionsroar.com/the-promise-of-nibbana/.

83. Dr. Henry Cloud and Dr. John Townsend, "Boundaries in Marriage." The Boundaries devotions are drawn from the *Boundaries* book series, which has transformed marriages, families, organizations, and individuals around the world. The *Boundaries* series is written by Dr. Henry Cloud and Dr. John Townsend. Copyright 2015 by Zondervan; all rights reserved. Learn more at BoundariesBooks.com.

84. Dr. Wayne Dyer, *I Can See Clearly Now.* (Hay House, Inc., Carlsbad CA 2014).

85. C.S. Lewis, *The Collected Letters of C.S. Lewis, Volume II: Books, Broadcasts, and the War 1931-1949.* © 2004 by C.S. Lewis Pte. Ltd. All rights reserved.

86. C.S. Lewis, *The Weight of Glory: And Other Addresses.* © 1949, 1976, 1980 by C.S. Lewis Pte. Ltd. All rights reserved.

87. C.S. Lewis, *The Collected Letters of C.S. Lewis, Volume III: Narnia, Cambridge, and Joy 1950-1963.* © 2006 by C.S. Lewis Pte. Ltd. All rights reserved.

88. James B. Nelson, *Between Two Gardens: Reflections on Sexuality and Religious Experience.* (The Pilgrim Press, New York 1983).

89. Dr. Wayne Dyer, "Love Is What's Left Over When Falling in Love Falls Away," from *Being In Balance, Forever Wisdom of Wayne Dyer*. (Hay House, Inc., P.O. Box 5100, Carlsbad, CA, 92018, 800-654-5126, www.DrWayneDyer.com).

90. *The Rice Seedling Sutra*, trans. Dharinasagara Translation Group. (*Buddhadharma*, Spring 2020).

91. Ramana Maharshi, http://www.arunachalasamudra.org/teachings_ramanamaharshi.html.

92. https://en.wikipedia.org/wiki/Nisargadatta_Maharaj.

93. Thich Nhat Hanh, "After the Honeymoon." (https://www.lionsroar.com/after-the-honeymoon, excerpted from *Fidelity*, © 2011 by Unified Buddhist Church, with permission of Parallax Press).

94. https://metta.lionsroar.com/the-four-highest-emotions/?utm_source=Lion%27s+Roar+Newsletter&utm_campaign=575be88632-EMAIL_CAMPAIGN_2018_05_01&utm_medium=email&utm_term=0_1988ee44b2-575be88632-21477953&mc_cid=575be88632&mc_eid=84a461539f.

95. C.S. Lewis, *The Screwtape Letters*. © 1942, 1996 by C.S. Lewis Pte. Ltd. All rights reserved.

96. Mark W. Muesse, Ph.D., Lecture 14, "Practicing Mindfulness: An Introduction to Meditation." (The Great Courses, The Teaching Company, LLC, 2011).

97. M. Gerard Fromm, "What Does 'Borderline' Mean?" (*Psychoanalytic Psychology*, Vol. 12, No. 2, Spring. 1995, pp. 233-45), from an interview conducted by Joshua Wolf Shenk in 2009 (http://www.austenriggs.org/blog-post/borderline-personality-disorder).

98. *The Kybalion*. (The Yogi Publication Society, Chicago 1912, 1940).

99. C.S. Lewis, *Surprised by Joy: The Shape of My Early Life*. © 1955 by C.S. Lewis Pte. Ltd. All rights reserved.

100. Thich Nhat Hanh, "The Doors of Liberation." (*Lion's Roar*, August 30, 2016).

101. C.S. Lewis, *The Great Divorce*. © 1946, 1973 by C.S. Lewis Pte. Ltd. All rights reserved.

102. Gelek Rimpoche, "Enlightenment in Female Form." (*Buddhadharma*, Summer 2006, Fall 2017).

103. C.S. Lewis, *The Horse and His Boy*. © 1954, 1982 by C.S. Lewis Pte. Ltd. All rights reserved.

104. Alan Lightman, *Einstein's Dreams*. (Warner Books, Inc., New York 1993).

105. Melvin McLeod, "The Ultimate Happiness: An exclusive interview with the Dalai Lama." (*Lion's Roar*, July 29, 2016).

106. Marianne Williamson, *A Return to Love: Reflections on the Principles of A COURSE IN MIRACLES.* (HarperOne, New York 1992).

107. John Welwood, "Intimate Relationship as a Spiritual Crucible." This essay is adapted from a talk given at the California Institute of Integral Studies in San Francisco. Copyright 2008 by John Welwood. All rights reserved.

108. Barbara O'Brien, "Ksanti Paramita: Perfection of Patience." (http://buddhism.about.com/od/ Paramitas/a/Ksanti-Paramita.htm).

109. C.S. Lewis, *The Magician's Nephew.* © 1955, 1983 by C.S. Lewis Pte. Ltd. All rights reserved.

110. C.S. Lewis, *The Voyage of the Dawn Treader.* © 1952, 1980 by C.S. Lewis Pte. Ltd. All rights reserved.

111. Timber Hawkeye, "New Year... New Identity." (http://www.buddhistbootcamp.com/p/blog.html).

112. Hank Wesselman, *The Re-Enchantment.* (Sounds True, Boulder 2016).

113. http://rzim.org/global-blog/the-death-of-truth-and-a-postmortem/.

114. https://www.lionsroar.com/awakening-the-bodhisattva/.

115. Blanche Hartman, "Good Evening, Bodhisattvas." (https://www.lionsroar.com/good-evening-bodhisattvas/).

116. Melissa La Flamme, *What You Are For: Inciting A Revolution In Your Soul.* (http://www.amazon. com/dp/1478753250). © Melissa La Flamme.

117. (a) https://www.youtube.com/watch?v=2Xy222pgZ_o, "7 Sneaky Things Narcissists Say to Get You Back." (b) https://www.youtube.com/watch?v=SnybyozFE6E, "Can A Narcissist Be Healed?" (c) https:// www.youtube.com/watch?v=rLCPDYtlwYk, "Narcissistic Abuse: An Unspoken Reality." (d) https:// www.youtube.com/watch?v=3TY9XtOUUQA, "6 Strong Signs You Have Narcissistic Abuse Syndrome." (e) https://www.youtube.com/watch?v=kivnDbpLyxw, "Can A Narcissist Be Cured?" (f) https://www. youtube.com/watch?v=SnybyozFE6E, "Can A Narcissist Be Healed?" (g) https://www.youtube.com/ watch?v=ZSc54LWSNlA, "Things Narcissists Don't Want You to Know."

118. https://www.hayhouseworldsummit.com/lessons/dodging-energy-vampires-an-empaths-guide-to-freedom.

119. https://www.hayhouseworldsummit.com/lessons/getting-into-the-vortex.

120. https://www.lionsroar.com/sisyphus-the-bodhisattva/?utm_source=Lion%27s+Roar+Newsletter&utm_campaign=f551f1b8c5-Weekly-June-12-2017&utm_medium=email&utm_term=0_1988ee44b2-f551f1b8c5-21477953&mc_cid=f551f1b8c5&mc_eid=84a461539f.

121. https://www.lionsroar.com/what-is-your-body-july-2013/?utm_source=Lion%27s+Roar+Newsletter&utm_campaign=0fb60a7f46-WR-Jun-23-2017&utm_medium=email&utm_term=0_1988ee44b2-0fb60a7f46-21477953&goal=0_1988ee44b2-0fb60a7f46-21477953&mc_cid=0fb60a7f46&mc_eid=84a461539f.

122. https://www.lionsroar.com/how-would-a-buddhist-monk-solve-the-classic-trolley-problem/?goal=0_1988ee44b2-5540aeeccf-21477953&mc_cid=5540aeeccf&mc_eid=84a461539f.

123. https://www.goodreads.com/work/quotes/2361393-walden-or-life-in-the-woods?

124. https://www.lionsroar.com/beyond-present-past-and-future-is-the-fourth-moment/?utm_source=Lion%27s+Roar+Newsletter&utm_campaign=ab37130ad4-Weekly-July-11-2017&utm_medium=email&utm_term=0_1988ee44b2-ab37130ad4-21477953&goal=0_1988ee44b2-ab37130ad4-21477953&mc_cid=ab37130ad4&mc_eid=84a461539f.

125. C.S. Lewis, *The Four Loves.* © 1960 by C.S. Lewis Pte. Ltd. All rights reserved.

126. "Forum: What Is Enlightenment?" (https://www.lionsroar.com/what-is-enlightenment-2/?goal=0_1988ee44b2-2c02a1a4a4-21477953&mc_cid=2c02a1a4a4&mc_eid=84a461539f).

127. Debra Flics, "What Meditation Can't Cure." (*Buddhadharma*, Summer 2017).

128. Kaia Roman, "Is That Your Intuition Talking (Or Just Your Fear)?" http://www.thesacredscience.com/is-that-your-intuition-talking-or-just-your-fear/.

129. Rochelle I. Frank, PhD and Joan Davidson, PhD; *The Transdiagnostic Road Map to Case Formulation and Treatment Planning.* (New Harbinger Publications, Inc. 2014).

130. Caroline Myss, www.worldpsychicsummit.com ©2017 Hay House, Inc. ©2017 Caroline Myss.

131. Joan Sutherland, "What Is Enlightenment?" (*Buddhadharma*, Spring 2013, Fall 2017).

132. http://www.thesacredscience.com/a-modern-day-shaman-shares-her-wisdom/.

133. https://www.brainpickings.org/2017/09/04/alan-burdick-why-time-flies-empathy/.

134. Mark Unno, "If It Sounds Too Good To Be True." (*Buddhadharma* July 18, 2017).

135. C.S. Lewis, *The Dark Tower and Other Stories*. © 1977 by C.S. Lewis Pte. Ltd. All rights reserved.

136. http://innertraditions.blogspot.com/2010/12/moth-and-candle-sufi-fable.html.

137. https://www.brainpickings.org/2017/11/30/seneca-on-the-tranquility-of-mind/?utm_source=Brain+Pickings&utm_campaign=6817afba37-EMAIL_CAMPAIGN_2017_12_01&utm_medium=email&utm_term=0_179ffa2629-6817afba37-238590357&mc_cid=6817afba37&mc_eid=85f9f38b9a.

138. Robert Alfred Vaughan, *Hours With The Mystics: A Contribution to the History of Religious Opinion*, Sixth Edition. (Gibbings & Co., Ltd.) and Ninth Edition. (George Routledge & Sons Ltd.). Originally published in 1856.

139. C.S. Lewis, *That Hideous Strength*. © 1945 by C.S. Lewis Pte. Ltd. All right reserved.

140. C.S. Lewis, *The Collected Letters of C.S. Lewis, Volume I: Family Letters 1905-1931*. © 2000 by C.S. Lewis Pte. Ltd. All rights reserved.

141. C.S. Lewis, *Perelandra*. © 1944 by C.S. Lewis Pte. Ltd. All right reserved.

142. https://www.lionsroar.com/buddhism-and-sexuality-its-complicated/?utm_source=Lion%27s+Roar+Newsletter&utm_campaign=a3ac4df129-EMAIL_CAMPAIGN_2018_02_13&utm_medium=email&utm_term=0_1988ee44b2-a3ac4df129-21477953&mc_cid=a3ac4df129&mc_eid=84a461539f.

143. http://experience.hayhouseu.com/dodgingenergyvampires-video2-protectyourselffromenergypredators/?utm_medium=email&utm_campaign=email_course_northrup_dev_2018_US&utm_source=quiz.

144. https://www.brainyquote.com/authors/stephen_hawking.

145. https://www.lionsroar.com/degrees-of-seeing/?utm_source=Lion%27s+Roar+Newsletter&utm_campaign=f25e06218c-EMAIL_CAMPAIGN_2018_03_15&utm_medium=email&utm_term=0_1988ee44b2-f25e06218c-21477953&mc_cid=f25e06218c&mc_eid=84a461539f.

146. https://plato.stanford.edu/entries/berkeley/.

147. Thich Nhat Hanh, "Understanding Our Mind: Fifty Verses on the Nature of Consciousness." (https://www.lionsroar.com/the-four-layers-of-consciousness/?utm_source=Lion%27s+Roar+Newsletter&utm_campaign=f25e06218c-EMAIL_CAMPAIGN_2018_03_15&utm_medium=email&utm_term=0_1988ee44b2-f25e06218c-21477953&mc_cid=f25e06218c&mc_eid=84a461539f).

148. Chögyam Trungpa, *Smile at Fear: Awakening the True Heart of Bravery.* Copyright 2009 by Diana J, Mukpo. Excerpted with permission from Shambhala Publications.

149. Ari Goldfield, https://www.lionsroar.com/forum-do-you-believe-in-miracles/.

150. C.S. Lewis, *Till We Have Faces*: *A Myth Retold.* © 1956, 1984 by C.S. Lewis Pte. Ltd. All rights reserved.

151. Zenju Earthlyn Manuel,_https://www.lionsroar.com/what-if-our-delusions-arent-a-barrier-to-enlightenment/?utm_source=Lion%27s+Roar+Newsletter&utm_campaign=946a1f11c5-EMAIL_CAMPAIGN_2018_04_03&utm_medium=email&utm_term=0_1988ee44b2-946a1f11c5-21477953&mc_cid=946a1f11c5&mc_eid=84a461539f.

152. Caroline Myss, https://www.soundstrue.com/store/science-medical-intuition-course/why-people-dont-heal?stsenddate=2018-04-04+00:05:54&stpromodays=20&sq=1&utm_source=bronto&utm_medium=email&utm_campaign=EvergreenSMI-2-WhyPeopleDontHeal_Video2&utm_content=Why+People+Don%25E2%2580%2599t+Heal.

153. Transcript of conversation with Neale Donald Walsch, www.hayhouseworldsummit.com, ©2018 Hay House, Inc. ©2018 Neale Donald Walsch.

154. C.S. Lewis, *An Experiment in Criticism.* © 1961 by C.S. Lewis Pte. Ltd. All rights reserved.

155. C.S. Lewis, *Letters of C.S. Lewis.* © 1966, 1988 by C.S. Lewis Pte. Ltd. All rights reserved.

156. "Do Buddhists believe in sin?" (https://www.lionsroar.com/do-buddhists-believe-in-sin/? mc_cid=d08148ba70&mc_eid=84a461539f).

157. Lama Tsultrim Allione, "The Sacred Feminine." (*Lion's Roar*, June 26, 2018). https://www.lionsroar.com/the-sacred-feminine/?utm_source=Lion%27s+Roar+Newsletter&utm_campaign=9a6014d664-TS-June-26-2018&utm_medium=email&utm_term=0_1988ee44b2-9a6014d664-21477953&goal=0_1988ee44b2-9a6014d664-21477953&mc_cid=9a6014d664&mc_eid=84a461539f.

158. Gelek Rimpoche, https://www.lionsroar.com/in-with-the-bad-air-out-with-the-good/?utm_source=Lion%27s+Roar+Newsletter&utm_campaign=02c8bbfb9b-WR-June-29-2018&utm_medium=email&utm_term=0_1988ee44b2-02c8bbfb9b-21477953&goal=0_1988ee44b2-02c8bbfb9b-21477953&mc_cid=02c8bbfb9b&mc_eid=84a461539f.

159. Sheng Yen, https://www.lionsroar.com/four-steps-to-magical-powers/?utm_source=Lion%27s+Roar+Newsletter&utm_campaign=b69db78716-WR-July-13-2018&utm_medium=email&utm_term=0_1988ee44b2-b69db78716-21477953&goal=0_1988ee44b2-b69db78716-21477953&mc_cid=b69db78716&mc_eid=84a461539f.

160. Caroline Myss, *Why People Don't Heal And How They Can.* (Three Rivers Press, New York 1997).

161. C.S. Lewis, *Reflections on the Psalms.* © 1958, 1968 by C.S. Lewis Pte. Ltd. All rights reserved.

162. Norman Fischer, "Life is Tough. Here Are Six Ways to Deal With It." (https://www.lionsroar.com/life-is-tough-six-ways-to-deal-with-it-march-2013/?mc_cid=291dd435fc&mc_eid=84a461539f).

163. John Coltrane, https://www.lionsroar.com/trane-of-no-thought-how-meditation-inspired-jazz-great-john-coltrane/.

164. Philip Glass, https://www.lionsroar.com/the-exquisite-moment/?utm_source=Lion%27s+Roar+Newsletter&utm_campaign=1a9c47ea16-WR-Aug-17-2018&utm_medium=email&utm_term=0_1988ee44b2-1a9c47ea16-21477953&goal=0_1988ee44b2-1a9c47ea16-21477953&mc_cid=1a9c47ea16&mc_eid=84a461539f.

165. Dainin Katagiri Roshi, "Alone in the Vastness of Existence." (*Buddhadharma*, Summer 2018, Vol. 16, No. 3).

166. Norman Fischer, https://www.lionsroar.com/the-problem-of-evil/?utm_source=Lion%27s+Roar+Newsletter&utm_campaign=74e3986c32-WR-Aug-24-2018&utm_medium=email&utm_term=0_1988ee44b2-74e3986c32-21477953&goal=0_1988ee44b2-74e3986c32-21477953&mc_cid=74e3986c32&mc_eid=84a461539f.

167. Mark Unno, "The Radical Thinkers of Pure Land." (https://www.lionsroar.com/the-radical-thinkers-of-pure-land/?mc_cid=ac686a6219&mc_eid=84a461539f).

168. Thanissaro Bhikkhu (Than Geoff), "The Real Reasons to Meditate." (*Lion's Roar*, July 2018).

169. Melvin McLeod, "6 Ways to Step in a Bucket." (*Lion's Roar*, July 2018).

170. Ajahn Amaro, https://www.lionsroar.com/the-sound-of-silence/?mc_cid=a5d965071c&mc_eid=84a461539f.

171. Joan Halifax, "Yes, We Can Have Hope." (*Buddhadharma*, Fall 2018). https://www.lionsroar.com/yes-we-can-have-hope/.

172. Margaret Wheatley, https://www.lionsroar.com/finding-hope-in-hopelessness/?mc_cid=b09169f458&mc_eid=84a461539f.

173. "Father Thomas Keating and Trungpa Rinpoche Talk About Egolessness."
This conversation took place during Naropa's 1983 Christian Buddhist Conference. *Speaking of Silence - Christians and Buddhists in Dialogue*, compiled and edited by Susan Szpakowski. (Kalapa Publications/ Vajradhatu Publications, Halifax 2005).

174. *The Nirvana Sutra*, Volume I, Fascicle IX, Chapter Four, "The Nature of the Tathāgata: Part 6" [The Parable of the Moon]. 416b-c, 421a.

175. C.S. Lewis, *Letters to Malcolm, Chiefly on Prayer*. © 1963, 1964, 1991, 1992 by C.S. Lewis Pte. Ltd. All rights reserved.

176. Kyle Idleman, https://www.biblegateway.com/blog/2018/11/idolatry-great-sin/?utm_source=Z-BG&utm_medium=email&utm_term=20181227&utm_campaign=Z-BG-122718b&spMailingID=580 26739&spUserID=OTA2Njk0NzIxMzIS1&spJobID=1541827768&spReportId=MTU0MTgyNzc2OAS2.

177. https://www.soundstrue.com/store/weeklywisdom?page=single&category=IATE&episode=13617&utm_source=bronto&utm_medium=email&utm_campaign=N190106-WW-Established-Listener&utm_content=This+Week:+Featuring+Damien+Echols+and+Father+Thomas+Keating.

178. John Welwood, https://www.lionsroar.com/on-spiritual-authority/.

179. John Welwood, https://www.lionsroar.com/the-perfect-love-we-seek-the-imperfect-love-we-live/.

180. Pema Chödrön, https://www.lionsroar.com/bodhichitta-the-excellence-of-awakened-heart/?mc_cid=b7b0893bf1&mc_eid=84a461539f.

181. https://www.cbsnews.com/news/first-black-hole-picture-event-horizon-telescope-first-image-black-hole-m-87-scientists-announce-today-2019-04-10/.

182. Dalai Lama, https://www.lionsroar.com/seeing-ourselves-clearly/?mc_cid=712a7a672a&mc_eid=84a461539f.

183. Sandra L. Brown, M.A. with Jennifer R. Young, L.M.H.C., *Women Who Love Psychopaths*. (Mask Publishing, Balsam Grove NC 2009-2018).

184. Gary Edmonds, https://www.huffpost.com/entry/agape-and-phileo-love-we-need-both_b_58a1e5d 6e4b0cd37efcfeb23.

185. Gabriel Garcia Marquez, *One Hundred Years of Solitude.* (Harper & Row, New York 1970).

186. Jennie Lee, *Breathing Love.* (Llewellyn Worldwide Ltd., Woodbury MN 2018).

187. https://www.biblegateway.com/blog/2019/09/niv-quest-study-bible-why-does-god-allow-bad-things-to-happen/.

188. from the *Tevijja Sutra* (Vanessa Zuisei Goddard, "The Four Immeasurables Leave Nothing Untouched." *Buddhadharma*, Winter 2019).

189. https://www.lionsroar.com/gautama-vs-the-buddha/?mc_cid=a2ade5687f&mc_eid=84a461539f.

190. Dalai Lama with Thubten Chodron, *Following in the Buddha's Footsteps.* (Adapted in *Buddhadharma*, Winter 2019).

191. https://www.lionsroar.com/through-the-lens-of-madhyamaka/?mc_cid=38f298f6b3&mc_eid=84a461539f.

192. Thanissaro Bhikkhu, "Things You Need for Your Journey." (https://www.lionsroar.com/things-you-need-for-your-journey/?mc_cid=483a19b686&mc_eid=84a461539f).

193. Krzesiński, Andrzej J., "Religion of Nazi Germany." (Rare Books and Manuscripts. 17, https://digital.kenyon.edu/rarebooks/17).

194. C.S. Lewis, *The Personal Heresy: A Controversy.* © 1939 by C. S. Lewis Pte. Ltd. All rights reserved.

195. Anne Bancroft, *Weavers of Wisdom: Women Mystics of the Twentieth Century.* (Arkana/Penguin Group, London 1989)

Most of the isolated quotes from Buddhist and Hindu scriptures and by various ancient and modern religious masters came from the Internet, from websites such as wikipedia.org, dharmanet.org, freebuddhistaudio.com, buddhanet.net, and others I cannot even begin to remember. In cases where I was able to identify the authors or translators of the quotes, I sought and obtained their permission to use their material. In some cases, however, I could not find the original source.

Unless otherwise attributed, all poems (and prose) contained herein were composed by Betty Hibod.

Subject Index

722, 723, 735, 777, 787, 792, 793, 808, 817, 832, 833, 846, 892, 907, 927, 952, 965, 971, 989, 993, 994, 1025, 1028, 1029, 1043, 1060, 1081, 1129, 1140, 1147, 1148, 1178, 1179, 1195, 1213, 1237, 1239, 1300, 1307, 1319, 1327, 1364, 1378, 1410, 1428, 1454

Martha and Rita – 562, 591, 635, 661, 714, 718, 725, 741, 746, 759, 779, 824, 828, 829, 932, 947, 957, 979, <u>1123</u>, 1124, 1162, 1321, 1355, 1359, 1388

Miracles, Epiphanies, Signs, Serendipities, and Synchronicities – <u>29</u>, 31, 58, <u>141</u>, 151, 199, <u>231</u>, <u>232</u>, 233, 234, 247, <u>250</u>, <u>256</u>, 258, 262, 266, 267, <u>268</u>, 269, <u>270</u>, 271, 272, 273, 313, 333, <u>340</u>, 347, 360, 368, 377, 381, 387, 395, 401, 415, 426, 456, 457, 459, <u>460</u>, 469, 484, 486, 489, 490, 501, 509, <u>539</u>, 558, <u>560</u>, <u>564</u>, 568, 569, <u>578</u>, 580, 583, 584, <u>594</u>, <u>604</u>, 611, 612, 635, 643, 649, <u>655</u>, 661, 662, 672, <u>688</u>, <u>689</u>, <u>693</u>, 701, 702, 752, <u>757</u>, 760, 820, 837, 838, 849, 854, 855, 860, 868, 875, 885, 887, 893, 895, 896, 916, 921, 924, 925, 929, 932, 944, 946, 947, 953, 982, 1011, <u>1026</u>, 1036, 1039, 1054, 1127, 1134, <u>1142</u>, 1161, 1176, 1186, 1187, 1199, 1200, 1221, 1241, 1242, 1256, 1268, 1284, 1287, 1292, 1297, 1337, 1382, 1404, 1413, <u>1423</u>, 1434, <u>1450</u>

Past, Present, and Future – 23, 92, 130, 136, 179, 182, 347, 371, 379, 393, 425, 441, 488, 531, 582, 660, 923, 1058, 1068, 1143, 1158, 1182, 1211, 1223

Poems – <u>14,</u> 42, 57, 72, 92, 94, 100, 140, 163, <u>268</u>, 275, 285, 333, 607, 624, 653, 681, 840, 846, 875, 1285, 1441, 1454

Pride, Ego, Trust, Unsupported Thought, and Surrender – 36, 37, 56, 67, 70, 144, 145, 147, 148, 149, 156, 157, 188, 208, 228, 356, 475, 590, 713, 743, 746, 847, 851, 934, 950, 972, 975, 991, 1004, 1007, 1009, 1012, 1020, 1033, 1041, 1049, 1073, 1109, 1174, 1175, 1212, 1220, 1248, 1264, 1283, 1313, 1325, 1345, 1367, 1374, 1379, 1397

Psychology – 465, 619, <u>637</u>, 645, 647, 656, 658, 667, 699, 717, 734, 740, 759, 771, 772, 774, 784, 807, 812, 813, 839, 872, 903, 934, 1002, 1016, 1048, 1053, 1086, 1097, 1099, 1107, 1111, 1128, 1159, 1164, 1178, 1180, 1218, 1225, 1229, 1232, 1302, 1402, 1409, 1437

Sex – 49, 51, 55, 74, 75, 77, 110, <u>117</u>, 118, 119, 121, 172, 203, 230, 255, 281, 343, 396, 409, 444, 510, 593, 600, 622, 676, 715, 746, 775, 801, 823, 848, 883, 905, 906, 969, 975, 980, 1081, 1094, 1102, 1135, 1245, 1273, 1340

Soul, Spirit, Buddha-nature, God-self – 79, 80, 82, 139, 403, 514, 609, 754, 985, 1093, 1249, 1252, 1360, 1418

Suffering, Submission, Rejection, and Sacrifice – 13, 71, 33, 91, 206, 366, 373, 397, 398, 419, 423, 428, 433, 471, 515, 551, 573, 603, 627, 743, 755, 770, 788, 795, 946, 1010, 1020, 1035, 1109, 1184, 1306, 1352, 1355, 1356

Sun, Moon, Nature, and Symbolism – 46, 72, 109, 144, 145, 168, <u>250</u>, <u>268</u>, 269, 272, 345, 360, 368, 377, 395, 432, 459, 469, 484, 509, 547, 558, <u>560</u>, 569, 570, <u>578</u>, 589, <u>594</u>, 612, 618, <u>688</u>, 713, <u>757</u>, 760, 787, 865, 885, 893, 895, 926, 949, 966, 983, 1027, 1052, 1134, 1200, 1201, 1207, 1212, 1221, 1252, 1256, 1268, 1285, 1295, 1350, 1362, 1379, 1386, 1393, <u>1423</u>

The Third Way, Triangulation, Resist not Evil – 968, 995, 1042, 1092, 1158, 1167, 1180, 1184, 1202, 1206, 1208, 1250, 1288, 1326, 1335, 1349, 1451

The Twins: Jean and Joan – <u>53</u>, 54, <u>60</u>, 61, 62, 63, 64, 65, 66, 68, 69, 79, 82, 83, 87, 88, 89, 104, 107, 108, 1104, 1190

The Unnamed One – 163, 165, 169, 174, 180, 184, 185, 186, 189, 190, 191, 192, 193, <u>194</u>, 195, 196, 197, 199, 200, 201, 202, 205, 207, <u>210</u>, 213, 214, 216, 217, 218, 223, 225, <u>231</u>, 235, 237, 240, 245, 246, 248, 249, <u>250</u>, 251, 253, 259, 265, 278, 280, 282, 284, 309, 310, 311, 319, 323, 332, 337, 339, 342, 344, 355, 361, 362, 366, 367, 373, 385, <u>388</u>, 394, 401, 402, 407, 420, 428, 431, 440, 445, 450, 451, 452, 454, 461, 465, 466, <u>468</u>, 470, 471, 472, 473, 478, 479, <u>487</u>, 503, 505, 507, 511, 513, <u>536</u>, 537, 548, 551, 555, 832, 1103

Truth, Justice, and Wisdom – 27, 361, 478, 481, 541, 542, 543, 549, 550, 553, 556, 557, 563, 794, 844, 858, 859, 862, 866, 869, 872, 873, 912, 915, 989, 1003, 1040, 1149, 1274, 1286, 1405, 1417, 1429, 1435, 1440

Words, Language, Knowledge, Thinking and the Mind – 28, 52, 59, 76, 84, 86, 90, 97, 150, 371, 391, 411, 424, 434, 523, 581, 614, 628, 630, 678, 727, 773, 798, 838, 889, 955, 964, 997, 999, 1023, 1145, 1146, 1155, 1160, 1210, 1235, 1254, 1285, 1286, 1287, 1288, 1289, 1294, 1296, 1299, 1300, 1310, 1313, 1333, 1342, 1344, 1348, 1349, 1357, 1389, 1411, 1412, 1439, 1445, 1452

The *fermata* ⌢ is a musical symbol that means "time stops."

Printed in the United States
by Baker & Taylor Publisher Services